NIGHT+DAY
D.C.

By Elise Hartman Ford
and Colleen Clark

PULSE GUIDES

Pulse Guides' **Night+Day D.C.** is an independent guide. We do not accept payment of any kind from events or establishments for inclusion in this book. We welcome your views on our selections. Please email us: **feedback@pulseguides.com**.

The information contained in this book was checked as rigorously as possible before going to press. The publisher accepts no responsibility for any changes that may have occurred since, or for any other variance of fact from that recorded here in good faith.

No part of this book may be reproduced in any form without permission in writing from the publisher, except by a reviewer who wishes to quote brief passages for a published review. This publication is a creative work fully protected by all applicable copyright laws, as well as by misappropriation, trade secrets, unfair competition, and all other applicable laws. The authors and editors of this work have added value to the underlying factual material herein through one or more of the following: unique and original selection, coordination, expression, arrangement, and classification (including the itineraries) of the information.

Distributed in the United States and Canada by National Book Network (NBN).
First Edition. Printed in the United States.
Copyright © 2006 ASDavis Media Group, Inc. All rights reserved.
ISBN-10:0-9766013-4-6; ISBN-13:978-0-9766013-4-0

Credits

Executive Editor	Alan S. Davis
Editor	Christina Henry de Tessan
Authors	Elise Hartman Ford, Colleen Clark
Copy Editor	Gail Nelson-Bonebrake
Maps	Chris Gillis
Production	Jo Farrell, Samia Afra

Photo Credits: (Front cover, left to right) Les Byerley (martini), courtesy of Kimpton Group (Firefly Restaurant), Laryn Bakker (National Museum of the American Indian); (Back cover, left to right) Ron Blunt (1789 Restaurant), David Phelps (Helix Lounge), courtesy of The Washington, DC Convention & Tourism Corporation (Capitol Dome), Maxwell MacKenzie (Zaytinya); (Inside cover, top to bottom) courtesy of Oya, David Phelps (Hotel Rouge), courtesy of Bombay Club; (p.4) Mary Lou D'Auray.

Special Sales

For information about bulk purchases of Pulse Guides (ten copies or more), email us at bookorders@pulseguides.com. Special bulk rates are available for charities, corporations, institutions, and online and mail-order catalogs, and our books can be customized to suit your company's needs.

NIGHT+DAY
the Cool Cities series from **PULSE**GUIDES

P.O. Box 590780, San Francisco, CA 94159
pulseguides.com

Pulse Guides is an imprint of ASDavis Media Group, Inc.

The Night+Day Difference

Pulse of the City

Our job is to point you to all of the city's peak experiences: amazing museums, unique spas, and spectacular views. But the complete *urbanista* experience is more than just impressions—it is grownup fun, the kind that thrives by night as well as by day. Urban fun is a hip nightclub or a trendy restaurant. It is people-watching and people-meeting. Lonely planet? We don't think so. Night+Day celebrates our lively planet.

The Right Place. The Right Time. It Matters.

A Night+Day city must have exemplary restaurants, a vibrant nightlife scene, and enough attractions to keep a visitor busy for six days without having to do the same thing twice. In selecting restaurants, food is important, but so is the scene. Our hotels, most of which are 4- and 5-star properties, are rated for the quality of the concierge staff (can they get you into a hot restaurant?) as well as the rooms. You won't find kids with fake IDs at our nightlife choices. And the attractions must be truly worthy of your time. But experienced travelers know that timing is almost everything. Going to a restaurant at 7pm can be a very different experience (and probably less fun) than at 9pm; a champagne boat cruise might be ordinary in the morning but spectacular at sunset. We believe providing the reader with this level of detail makes the difference between a good experience and a great one.

The Bottom Line

Your time is precious. Our guide must be easy to use and dead-on accurate. That is why our executive editor, editors, and writers (locals who are in touch with what is great—and what is not) spend hundreds of hours researching, writing, and debating selections for each guide. The results are presented in four unique ways: The *99 Best* with our top three choices in 33 categories that highlight what is great about the city; the *Experience* chapters, in which our selections are organized by distinct themes or personalities (Chic, Hip, and Classic); a *Perfect Plan* (3 Nights and Days) for each theme, showing how to get the most out of the city in a short period of time; and the *D.C. Black Book*, listing all the hotels, restaurants, nightlife, and attractions, with key details, contact information, and page references.

Our bottom line is this: If you find our guide easy to use and enjoyable to read, and with our help you have an extraordinary time, we have succeeded. We review and value all feedback from our readers, so please contact us at **feedback@pulseguides.com**.

From the Publisher

I've had the travel bug ever since my first summer job during college—escorting tour groups around Europe to evaluate them for my parents' travel company. When I retired from the paper business ten years ago, I set out on a journey to find the 100 most fun places to be in the world at the right time. The challenge of unearthing the world's greatest events—from the Opera Ball in Vienna to the Calgary Stampede—led me to write a guidebook.

In Union Station

The success of *The Fun Also Rises,* named after Ernest Hemingway's *The Sun Also Rises,* which helped popularize what has become perhaps the most thrilling party on earth (Pamplona's Fiesta de San Fermín, also known as the Running of the Bulls), persuaded me that there were others who shared my interest in a different approach to travel. Guidebooks were neither informative nor exciting enough to capture peak experiences—whether for world-class events or just a night on the town.

My goal is to publish *extraordinary guides for extraordinary travelers.* **Night+Day**, the first series from Pulse Guides, is for Gen-Xers to Zoomers (Boomers with a zest for life), who know that if one wants to truly experience a city, the night is as important as the day. **Night+Day** guides present the best that a city has to offer—hotels, restaurants, nightlife, and attractions that are exciting without being stuffy—in a totally new format.

Pulse Guides abides by one guiding principle: *Never settle for the ordinary.* We hope that a willingness to explore new approaches to guidebooks, combined with meticulous research, provides you with unique and significant experiences.

When we chose D.C. as one of our cool cities, there were many skeptics. No doubt D.C. is a great place to visit, but a cool city? Behold the undiscovered and underreported D.C.—a city that I believe joins the ranks of the world's most vibrant. I'm confident you'll feel the same after reading **Night+Day D.C.**

Wishing you extraordinary times,

Alan S. Davis, Publisher and Executive Editor
Pulse Guides

P.S. To contact me, or for updated information on all of our Night+Day guides, please visit our website at **pulseguides.com**.

TOC

INTRODUCTION 9
Night+Day's D.C. Urbie 12

THE 99 BEST OF D.C. 15
    Always-Hot Tables 16
    American Originals 17
    Art Museums 18
    Brunches 19
    Chef's Tables 20
    Dance Clubs 21
    Drinks with a View 22
    Fine Dining 23
    Gay Bars 24
    Hot Chefs 25
    Hotel Bars 26
    Indian Restaurants 27
    Insider D.C. Experiences 28
    International Scenes 29
    Live Music 30
    Local Favorites 31
    Luxury Spas 32
    Monumental Sculptures 33
    Only-in-D.C. Restaurants 34
    Outdoor Activities 35
    Outdoor Drinking 36
    Patriotic Adventures 37
    Politico Sightings 38
    Power Lunch Spots 39
    Rainy Day Experiences 40
    Restaurant Lounges 41
    Romantic Dining 42
    Romantic Trysts 43
    Sexy Lounges 44
    Singles Scenes 45
    Trendy Tables 46
    Vegetarian Restaurants 47
    Views of D.C. 48

EXPERIENCE D.C. 49
Chic D.C. 50
- The Perfect Plan (3 Nights and Days) 51
- The Key Neighborhoods 55
- The Shopping Blocks 56
- The Hotels 57
- The Restaurants 60
- The Nightlife 69
- The Attractions 77

Hip D.C. 82
- The Perfect Plan (3 Nights and Days) 83
- The Key Neighborhoods 87
- The Shopping Blocks 88
- The Hotels 89
- The Restaurants 92
- The Nightlife 100
- The Attractions 108

Classic D.C. 115
- The Perfect Plan (3 Nights and Days) 116
- The Key Neighborhoods 120
- The Shopping Blocks 121
- The Hotels 122
- The Restaurants 124
- The Nightlife 132
- The Attractions 137

PRIME TIME D.C. 143
Prime Time Basics 144
- Eating and Drinking 144
- Weather and Tourism 144
- National Holidays 145

The Best Events Calendar 146
The Best Events 147

HIT THE GROUND RUNNING 155
City Essentials 156
- Getting to D.C.: By Air 156
- Getting to D.C.: By Land 162
- D.C.: Lay of the Land 163
- Getting Around D.C. 163

Other Practical Information (Money Matters; Numbers to Know; Safety; Security; Gay and Lesbian Travel; Traveling with Disabilities; Print Media; Radio Stations; Shopping Hours; Attire; Size Conversion; When Drinking Is Legal; Smoking; Drugs; Time Zone; Additional Resources for Visitors) 166
Party Conversation—A Few Surprising Facts 172
The Cheat Sheet (The Very Least You Ought to Know About D.C.)
(Neighborhoods, Theaters, Great Parks and Gardens, Major Traffic Circles, Sports Teams, Subway Lines, Concert Venues, Skyscrapers, Rivers, Singular Sensation, and Coffee) 173
Just for Business and Conventions 182

D.C. Region Map 184

LEAVING D.C. 185
Overnight Trips
Baltimore, Maryland 186
The Maryland and Delaware Beaches 188
Maryland's Eastern Shore along the Chesapeake Bay 190
Virginia Wine Country 192
Washington, Virginia 194
Day Trips
Annapolis, Maryland 196
Great Falls Park, Maryland 197
Harper's Ferry, West Virginia 198
Leesburg and Middleburg, Virginia 199
Old Town Alexandria and Mount Vernon, Virginia 200

D.C. BLACK BOOK 201
D.C. Black Book 202
D.C. Black Book by Neighborhood 217
D.C. Unique Shopping Index 221

Action Central D.C. Map 222
D.C. Neighborhoods Map 223

About the Authors

Elise Hartman Ford is a freelance writer based in the Washington, D.C., area. She is the author of several guidebooks, including, since 1998, the annually published *Frommer's Guide to Washington, D.C.* Her writing has appeared in the *Washington Post*, *Washingtonian* magazine, the London-based *Bradman's North America Guide*, and other national, regional, and trade publications.

Colleen Clark made stops in Pennsylvania, England, and Kenya before setting into the U Street neighborhood of D.C. By day she covers travel for usatoday.com, and by night she uses freelance gigs as an excuse to see concerts and drink cocktails. Her writing has appeared in *USA Today*, *DCist*, and *Two Mundos*.

Acknowledgments

This book was a blast to write, so first I must thank Alan Davis for taking me on, and my editor, Christina Henry de Tessan, who convinced him he should. I'm especially grateful to Christina, who was a delight to work with and get to know, and who alternately revved me up, calmed me down, or patiently prodded me, as the book progressed.

Thank you to my cowriter, Colleen Clark, my partner in panic and in fun, whose tales of D.C. nightlife I intend to dine out on for years to come.

Certain Washington sources were particularly helpful, and they include Rebecca Pawlowski, media relations manager for the Washington Convention & Tourism Corporation; Heather Freeman, of Heather Freeman Media and Public Relations, LLC; Thea Bowers, head of Bowers Communications; and Sarah Crocker, public relations manager for Kimpton Hotels in Washington, D.C. Many thanks.

To my intrepid husband, ultimate best source, and biggest supporter Jim, and to my good-sport girls, Caitlin and Lucy, whose keen observations I find indispensable, and who have become, perhaps, a little too accustomed to doing homework at restaurant tables, my greatest love and thanks. **Elise Hartman Ford**

I'd like to thank Hillary, Colleen, Emily, and Molly for their energy support, and good humor; Elise and Christina for their guidance; and Dad, Mom, Erin, and Katie for their love and patience. I would also like to thank my liver for staying with me through all 120 stops on this five-month bar crawl. From Chimay at Saint-Ex to Grey Goose with Jenna Bush, you were with me every step of the way. **Colleen Clark**

Introduction

As world capitals go, Washington, D.C., (affectionately referred to by locals as "D.C.") is young and beautiful. Her 67 square miles are lush with green parkland and gardens, the lovely Potomac River forming her western embrace. A network of grand avenues and circles directs not only the flow of traffic through the city but one's attention, toward architectural supermodels, like the Capitol and the Washington Monument, preening in the low skyline. Famous for its federal role, the city now pulses in its dual role as a lively center for hip restaurants, hot bars, trendy shops, groundbreaking music, and captivating art.

D.C.: What It Was

Histories of the city tend to pick up the story in the late 18th century, when the locale was chosen as the site of the nation's capital. Of course, the land itself, and other people, were here first, as far back as 13,000 years ago. Archaeologists believe that early peoples settled and prospered here as the Ice Age waned, the climate warmed, plant and animal life flourished, and glaciers melted, creating today's Potomac and Anacostia rivers and the Chesapeake Bay. The woodland known now as Rock Creek Park has proven to be a treasure trove of artifacts for archaeologists, whose discoveries there include pointed weapons and stone tools that date from thousands of years ago. More-exact information derives from the accounts of European explorers in the 1500s and 1600s. Captain John Smith, in particular, is credited with giving the shout-out to his English countrymen about the New World after his trip in June 1608, when he and 14 Jamestown colonialists explored the Potomac River as far as Great Falls. Smith and company encountered Nacotchtank and Piscataway Indians, who initially welcomed the colonists. By 1697, however, encroaching settlement chased away these Native Americans.

Early settlers, mostly from Great Britain, continued to migrate to this territory, attracted by its position on the Potomac River, easily accessed via the Atlantic Ocean and Chesapeake Bay. In 1751, immigrants founded Georgetown and proceeded to develop it into a thriving port town for shipping tobacco grown on nearby plantations. In those days,

> **George Washington and Thomas Jefferson convinced Congress to create a brand-new capital city for the young country, one situated halfway between the North and the South on the Potomac River.**

the Potomac reached as far as N and Prospect streets; wealthy ship owners and merchants lived on a bluff overlooking the harbor, in many of the grand houses that remain intact today. Meanwhile, across the Potomac River, Scottish immigrants had staked out the port village of Alexandria in 1749, and hired a 17-year-old local named George Washington to survey the town. Like Georgetown, Alexandria is alive in its numerous historic mansions, taverns, and streets preserved from those earlier days.

When independence-minded colonists threw off the yoke of imperial England during the American Revolution (1775–83), they founded a new nation, and then looked about for a worthy capital city. New York? Philadelphia? Annapolis? Then, as now, members of Congress were an argumentative bunch, with Northern and Southern factions vying to place the capital in their particular locations. President George Washington and his secretary of state Thomas Jefferson convinced Congress to approve a grander idea: to create a brand-new capital city for the young country, one situated halfway between the North and the South on the Potomac River. In 1790, Congress authorized Washington to carve a ten-mile-square chunk of land out of Maryland and Virginia: The District of Columbia and the nation's capital were born.

The site was not an obvious choice. From 1790 to the mid-1800s, both the capital and the country were getting off the ground in a place that was mostly a muddy morass. This was a time of construction, as slaves and immigrants from Ireland, Scotland, and other countries labored to raise up a city from its roots. In the meantime, Congress and the president operated out of Philadelphia. One by one, the White House (the oldest federal structure in Washington), the Capitol, the Treasury building, and other buildings were erected, fleshing out the breathtakingly elegant 1791 design of the brilliant Frenchman, Pierre Charles L'Enfant. By 1800, second president John Adams and wife Abigail had moved into the White House and Congress into the Capitol, everyone making do in half-built structures. By the 1840s, the city was still a mess, with only a handful of grand facades to represent the city's and the nation's potential.

In the 1860s, the Civil War transformed Washington into a military camp and its federal buildings, including the Capitol and the Patent Office (now the National Portrait Gallery), into hospitals. The population jumped from 60,000 to 200,000, as military personnel, former slaves, merchants, and laborers arrived on the very chaotic scene. In the war's aftermath, these newcomers stayed on, then spread out to live and work in nearby towns, a circumstance made possible by the burgeoning railroad system that expanded Washington's horizons by connecting the city to outlying areas.

The capital was at last starting to take shape. In the 1870s, a public works official named Alexander "Boss" Shephard led the charge to construct and pave streets and bridges, install operable water and sewer systems, lay sidewalks, plant trees, and illuminate the city with streetlights. The Washington Monument, begun in 1848, was finally completed in 1884. The first of the Smithsonian buildings, the National Museum (now called the Arts and Industries Building), opened on the Mall in 1881. A beautification program continuing into the 20th century included the planting of the famous cherry trees along the Tidal Basin and the creation of the Lincoln Memorial at the west end of the Mall.

In the world at large, momentous events were taking place: The automobile was becoming a fixture on the roads; airplanes were taking to the skies; World War I, the Great Depression, and World War II followed in close succession. Washington, the American capital, was no longer the new kid on the block, but a global power. Washington, the city, was undergoing a population explosion, with African Americans especially increasing their ranks. The 1920s and 1930s nurtured a black renaissance in the neighborhood surrounding Howard University, giving rise to jazz greats Duke Ellington, Cab Calloway, and Pearl Bailey—who performed in theaters along U Street, "Black Broadway," as it was called—and to writers like Langston Hughes and Zora Neale Hurston. By the 1960s, it was only natural that the civil rights move-

Key Dates

1608	Captain John Smith explores the Potomac River and land near present-day D.C.
1790s	Congress approves the site for the capital. Construction begins on the Capitol and White House.
1800	Congress and the president move into the unfinished Capitol and White House.
1861–65	The Civil War turns the capital into a staging area and military camp, and soldiers and laborers crowd into the city.
1870s	The capital starts to take shape as sewers, streetlights, and paved roads are installed.
1884	The Washington Monument, begun in 1848, is completed.
1912	The capital receives a gift of cherry trees from the Japanese and plants them all along the Tidal Basin.
1963	Dr. Martin Luther King, Jr., delivers his "I Have a Dream" speech at the Lincoln Memorial; more than 200,000 march for civil rights.
2001	Terrorists attack the Pentagon and New York on 9/11.

Night+Day's D.C. Urbie

Night+Day cities are chosen because they have a vibrant nightlife scene, standard-setting and innovative restaurants, cutting-edge hotels, and enough attractions to keep one busy for six days without doing the same thing twice. In short, they are fun. They represent the quintessential *urbanista* experience. This phenomenon wouldn't exist but for the creativity and talents of many people and organizations. In honor of all who have played a role in making D.C. one of the world's coolest cities, Pulse Guides is pleased to give special recognition, and our Urbie Award, to one couple whose contribution is exemplary.

THE URBIE AWARD: Abe and Irene Pollin

D.C.'s Penn Quarter neighborhood today is a far, far cry from what it was just one decade ago, when this downtown district was a place of office buildings and not much else. Come sundown, most folks got the heck out of Dodge. Around that time, a couple named Abe and Irene Pollin, owners of the Washington Wizards basketball team and the Washington Capitals ice hockey team, decided to build a new sports center in the heart of downtown, financing the $200 million cost themselves. The MCI Center, now called the Verizon Center, opened on December 2, 1997, to a sellout crowd. "I had two goals when I decided to build this building," says Abe Pollin. "The first was that if I was building in downtown Washington, the nation's capital, it had to be the best building of its kind in the country. The second was to be the catalyst that turned the city around."

And that's exactly what happened. By constructing their sports arena in the middle of D.C.'s desolate downtown, the Pollins gave office workers an enticement to stay on after dark, and Washingtonians in other parts of the city good reason to head here. Entrepreneurs took notice of all this activity and started to set up shop; one savvy shop led to the next fine restaurant, which led to the next hot bar, which led to the next chic hotel, and pretty soon, an enormous new convention center had been built, sealing D.C.'s fate as a top-draw city. Visit the Penn Quarter today, and you'll find yourself on the pulse of the capital's hippest neighborhood, where fashionistas, urbanistas, and happy revelers fill the streets night and day. Abe and Irene Pollin, whose achievements in business, philanthropy, and public service are both legion and legendary, may perhaps be best known for building the Verizon Center and in so doing, spearheading Washington's phoenixlike transformation from a deteriorating ruin into an urban star.

ment taking hold throughout the country should gain strength in the nation's capital, where 75% of the residents were now black. But it was a mix of blacks and whites who marched on Washington on August 28, 1963, to demand that Congress pass the Civil Rights Act, and to listen to Dr. Martin Luther King, Jr.'s, famous "I Have a Dream" speech, delivered from the steps of the Lincoln Memorial.

> **The attacks had a profound effect upon the capital, but not the one anticipated by the terrorists: The city is vibrant with fresh purpose and enterprise, and renewed zest for sharing the best American experiences.**

As the 20th century headed to the finish line, Washington was the site of rioting after the assassination of Dr. King in April 1968, and protests during the Vietnam War. The capital was rocked by the presidential political scandals of Richard Nixon's Watergate in the 1970s and of Bill Clinton's Monica Lewinsky incident in the 1990s, as well as by the local political scandal of Mayor Marion Barry's corrupt administration and drug charges in 1990. In the midst of all this, D.C. continued to blossom, gaining a delegate, though not a voting member, in Congress; a world-class subway system; the grand John F. Kennedy Center for the Performing Arts; a superbly renovated Union Station; and bedroom communities to accommodate the baby boomer generation and increasing numbers of immigrants. By the end of the 20th century, Washington had evolved from a provincial town into a cosmopolitan city.

The 21st century opened with the terrorist attacks in New York and at the Pentagon, on September 11, 2001. Those attacks have had a profound effect upon the capital, but not perhaps the one anticipated by the terrorists: Security precautions are in place at many sightseeing attractions, yes, but the city is vibrant with fresh purpose and enterprise, and renewed zest for sharing the very best of American experiences.

D.C.: What It Is

Washington, D.C., today is a city of more than 550,000 people, about 60% African American, 27% white, and the remaining percent mainly a mix of Latinos and Asians. The federal government is the city's largest employer, but the tourism industry runs a close second, with studies showing that some 18 million Americans and 1 million international tourists visit Washington annually.

> D.C. is a cosmopolis brimming with hip artists and musicians, young entrepreneurs and high-spirited visionaries, who are reinvigorating the town.

Washington, D.C., represents "the American Experience," say city tourism officials. The name suits. Think patriotic, and you've got your traditional adventures, whether a tour of the Capitol or a stroll by the White House. Think playful, and the city's personality unfolds: Historic Georgetown teems with fashionistas, chic shops, and cool bars; the newborn Penn Quarter, where Walt Whitman once rambled, is home to sexy new restaurant lounges and flocks of the young and restless; and the U Street neighborhood, where Duke Ellington once performed, is a place of late-night clubs that draw a music-loving crowd. From the politico hangouts on Capitol Hill to the salsa clubs in Adams Morgan, from the boutiques and bistros of Dupont Circle to the power pow-wow restaurants near the White House, Washington is a go-to place for a fun time. It's a cultural cocktail, too, offering a heady mix of art museums, world-renowned theater, and multiethnic restaurants.

In a little over two centuries, a remarkable transformation has taken place. Federally speaking, the city is full of hopeful Mr. and Ms. Smiths who've gone to Washington to make a difference. Municipally speaking, Washington is a cosmopolis brimming with hip artists and musicians, young entrepreneurs and high-spirited visionaries, who are reinvigorating the town. There's simply never been a better time to check out this vibrant and dynamic city.

Welcome to fabulous D.C. ...

THE 99 BEST of D.C.

Who needs another "Best" list? You do—if it comes with details and insider tips that make the difference between a good experience and a great one. We've pinpointed the 33 categories that make D.C. exciting, magnetic, and unforgettable, and picked the absolute three best places to go for each. With a little help from Night+Day, the nation's capital is yours for the taking.

Best

Always-Hot Tables

#1–3: Politics controls an awful lot in this town, including, at times, the popularity of restaurants. Not these three, though. Each of these establishments exudes its own particular exuberance, and is always at the top of everybody's lists, no matter what political wind blows.

Bistro Bis
Hotel George, 15 E St. NW, Capitol Hill, 202-661-2700 • Chic

The Draw: Proximity to the Capitol, and the fact that it's open daily for all three meals, means that stylish and sophisticated Bis is always a spectacle.

The Scene: Politicians, lobbyists, and the press consider Bis a godsend on the restaurant-scarce Hill. All of these types fill the dining room and bar, with everyone trying to use the food and the ambience to his own advantage. *Daily 7-10am, 11:30am-2:30pm, 5:30-10:30pm.* $$ B≡

Hot Tip: Pop in on a Friday evening after 7pm. Leaders, lawyers, reporters, and lobbyists who are supposed to be headed home very often wind up here for one last chance at cinching the deal, getting the story, or convincing the senator.

Cashion's Eat Place*
1819 Columbia Rd. NW, Adams Morgan, 202-797-1819 • Chic

The Draw: The intimate setting—a curving bar and a sliver of a dining room—and Ann Cashion's deeply satisfying food on the plate.

The Scene: When the weather cooperates, Cashion's opens up its glass front to the sidewalk, extending tables outdoors, which lightens up and enlarges the place. Otherwise, the dimly lit dining room and its slightly elevated bar are usually crowded with neighborhood regulars and others who simply wish they were. *Sun 11:30am-2:30pm and 5:30-10pm, Tue 5:30-10pm, Wed-Sat 5:30-11pm.* $$ B≡

Hot Tip: Try to dine here on a Friday, the night that the chef typically introduces a new extra-special something on the menu; arrive after 7:30pm to experience the best ready-for-the-weekend frisson.

Galileo
1110 21st St. NW, West End, 202-293-7191 • Classic

The Draw: Exquisite Piedmontese cuisine and a see-and-be-seen crowd.

The Scene: Doesn't matter that the seats are worn, or that even with reservations there's a wait, or that your waiter does not speak English. It's all part of the experience. And though you may not recognize them, your fellow diners include some VIPs. *Sun 5-10pm, Mon-Thu 11:30am-2:15pm and 5:30-10pm, Fri 11:30am-2:15pm and 5:30-10:30pm, Sat 5:30-10:30pm.* $$$ B≡

Hot Tip: Galileo has a chef's table, which seats up to eight people who get to watch the chef Amy at work (you don't have to reserve the entire table).

THE 99 BEST OF D.C.

 ## American Originals

#4–6: There's no mistaking an American original, whether it's Mark Twain, Duke Ellington, or Oprah. In terms of cuisine, it comes down to the perfect mélange of fresh ingredients, American ingenuity, and technique, informed by the best tastes of a particular culture or region.

Acadiana
901 New York Ave. NW, Penn Quarter, 202-408-8848 • Chic

The Draw: An abundance of Southern charm, elegant ambience, and a decadent menu that is a fitting tribute to New Orleans' proud culinary heritage.

The Scene: The only thing more welcoming than the waitstaff is the flaky biscuits slathered in Creole cream cheese and pepper jelly that greet you on arrival. The Southern hospitality makes the somewhat cavernous dining room feel downright cozy. *Mon-Thu 11:30am-2:30pm and 5:30-10:30pm, Fri 11:30am-2:30pm and 5:30-11pm, Sat 5:30-11pm. $$*

Hot Tip: If you haven't reserved ahead, try your luck at the bar, where a convivial crowd gathers after work.

Johnny's Half-Shell
2002 P St. NW, Capitol Hill, 202-296-2021 • Hip

The Draw: Its move from funky Dupont Circle to bigger digs on Capitol Hill only means there's more room to enjoy Johnny's special, good-mood vibe. Most everything else—the friendly service, Chesapeake Bay classics, and laid-back ambience—is the same.

The Scene: Customers are of all persuasions, political and otherwise, filling the tables on the terrace outside and the booths and long bar inside. *Mon-Thu 11:30am-10:30pm, Fri-Sat 11:30am-11pm. $$*

Hot Tip: A new feature is a taqueria carryout, open 7am-3pm weekdays and serving breakfast and lunch tacos.

Zola*
800 F St. NW, Penn Quarter, 202-654-0999 • Chic

The Draw: Teasing takes on American cuisine (yes, that would be single malt scotch you taste in the butterscotch pudding), a sexy dining room that plays on intrigue, and a great location add up to a hard-to-beat first stop on a night out.

The Scene: Housed within the same building as the International Spy Museum, Zola's décor thickens the plot with black-and-white images of spies and decoded KGB documents. A crush of exuberantly cruising singles fills the bar nightly, while in the dining room love affairs bloom and parties get under way. *Sun 5-9pm, Mon-Thu 11:30am-3pm and 5-10pm, Fri 11:30am-3pm and 5-11pm, Sat 5pm-11pm. $$*

Hot Tip: Come on a Saturday night and ask for tables 703 or 704.

Art Museums

#7–9: Washington art museums invite exploration by staging gospel brunches, singles nights, and jazz concerts, not to mention special sales of killer merchandise in their shops. Oh, and the art's pretty hot, too.

Corcoran Gallery of Art
500 17th St. NW, White House, 202-639-1700 • Classic

The Draw: The city's oldest art museum is a marble paean to Beaux Arts architecture, famous for its vast permanent collection of American art. Keep an eye out for blockbuster temporary exhibits as well.

The Scene: The Gallery is also home to an art school, whose students, with their cockscomb haircuts and outré outfits, often loll on the grand stone steps at the museum entrance. Galleries and a cafe stem off the magnificent, skylit double atrium. *Wed, Fri-Sun 10am-5pm, Thu 10am-9pm. $-*

Hot Tip: Tour the gallery on a Thursday evening, when the cafe stays open until 8pm, the crowds have thinned out, and, with advance reservations, you can attend a musical performance, cohosted by the gallery and an embassy.

Hirshhorn Museum and Sculpture Garden
Independence Ave. SW, at Seventh St., National Mall, 202-633-1000 • Chic

The Draw: One of the country's premier modern international art institutions, best known for its 20th-century Picassos and Warhols, Rodins and Henry Moores, but also for more contemporary works, the Hirshhorn is housed in a striking, cylindrical building.

The Scene: Modern art enthusiasts roam wide-eyed through the Hirshhorn. The museum's windowed interior walls overlook its central, open courtyard, capturing abundant daylight with which to view the Giacomettis, Calders, and de Koonings. *Museum: daily 10am-5:30pm; Sculpture Garden: daily 7:30am-dusk.*

Hot Tip: You must tour the sunken Sculpture Garden across Jefferson Drive, and be sure not to miss the sculpture displayed en route, on the Hirshhorn's plaza.

National Gallery of Art and Sculpture Garden
Constitution Ave. NW at Seventh St., National Mall, 202-737-4215 • Classic

The Draw: This is the crème de la crème of the capital's art museums, covering medieval to 21st-century Western art.

The Scene: The museum is vast. Allow plenty of time and don't try to see everything that's on display. *Sun 11am-6pm, Mon-Sat 10am-5pm; Summer hours: Sun 11am-7pm, Mon-Thu, Sat 10am-7pm, Fri 10am-9:30pm.*

Hot Tip: In the summer, the Sculpture Garden hosts free jazz performances on Friday evenings; in winter, the garden's pool turns into an ice rink for skating.

Brunches

#10–12: Brunch appeals to all types in D.C.—Capitol Hill aides and administration grunts indulging and fortifying themselves for the long week ahead, sleepy hipsters recovering from a late night, and Boomer and Gen-X families using it as an excuse for a social outing.

Café Atlantico
405 Eighth St. NW, Penn Quarter, 202-393-0812 • Chic

The Draw: Café Atlantico's Latino dim sum is the city's coolest brunch, serving tapas-sized portions of some 33 dishes. You can order à la carte or stuff yourself senseless by ordering the tasting menu.

The Scene: People are still waking up as they wander in, but by noon or so, the place picks up. The second floor of the spiraling multilevel restaurant is the liveliest, since the open kitchen is at one end, the bar at the other. Though the food is upscale-sumptuous, the ambience is chill. *Sun-Thu 11:30am-2:30pm and 5-10pm, Fri-Sat 11:30am-2:30pm and 5-11pm. $$*

Hot Tip: To experience it at its best, come at 12:30pm on a Sunday.

Lafayette Room
Hay-Adams Hotel, One Lafayette Sq., White House, 202-638-2570 • Classic

The Draw: This is the ultimate in traditionally elegant brunches, with a seasonally fresh, weekly changing menu, à la carte or buffet; a view of the White House through the windows; and a pianist playing classical and jazz standards.

The Scene: People come straight from services at St. John's Church ("Church of the Presidents") right across the street, or from Mass at nearby St. Matthew's Cathedral, or to celebrate a special anniversary or birthday. It draws hotel guests during the week, but at brunch, it's mostly locals—the sophisticated-in-pearls, rather than the flashy-diamonds set. *Sun 7-11am, Mon-Fri 6:30-11am, 11:30am-2pm, and 5:30-10pm, Sat 7-11am and 11:30am-2pm. $$$*

Hot Tip: Ask for table 8, which is by the fireplace, or table 18, which overlooks Lafayette Park and the White House.

Perrys
1811 Columbia Rd. NW, Adams Morgan, 202-234-6218 • Hip

The Draw: A playful vibe and delicious food at the raucous Sunday drag brunch.

The Scene: The velvety couches grouped among tables in the sunny second-floor room make Perrys ideal for groups of friends. Sassy drag queens ham it up while diners nosh on buffet fare from smoked salmon to sushi to crème brûlée. *Sun-Thu 5:30-10:30pm, Fri-Sat 5:30-11:30pm, Sun 10:30am-2:30pm. $$*

Hot Tip: The wait for a table is sometimes a blessing in disguise—it gives you time to load up on mimosas at the bar as Marilyn, Madonna, and Aretha shamelessly flirt on their path to performance.

Chef's Tables

#13–15: Open kitchens are a clever idea, for chefs and diners to get a good peek at each other. Chef's tables are that much more fun, especially when you're talking the best chefs in town. It's dinner theater in the 21st century.

Laboratorio del Galileo
1110 21st St. NW, West End, 202-293-7191 • Classic

The Draw: Star chef Roberto Donna is a hardworking magician, intense and focused as he's cooking, jovial in between courses, bantering with those seated up close, and then voilà, he presents his masterpieces.

The Scene: Unlike most chef's table situations, this one is a stand-alone restaurant within a restaurant. The kitchen and its eight tables of four people are in a separate room at the back of the larger restaurant (Galileo). The atmosphere within varies night to night, depending on the mood of the patrons as well as Donna. The 10- to 12-course feast lasts three to four hours. *Schedule varies, but usually Thu-Sat 7:30pm. $$$$*

Hot Tip: Ask for tables 7 and 8, which are closest to the counter, if you want the best seats for watching and chatting with Donna.

Minibar at Café Atlantico
405 Eighth St. NW, Penn Quarter, 202-393-0812 • Hip

The Draw: Two of D.C.'s top chefs take adventurous diners on a two-hour tour through 32 new-wave dishes.

The Scene: Located on the second floor of Café Atlantico, the understated six-person bar puts foodies face to face with culinary nirvana. The chefs will offer insight into the preparation of and philosophy behind dishes like lobster américaine and maracuya marshmallows. *Tue-Sat seatings at 6 and 8:30pm. $$$$*

Hot Tip: Because the bar can only accommodate two six-person seatings a night, reservations are a must. Call at 9am a month ahead of the day you'd like to dine.

Teatro Goldoni
1909 K St. NW, White House, 202-955-9494 • Chic

The Draw: The maître d' coddles you, explains the ingredients and history of each dish, and tells you about the wine pairings, leaving the chef to create one magnificent course after another of Venetian specialties until you say "Stop!"

The Scene: The chef's table here is a semicircular booth in the glass-enclosed kitchen. For five lucky diners, this is an intimate, up-close gastronomic adventure. *Chef's table hours: one seating for lunch at noon and for dinner at 6pm, but call to request your preferred time. $$$*

Hot Tip: Your booth companions, and the restaurant at large, are likelier to be livelier on weeknights.

THE 99 BEST OF D.C.

 Best

Dance Clubs

#16–18: Nowhere is D.C.'s work-hard, play-hard mentality more evident than on the dance floors where the city unwinds. From mega-clubs to cozy Latin lounges, D.C. draws stellar DJs that know how to get the District moving.

Five
1214 B 18th St. NW, Dupont Circle, 202-331-7123 • Hip

The Draw: While the rest of the city's bartenders are yelling "last call," Five is just getting warmed up. Internationally known house and hip-hop DJs keep the dance floor moving until 5am.

The Scene: Bubbled panels of light glow on the walls. Amber orbs hover over the bar. Brightly striped walls curve up over the second-floor lounge. And in the summer, you can catch the sunrise from the open-air rooftop tiki bar. *Sun 9pm-3am, Wed 9pm-3am, Thu 10pm-2am, Fri-Sat 9pm-5am.*

Hot Tip: Lines vary wildly depending on the night's DJ or special performer. Check out fivedc.com or call ahead to make sure you're not left waiting outside.

Habana Village
1834 Columbia Rd. NW, Adams Morgan, 202-462-6310 • Classic

The Draw: If you'd prefer to trade hip-hop and house for some Latin flavor, Habana Village is the place to be. Live bands play on all three levels, and ladies are seldom at a loss for a partner.

The Scene: Habana Village may not be as flashy as other D.C. clubs, but that's because the focus is less on posing and more on getting people moving. D.C.'s best mojitos—served properly with a stick of sugar cane—help, as does a friendly atmosphere in which young and old, Cuban and American mix on the dance floor. *Wed-Sat 6:30pm-3am.* Men

Hot Tip: Can't tell a mambo from a mojito? Lessons run Wednesday through Saturday 7:30-9:30pm.

Love
1350 Okie St. NE, Northeast, 202-636-9030 • Chic

The Draw: This is the ultimate nightlife experience from valet to VIP. If you're ready to spend, Love is the place to do it.

The Scene: Four floors of granite bars, plush couches, mahogany walls, and mammoth dance floors. Expect a high-rolling crowd from jet-setters to hip-hop stars, pro athletes to fashionistas. *Thu 9pm-3am, Fri-Sat 9pm-4am.*

Hot Tip: In a club this big, you need a home base. Reserve a table ahead of time and a concierge will be there on arrival to show you to your table and introduce you to the club.

Best Drinks with a View

#19–21: Cocktail bars and national art institutions alike cash in on the spectacular views made possible by the spacious layout of the National Mall and the District's low skyline. These bars let you take the high road to nightlife nirvana.

The Kennedy Center Roof Terrace Restaurant & Bar
2700 F St. NW, Foggy Bottom, 202-416-8555 • Classic

The Draw: With more than 3,000 world-class performances a year, it would be easy to overlook the Kennedy Center's other great asset—expansive views of the Potomac, Georgetown, and Roosevelt Island. However, the floor-to-ceiling windows and sprawling terrace ensure that the city gets the bravos it deserves.

The Scene: An older moneyed crowd drinks and dines inside, while performing-arts lovers of all ages hang at the KC Jazz Bar and the seasonal outdoor wine and martini bar. *Sun 11am-2pm, Mon-Wed 5-8pm, Thu-Sat 5-8:30pm, and after performances.*

Hot Tip: Dine on Marcel's pretheater menu, and they'll give you complimentary limo service to the Kennedy Center.

Sky Terrace at the Hotel Washington
2800 Pennsylvania Ave. NW, White House, 202-342-0444 • Classic

The Draw: Hitching a ride in the president's helicopter is the only way to score views of the National Mall and White House to rival those from the terrace of the Hotel Washington.

The Scene: These vistas have universal appeal, so expect to find young professionals, older couples, politicians, and tourists alike. Dress and menu are both casual. *Apr-Oct daily 11:30am-12:30am.*

Hot Tip: Washingtonians are notoriously bad at coping with cold weather, and the Hotel Washington is no exception. The roof terrace goes into hibernation each winter from late October until late March.

Tabaq Bistro*
1336 U St. NW, U Street Corridor, 202-265-0965 • Chic

The Draw: The glass walls and retractable roof of this chic restaurant lounge ensure sparkling nighttime vistas throughout the year.

The Scene: Expect an international crowd sipping martinis and sharing mezze from the subterranean hookah lounge to the red room bar to the glass terrace. It takes several flights of stairs to get to the top, but that doesn't stop women from making the climb in sky-high stilettos. Men opt for button-downs and dress pants. *Sun 11am-4pm and 5-11pm, Mon-Thu 5-11pm, Fri 3pm-midnight, Sat 11am-4pm and 5pm-midnight.*

Hot Tip: Get there in time to see the sunset, and you'll have enough space to enjoy yourself without being jostled by the crowds.

Fine Dining

#22–24: Washington wasn't always a restaurant town, nor was fine dining always a matter of great choice. Today, at long last, the capital offers quite a number and variety of these white-tablecloth, haute cuisine establishments.

Marcel's
2401 Pennsylvania Ave. NW, Foggy Bottom, 202-296-1166 • Classic

The Draw: Superb French cooking is nothing new to the capital, but French cooking with a Flemish flair sets Marcel's apart.

The Scene: With its stone walls and Provençal furnishings, Marcel's puts one in a South of France frame of mind, even as one glances around the room to note Washington figureheads, global bankers, and couples who appreciate Marcel's rather old-fashioned (in a good way) emphasis on graciousness. *Sun 5:30-9:30pm, Mon-Thu 5:30-10pm, Fri-Sat 5:30-11pm.* $$$

Hot Tip: Marcel's chef/owner Robert Wiedmaier is best known for his boudin blanc, a delicate white sausage served with truffle red wine essence and celery root puree.

Obelisk
2029 P St. NW, Dupont Circle, 202-872-1180 • Classic

The Draw: The nightly prix-fixe menu presents only two or three choices for each of five courses, but regulars know that any one of these choices assures a taste of perfection.

The Scene: A simply decorated, one-room, second-floor townhouse restaurant might seem an unlikely setting for a temple of fine dining, but that's exactly purist-owner Peter Pastan's point: It's all about the food—and about relaxing enough to enjoy it. *Tue-Sat 6-10pm.* $$$

Hot Tip: Obelisk specializes in intriguingly rewarding Italian vintages not found on other wine lists. Take advantage of the unusual offerings.

Tosca
1112 F St. NW, Penn Quarter, 202-367-1990 • Chic

The Draw: Tosca's elegant décor and chef Cesare Lanfranconi's hallmark northern Italian dishes serve as the perfect antidote to the world worries that rage just outside the door.

The Scene: Lawyers and other downtown professionals frequent this oasis for lunch, and couples and livelier parties join them for dinner. *Mon-Thu 11:30am-2:30pm and 5:30-10:30pm, Fri 11:30am-2:30pm and 5:30-11pm, Sat 5:30-11pm.* $$$

Hot Tip: For privacy and romance, ask for table 50, Tosca's only alcove.

Gay Bars

#25–27: With one of the largest gay communities in the country, D.C. has always had a vibrant same-sex nightlife scene. From cruising along the "P Street Beach" south of Dupont Circle to dancing at clubs in the 17th Street "Gayberhood," nightlife options run the spectrum from casual haunts to wild scenes.

Cobalt
1639 R St. NW, Dupont Circle, 202-462-6569 • Chic

The Draw: Cobalt's motto? "We feed you the beat, and what you do with it is your own business." It's fitting for a bar known for its weekly "best package" contests (on Thursdays) and its wild weekend dance parties.

The Scene: Cruise downstairs in the 30 Degrees cocktail lounge before heading upstairs to dance to retro remixes. The crowd tends to be slightly younger than at other gay bars along the 17th Street strip. *Sun 6pm-1:30am, Mon 5pm-1:30am, Tue-Thu 5pm-2am, Fri-Sat 5pm-3am.*

Hot Tip: The party doesn't get started until after 11pm. Grab cocktails on the patio downstairs at Food Bar D.C.

Duplex Diner
2004 18th St. NW, Adams Morgan, 202-265-7828 • Hip

The Draw: A menu of childhood favorites like grilled cheese and tomato soup lends a playful and laid-back vibe to an otherwise chic restaurant and bar.

The Scene: Bright colors splash over the walls and booths. Martini glasses and a disco ball replace the crystals on an old chandelier. The light, friendly vibe matches the crowd. *Sun-Mon 6-11pm, Tue-Wed 6pm-12:30am, Thu 6pm-1am, Fri-Sat 6pm-1:30am.*

Hot Tip: If you're looking to meet people, hold off until later in the evening when patrons shift from dining to drinking.

Halo
1435 P St. NW, U Street Corridor, 202-797-9730 • Chic

The Draw: Some of the best cocktails in the District (try the blueberry mojito), a suave space, and a grown-up crowd.

The Scene: Halo is configured for conversation: Ultramod banquettes line the walls, and you never have to scream over the jazzy lounge music to make yourself heard. It's a sophisticated space for a sophisticated crowd. *Sun-Thu 5pm-1:30am, Fri-Sat 5pm-2:30am.*

Hot Tip: Friday postwork and Saturday late-night lines are inevitable and unavoidable. Arriving early is the only answer.

Best — Hot Chefs

#28–30: Highly skilled though many chefs may be, rare's the one who rightly wears the artist's crown. Rarer still are chefs whose artistry is as delicious as it is inventive. These restaurants and the wizards behind them are renowned throughout the culinary world.

Citronelle
3000 M St. NW, Georgetown, 202-625-2150 • Classic

The Draw: A passionate chef with a creative streak who consistently turns out inventive French cuisine that creates excitement in the dining room.

The Scene: This is the first place local foodies take visitors to impress them. Politicians, celebs, and executives fill the dining room nightly, though Saturday is busiest. *Daily 6:30-10:30am, Sun 6-9pm, Mon-Sat and 6-9:30pm.* $$$$ B=

Hot Tip: Michel Richard offers a chef's table experience nightly, but you must have a minimum of six people to reserve it. If you're not in a group, ask for a table with a kitchen view and you'll at least be able to see Richard at play.

CityZen
1330 Maryland Ave. SW, Southwest, 202-787-6006 • Chic

The Draw: CityZen tapped famed French Laundry chef de cuisine Eric Ziebold to open its restaurant in 2004, and he offers plenty of "chef surprises" between sophisticated courses.

The Scene: Come Thursday through Saturday to dine in this minimalist cathedral-like dining room, whose banquettes and dimly lit tables are filled with locals and visiting celebs. *Tue-Thu 6-9:30pm, Fri-Sat 5:30-9:30pm.* $$$$ B=

Hot Tip: For intimate dinners, ask whether the private party area is available; when the space has not been reserved, its few tables are open to couples.

Palena
3529 Connecticut Ave. NW, Upper Northwest, 202-537-9250 • Chic

The Draw: Onetime White House chef Frank Ruta wins over everyone with his range of exuberant tastes, from fine dining to cafe entrées.

The Scene: Sensing they're walking into someplace special, diners dress at least one notch up from casual, even though Palena doesn't care. The old-world décor of the main dining room feels romantic and celebratory, so couples and parties head there. Younger, more spontaneous walk-ins prefer the room upfront. *Tue-Sat 5:30-10pm.* $$$ B= *Cafe: Mon-Sat 5:30-10pm.* $-

Hot Tip: Palena's Monday nights are one of the city's coolest, though most crowded, dining scenes: Only the nonreservable front room and bar and the cafe menu are available, which draws a standing-room-only mob of 20-somethings hungry for Palena's famous cheeseburger and fried lemons.

Hotel Bars

#31–33: Back in the day, many politicians lived in local hotels while Congress was in session. As such, hotel watering holes have a rich history as a meeting place for D.C.'s power players. Today's hotel bars, which cater to a much more diverse clientele, get the ambience and cocktail list just right.

Degrees
3100 South St. NW, Georgetown, 202-912-4100 • Chic

The Draw: Ritz Carlton is synonymous with indulgence, and the ambrosial cocktails served here are no exception.

The Scene: Star athletes occupy velvety couches alongside black-tie–bedecked politicos, rich rock stars, and an otherwise fashionable clientele. The bar draws inspiration from its past life as an incinerator with exposed brick walls and fiery hues. *Sun-Thu 2:30pm-midnight, Fri-Sat 2:30pm-2am.*

Hot Tip: You're likely to fall in love with the 1940s-style etched barware. Enough people have requested them that the striped orange and red polka-dotted glasses are available for purchase at the bar.

Helix Lounge*
1430 Rhode Island Ave. NW, Dupont Circle, 202-462-9001 • Hip

The Draw: Your Coco Chanel cocktail arrives on a glow-in-the-dark tray. Your white pod stool lights up when you sit down. Kookiness reigns at the Hotel Helix's lounge.

The Scene: If you dig pop art and *People*, you'll fall for Helix's nouveau Austin Powers vibe. The silliness of the setup encourages playfulness among the hipsters and visitors alike. The summertime cabanas are an added bonus—oversized sunglasses are a must. *Sun-Thu 5-11:30pm, Fri-Sat 5pm-1:30am.*

Hot Tip: Don't miss out on the greasy goodness of bar menu items like beer cheese dip and potato martini (mashed, not stirred, with blue cheese butter).

Round Robin
1401 Pennsylvania Ave. NW, Downtown, 202-628-9100 • Classic

The Draw: The well-heeled from around the world swill at the same bar that has served politicians and poets alike, and that inspired verse from Walt Whitman and prose from Nathaniel Hawthorne.

The Scene: Portraits of illustrious former patrons adorn the hunter green walls surrounding the round mahogany bar. Suits sip old-school cocktails like sidecars and gin rickeys. But no cocktail is more revered than the mint julep, which is still made according to the recipe orator Henry Clay wrote in the 1850s. *Sun noon-midnight, Mon-Sat noon-1am.*

Hot Tip: Bartender and Washington history buff Jim Hewes relates stories from the bar's past and creates themed menus like "All the Presidents' Cocktails."

THE 99 BEST OF D.C.

Indian Restaurants

#34–36: Locals have always known where to go for a serviceable curry. Until recently, that's all they ever wanted. But at these sparkling new Indian restaurants that have exploded onto the scene, you'll find hot hangouts, exotic drinks, and seductive cuisine.

The Bombay Club
815 Connecticut Ave. NW, White House, 202-659-3727 • Classic

The Draw: This perennial favorite put Indian food on D.C.'s map, paving the way for the current craze. With its rajahlike service, imperial setting, and mouthwatering tandooris, the Bombay Club never fails to get its highbrow crowd purring.

The Scene: The Bombay Club at lunch seats ambidextrous professionals simultaneously working their Blackberries and flourishing forks. Nighttime and weekends, the same sorts return, somewhat calmer and more relaxed. *Sun 11:30am-2:30pm and 5:30-9pm, Mon-Thu 11:30am-2:30pm and 6:30-10:30pm, Fri 11:30am-2:30pm and 6-11pm, Sat 6-11pm.* $$

Hot Tip: Bombay Club is a good bet for vegetarians.

Indique
3512-14 Connecticut Ave. NW, Upper Northwest, 202-244-6600 • Chic

The Draw: Purists will tell you this is the truest Indian cuisine in town, but that's not what jams the place on weekends. This uncommonly attractive restaurant has that extra bit of buzz that draws urbanites from all over town.

The Scene: Indique's crowd is a mix of neighborhood and embassy regulars weekdays and early evenings. Make the scene on a Friday or Saturday night sans reservation and you're in for a three-pomegranate-martini wait, but you'll be in good, pumped-up company. *Sun-Thu noon-3pm and 5:30-10:30pm, Fri-Sat noon-3pm and 5:30-11pm.* $

Hot Tip: Just because it's not on the menu doesn't mean it can't be done, so if you have a favorite Indian dish you don't see listed, ask!

Mitsitam
National Museum of the American Indian, Independence Ave. SW, National Mall, 202-633-1000 • Hip

The Draw: When is Indian cuisine not curries and tandooris? When it's salmon cakes from the Pacific Northwest and buffalo burgers from the Great Plains. Though the restaurant is in a museum, the food's delicious.

The Scene: Hungry tourists and staff from neighboring museums fill the cafeteria on the first floor of the National Museum of the American Indian. *Daily 10am-5:15pm, full menu 11am-3pm.* $-

Hot Tip: Don't leave without trying the fry bread with cinnamon and honey.

Insider D.C. Experiences

#37–39: If you're lucky, you've got a D.C. buddy who's more than happy to cruise around town, introducing you to his favorite insider haunts for a taste of local color. But if he's still sleeping off last night's indoctrination, or you're otherwise on your own, go native with one of these experiences.

Dupont Circle
Intersection of Massachusetts, Connecticut, and New Hampshire Aves. • Chic

The Draw: Washingtonians of all stripes flock to this neighborhood for its wide array of diversions—art galleries, small museums, and boutiques. Above all, it excels as a place to hang out, whether on the grassy circle or in the cafes, bookstores, bars, and coffeehouses that line the streets radiating off the circle.

The Scene: Beckoning galleries and shops pull in and relinquish the lazy, brazen, pierced, and chic, mostly but not entirely youngish, crowd.

Hot Tip: Don't miss Kramerbooks & Afterwords (1517 Connecticut Ave.), especially if you're out late on the weekend: The bookstore, cafe, and live music venue stays open straight through from Friday morning until Sunday night.

Eastern Market
Seventh St. SE, at North Carolina Ave., Capitol Hill, 202-544-0083 • Hip

The Draw: Historic Capitol Hill has a small-town feel to it, best appreciated at this 133-year-old treasure, whose high-quality fresh produce and other foods make going to market an almost (it's closed Mondays) daily ritual for the young families, low-salaried singles, and neighborhood elders who live nearby.

The Scene: Inside South Hall, vendors at permanent stalls sell produce, meats, fish, flowers, baked goods, cheese, and everything else you can imagine to an endless flow of chatty customers of all ages, races, and persuasions. The market extends to outdoor stalls on the weekend, including a Sunday flea market. *Indoor market: Sun 9am-4pm, Tue-Sat 7am-6pm; outdoor market: Sat-Sun 7am-4pm (farmers market) and Sun 9am-6pm (flea market).*

Hot Tip: The Market Lunch counter's blueberry pancakes are legendary.

Union Station
50 Massachusetts Ave. NE, Capitol Hill, 202-289-1908 • Classic

The Draw: Though Union Station's primary purpose is as a hub for train and subway travel, its lofty architecture and two levels of fabulous chain and homegrown shops make a visit here a pleasure.

The Scene: Night and day, Union Station is a major thoroughfare for commuters. Stay out of their way, and enjoy the abundant shopping opportunities. *24/7, stores Sun noon-6pm, Mon-Sat 10am-9pm.*

Hot Tip: Find specialty shops Destination: D.C. and Making History to score some of the city's best souvenirs.

THE 99 BEST OF D.C.

International Scenes

#40–42: From sipping tej in Little Ethiopia to eating pupusas in Mount Pleasant and dancing with diplomats from the more than 175 embassies, D.C. has one of the most vibrant international scenes in the world. These bars encourage cultural diplomacy in the form of cocktails and conversation.

Agua Ardiente*
1250 24th St. NW, Foggy Bottom, 202-833-8500 • Chic

The Draw: The sexy blend of Euro cool and Latin American heat ensures that at Agua, seduction won't get lost in translation.

The Scene: From bhangra to salsa, Agua's DJs pack the dance floor with swaying hips and wandering eyes. Couples flirt in candlelit alcoves, and groups slip past gauze curtains to the VIP lounge. *Mon-Wed 5:30-10:30pm, Thu-Fri 5:30-11pm, Sat 6-11pm.*

Hot Tip: If you're feeling adventurous, try the Latin American liqueur after which the restaurant lounge is named. It's roughly translated as "fire water," and tastes like it too.

Maté
3101 K St. NW, Georgetown, 202-333-2006 • Chic

The Draw: Exotic cocktails made with South American yerba mate tea—known for its Red Bull–like qualities—mix well with the exotic crowd draped on the chic lounges.

The Scene: The '60s-inspired décor could be a nod to the jet-set lifestyle that much of Maté's clientele lives. The pretty people nosh on Latin-Asian sushi while a DJ hovering above the crowd spins downtempo lounge with Brazilian beats. *Sun-Thu 5pm-2am, Fri-Sat 5pm-3am.*

Hot Tip: Doormen make sure you dress the part: Tailored blazers over graphic tees should work for men. Ladies, go funky with Miu Miu or Missoni.

Russia House
1800 Connecticut Ave. NW, Dupont Circle, 202-234-9433 • Classic

The Draw: The stately décor and private dining rooms give visitors a window into the diplomat's life.

The Scene: Decadence reigns in the marble, silks, and dark wood. Expect an eclectic crowd of Russian expats, cultured couples, and hipster kids with a penchant for strong booze and Tolstoy. *Mon-Thu 5pm-midnight, Fri 5pm-2am, Sat 6pm-2am.*

Hot Tip: If you're exploring the vodka menu, plan a few shots ahead and the bartender will prechill the liquor for you.

Live Music

#43–45: Today's hip-hop scene thrives on the same blocks that once hosted legendary jazz greats like Duke Ellington and Sarah Vaughan. A new generation of indie rockers carries the torch of the famous punk label Dischord. Want an entrée into D.C.'s rich musical history? Try one of these clubs.

The Black Cat
1811 14th St. NW, U Street Corridor, 202-667-7960 • Hip

The Draw: Black Cat wants you to get intimate with rockers: The 7,000-square-foot concert hall hosts acts that in other East Coast cities normally play massive venues.

The Scene: See the latest Pitchfork darlings, local punk acts, and poetry nights. On the weekends, DJs throw Brit pop, indie rock, '80s alt-pop, and hip-hop dance parties. *Sun-Thu 8pm-2am, Fri-Sat 7pm-3am.* C≡

Hot Tip: Those in the know turn down the faux-hip PBR for the equally cheap but exponentially better house beer, the Red Room Ale.

Blues Alley
1073 Wisconsin Ave. NW, Georgetown, 202-337-4141 • Classic

The Draw: The candlelit tables and tiny stage will transport you to the supper clubs of the 1930s.

The Scene: Contrary to the name, Blues Alley is a straight-up jazz club, located down an alley between a T-shirt store and a sushi joint. Jazz hounds eat Cajun dishes while top-name musicians play two sets per night. *Daily 6pm-12:30am.* C≡

Hot Tip: Music lovers covet the chance to see nationally known acts in this intimate setting, so be forewarned that talking over the music is a big no-no.

Madam's Organ
2461 18th St. NW, Adams Morgan, 202-667-5370 • Hip

The Draw: The 25-foot-tall busty madam's mural lures 18th Street revelers from blocks away. But this quirky bar doesn't need a sexy painting to sell the nightly drunken throwdowns to blues, Latin, and funk.

The Scene: The interior resembles a cross between a gin joint and an antique store with a hodgepodge of trombones, vintage bikes, nun pictures, and bear heads. A rowdy crowd of music lovers dances on the ground floor, sits around the balcony's roaring fireplace, and throws back whiskey on the roof deck. *Sun-Thu 5pm-2am, Fri-Sat 5pm-3am.* C≡

Hot Tip: Redheads always get half-price Rolling Rocks.

Local Favorites

#46–48: There's something to be said for the local watering hole, for pretension-free imbibing that eschews door policies and VIP sections in favor of good beer and friendly people. These bars have won the hearts and bar tabs of the locals.

The Brickskeller Saloon
1523 22nd St. NW, Dupont Circle, 202-293-1885 • Hip

The Draw: More than 1,300 varieties of beers from 57 different countries. 'Nough said.

The Scene: The walls of the labyrinthine downstairs bar are packed with beer memorabilia. The higher ceilings and newer finish of the upstairs bar make for more pleasant if louder drinking quarters. *Sun 6pm-2am, Mon-Thu 11:30am-2am, Fri 11:30am-3am, Sat 6pm-3am.*

Hot Tip: Knock back one too many? Crash upstairs at the Mariflex Hotel.

Café Saint-Ex*
1847 14th St. NW, U Street Corridor, 202-265-7839 • Hip

The Draw: With sunny sidewalk brunches, cozy bistro dinners, and late-night dancing, Café Saint-Ex is a neighborhood go-to place for good food, good beer, and good people.

The Scene: The pressed-tin ceilings, basement lounge (dubbed Gate 54), and antique bar have a Latin-Quarter brasserie feel. The crowd skews arty during the week, cocktail-swilling on the weekends. *Sun, Tue-Thu 11am-1:30am, Mon 5pm-1:30am, Fri-Sat 11am-2:30am.*

Hot Tip: The basement lounge gets uncomfortably crowded Friday and Saturday. Stick to the upstairs, and check out the stellar downstairs DJs Sunday through Thursday nights.

The Wonderland Ballroom
1101 Kenyon St. NW, Upper Northwest, 202-232-5263 • Hip

The Draw: The come-as-you-are vibe of this neighborhood dive is infectious.

The Scene: The first floor—decorated with vintage album covers and furnished with a Pac-Man table and bench seats from a minivan—is host to one of D.C.'s best jukeboxes. Bands and DJ rule the second floor. *Sun-Thu 5pm-2am, Fri-Sat 5pm-3am.*

Hot Tip: Check your pretensions at the door, and don't disobey the directive on the jukebox: "Free your mind and your ass will follow, so please shoot for dance music after 11pm. Thanks, George Clinton." If George Clinton is telling you to get down, you best be getting down.

> Best

Luxury Spas

#49–51: Beneath their straitlaced Brooks Brothers suits and no-nonsense navy blue ensembles, Washington men and women are buffed and oiled to a fare-thee-well. See for yourself by visiting the same full-treatment spas they frequent.

I Spa at the Willard
1401 Pennsylvania Ave. NW, Downtown, 202-942-2700 • Classic

The Draw: The outdoor relaxation deck overlooking the hotel courtyard and services like the Jet Lag body treatment add a touch of resort to this luxurious spa.

The Scene: The Willard's elite hotel guests are delighted first customers, though upscale downtown execs are starting to stop in for Orange Blossom pedicures and Lemon Sugar body polishes. Treatments include those for couples, who have their own room and secluded outdoor deck, and men, for whom there is a Gentleman's Escape package. *Sun 9am-5pm, Mon-Sat 9am-7pm.* $$$$

Hot Tip: Get a kick from champagne: I Spa's exclusive Body Champagne by Algotherm treatment douses you with champagne, then wraps you in seaweed.

SomaFit Spa and Fitness Center
2121 Wisconsin Ave. NW, Upper Georgetown, 202-965-2121 • Chic

The Draw: The main highlight of this spa is its wide range of options—from yoga class to massage, to fitness training, to facial—and the fact that it's open to all, no club membership required.

The Scene: The spa's got that white-on-white look that's so popular now. Its demographic includes *Washington Post* A-section newsmakers and lissome beauties in their 20s, here as much to hide out as to work out. *Sun 10am-6pm, Mon-Fri 6am-9pm, Sat 8am-6pm.* $$$$

Hot Tip: If your raft of Georgetown purchases gives you shopper's shoulder, hail a taxi for the short ride up Wisconsin Avenue to SomaFit for a pick-me-up 10- or 20-minute massage. (Best call first to make sure a masseuse is available.)

Spa at the Mandarin Oriental
1330 Maryland Ave. SW, National Mall, 202-787-6100 • Chic

The Draw: Lit candles and smells of cinnamon lead you along the winding hallway to this most luxurious of Washington spas, which has a treatment for every ancient tradition: Chinese, Ayurvedic, Balinese, Thai, Mediterranean, Arabic; and a massage for every body need: aromatherapy, deep tissue, shiatsu, Reiki, oriental foot, and maternity.

The Scene: This 10,500-square-foot spa is often booked, especially on weekends, when Washington's weary social set arrives to reboot its hard drives with a massage and the holistic foot and nail treatment with hot stones, a specialty for which the spa is known. *Sun 9am-7pm, Mon-Sat 9am-9pm.* $$$$

Hot Tip: Consider trying the aqua yoga offered here.

Best

Monumental Sculptures

#52–54: In a city so adorned with stone-carved buildings, equestrian statues, historic figures, and other marble embellishments, it's sometimes hard to distinguish the notable from the hoi polloi. You'll have no trouble with these three.

Jefferson Memorial
Ohio Dr. SW, south shore of the Tidal Basin, Southwest, 202-426-6841 • Classic

The Draw: To call on Jefferson here is to remember and pay tribute to the man whose words declared our country's independence and whose actions as founding father and third president helped solidify that freedom.

The Scene: The 19-foot-high statue wears a full-length, fur-collared coat and stands gracefully erect with eyes straight ahead. The Jefferson Memorial sits on the banks of the Tidal Basin facing the Washington Monument.

Hot Tip: Don't drive here. Arrive at a more relaxed pace by walking along the pathway bordering the Tidal Basin that leads from the nearby FDR Memorial to the Jefferson.

Lincoln Memorial
Western end of the Mall, National Mall, 202-426-6842 • Classic

The Draw: Citizens of the world find inspiration and pleasure in visiting this memorial to contemplate the life and spirit of the nation's 16th president, the man who forged a peace out of the Civil War and united the country behind Thomas Jefferson's words in the Declaration of Independence, "... that all men are created equal."

The Scene: The luminous white marble temple that houses the seated statue of Abraham Lincoln stands at the far end of the National Mall. This is a must for anyone visiting the city for the first time.

Hot Tip: In a vault beneath the memorial is a small museum providing a bit of history and—more to the point, perhaps—bathrooms.

Washington Monument
On the Mall, at 15th St. NW, National Mall, 202-426-6841 • Classic

The Draw: Sorry, Mr. President, but it's the stellar 360-degree view that is the real draw here: of the city, and 60 miles beyond when the skies are all clear.

The Scene: To make it to the top of the 555-plus-feet-tall obelisk requires standing in line, first to obtain a ticket, then to gain admission to the elevator that takes you to the tip of the city's tallest building. Your traveling companions will form a global microcosm, whom you may come to know very very well, depending on the length of the line. *Daily 9am-5pm.*

Hot Tip: Admission is free, but do yourself a favor and spend the $1.50 to order an advance ticket.

Only-in-D.C. Restaurants

#55–57: Very few restaurants are real Washington institutions, by dint of history, clientele, character, and locale. Each is so much a part of the fabric of the city that if you took either one away from the other, neither the restaurant nor the city would be the same.

Ben's Chili Bowl
1213 U St. NW, U Street Corridor, 202-667-0909 • Hip

The Draw: Not even the 1968 riots that devastated the District were able to close down this Washington institution. You can still sit at the same counter that has fed Ella Fitzgerald, Nat King Cole, and countless D.C. denizens since its 1958 opening.

The Scene: Expect the hallmarks of a classic diner: grease, neon, and regulars. Afternoons tend to attract folks from the area, while late nights feed an eclectic mix of partiers. *Sun noon-8pm, Mon-Thu 6am-2am, Fri-Sat 6am-4am.* $-

Hot Tip: You can't go wrong with a classic like the chili-smothered half smokes.

The Monocle
107 D St. NE, Capitol Hill, 202-546-4488 • Classic

The Draw: Sup at the Monocle and you'll feel like a player in backroom politicking as senators, representatives, and staff from both sides of the aisle, as well as lobbyists and the occasional Supreme Court justice, dine here at lunch and dinner. The bar is a lively after-hours watering hole for congressional staff.

The Scene: When Congress is in session, these rooms are packed weekdays with suited-up men and women, sitting at small tables, checking their Blackberries as they exchange Hill gossip. A collegial atmosphere reigns despite political differences. *Mon-Fri 11:30am-midnight.* $$

Hot Tip: When Congress is out, look elsewhere.

The Willard Room
1401 Pennsylvania Ave. NW, Downtown, 202-637-7440 • Classic

The Draw: Those who miss grace and refinement in today's society know they will find it in the historic Willard Hotel's Edwardian dining room, whose décor recalls old-world grandeur and whose staff treat guests like royalty.

The Scene: Real-life kings, queens, and the otherwise powerful sit at elaborately set tables well spaced between tall scagliola columns, in a lofty dining room with paneled walls and crystal chandeliers. It looks like a movie set and is often used as one. *Mon-Thu 7:30-10am, 11:30am-2pm, and 6-10pm, Fri 7:30-10am, 11:30am-2pm, and 5:30-10pm, Sat 5:30-10pm.* $$$$

Hot Tip: A drink, specifically a mint julep, in the Willard's Round Robin bar is a must preceding or following your meal.

THE 99 BEST OF D.C.

 Best

Outdoor Activities

#58–60: While its political and cultural institutions might keep you endlessly entertained indoors, the capital's assorted outdoor attractions hold their own refreshing allure.

National Mall
Bounded by Constitution and Independence Aves. and the Lincoln Memorial and the Capitol.

The Draw: Promenade the two-mile length of this green sweep of the Mall, between the Capitol and Lincoln Memorial. Fly a kite on the Washington Monument grounds. Or order paninis from the National Gallery of Art's Pavilion cafe and picnic in the Sculpture Garden.

The Scene: Events take place here year-round, whether it's the Smithsonian Kite Festival in spring or the Library of Congress National Book Festival in September. The Mall is a central pedestrian axis used by locals and visitors in pursuit of exercise, a shortcut to work, tourist attractions, and a beautiful stroll.

Hot Tip: Keep your eyes peeled for your senator or representative trotting past you on the path. A number of congressional members are known to take their morning or evening constitutional along this stretch.

Pedal Boats
Raoul Wallenberg Pl./15th St. SW off Independence Ave., Southwest, 202-479-2426 • Hip

The Draw: On a pretty day, it's a lark to pedal yourself silly around the Tidal Basin, with the Jefferson Memorial, the Washington Monument, and the blooming (or not) cherry trees cheering you on.

The Scene: This is a popular diversion during the summer. Expect long lines, especially on weekends. *Daily mid-Mar–Labor Day, Wed-Sun Labor Day-Columbus Day weekend 10am-6pm, weather permitting.* $-

Hot Tip: Lather up with sunscreen, for the Tidal Basin is totally exposed.

Rock Creek Park
From the Potomac River near the Kennedy Center, northwest through the city into Maryland, 202-895-6070 • Classic

The Draw: Rock Creek Park is a heavenly refuge of nearly 2,000 acres, for anyone who wants to bike, hike, ride horses, picnic, or escape from pavement.

The Scene: Rent a bike and pedal along the flat pathway that parallels the Potomac River. Cycle south to connect with the Mall; cycle north to remain in Rock Creek Park, whose path winds 11 miles through woods into Maryland.

Hot Tip: Thompson's Boat Center (2900 Virginia Ave. NW, 202-333-4861), across from the Kennedy Center, rents bikes as well as boats.

Outdoor Drinking

#61–63: Washingtonians have never dealt well with winter, so when the first traces of spring sunshine appear sometime in April, bar-goers are quick to welcome it on the city's patio, deck, and rooftop watering holes.

Gazuza
1629 Connecticut Ave. NW, Dupont Circle, 202-667-5500 • Chic

The Draw: The pretty people lounge on low-slung beds on the all-weather patio and watch vintage films flickering on neighboring brick walls.

The Scene: Gazuza mishmashes a globe's worth of influences: from a Spanish name, to a Japanese sushi menu, to Latin music mixed with Arabic beats. The chichi crowd is a similar mélange of styles. *Daily 5pm-last call (often around 1:30am).*

Hot Tip: Everyone obsesses over the second-floor patio, but the inside lounge's sleek candlelit seating area is another perfect place to share a hookah and flirt over exotic cocktails.

Local 16
1604 U St. NW, U Street Corridor, 202-265-2828 • Chic

The Draw: The only views from Local 16's rooftop are of the stars. Sightlines obscured by plants and neighboring buildings give the bar the feel of an exclusive private fête.

The Scene: Dark wood, sumptuous fabrics, and candlelit corners set the mood for seduction in the first- and second-floor bars. The fashionable crowd complements the scene with plunging necklines and tailored shirts. *Sun-Thu 5:30pm-2am, Fri-Sat 5:30pm-3am.*

Hot Tip: Reserve a rooftop table for early evening tapas in order to avoid the often interminable waits that come with nice weather.

Sequoia
3000 K St. NW, Georgetown, 202-944-4200 • Chic

The Draw: Summers find the four-level riverfront patio of Sequoia packed with the rich and single from happy hour until last call.

The Scene: Margaritas in hand and ready to mingle, a flirtatious crowd of young professionals enjoys Sequoia's views of Roosevelt Island and the Kennedy Center. The classiness of the attached restaurant and bar—a towering structure of glass and warm cherry wood—ensures a more upscale clientele than in some of the more frat-like neighboring bars. *Sun 10:30am-12:30am, Mon-Thu 11:30am-12:30am, Fri-Sat 11:30am-1:30am.*

Hot Tip: The food at Sequoia can be so-so. Stop off before or after at the dumpling bar at nearby Bangkok Joe's or the Latin sushi lounge Maté.

Patriotic Adventures

#64–66: Where else can you see the original Declaration of Independence, Congress debating a bill, and the world's largest collection of American art? Visit these sites for a greater sense of American history, democratic principles, and culture.

National Archives
Constitution Ave. NW. bet. Seventh and Ninth Sts., National Mall, 202-357-5000 • Classic

The Draw: On display at the National Archives are the 1776 Declaration of Independence, 1787 Constitution, and 1789 Bill of Rights.

The Scene: Inside the Rotunda, wall murals re-create historical scenes and glass cases display the Charters of Freedom. A hushed atmosphere prevails as visitors read the inked words penned by Thomas Jefferson and fellow founding fathers. *Labor Day–late-Mar 10am-5:30pm, Apr-Memorial Day weekend 10am-7pm, Memorial Day–Labor Day 10am-9pm.*

Hot Tip: Reservations, made at least six months in advance, are recommended; you can reserve a space to tour on your own or with a docent.

Smithsonian American Art Museum / National Portrait Gallery
F St. NW, bet. Eighth and Ninth Sts., Penn Quarter, 202-275-1500 • Chic

The Draw: The world's largest collection of American art and portraiture is finally back in the public eye after six long years of museum renovation.

The Scene: Inside, portraits of 42 American presidents and art by Edward Hopper and Georgia O'Keeffe hang in dazzling vaulted, skylit galleries; outside, the scene swirls with bars, clubs, and restaurants. *Daily 11:30am-7pm.*

Hot Tip: If you're hungry, all you have to do is make a mad, 30-second dash across F Street to Zola, Poste, or the Spy Café, splendid eating options all.

U.S. Capitol
East Capitol St. at First St. NE/NW, Capitol Hill, 202-225-6827 • Classic

The Draw: The nation's past, present, and future are on display in the august halls and chambers of this building. Try to attend a session of Congress to view on- and off-camera legislative proceedings.

The Scene: Security procedures encumber the touring process, so expect lines to obtain tour passes and lines to take your turn on the tour. Guided tours go to the stupendous Rotunda and National Statuary Hall. With passes obtained from your senator or representative, you can visit the Senate or House gallery to watch a live session of Congress. *Mon-Sat 9am-4:30pm.*

Hot Tip: Contact your senator or representative in advance to obtain gallery passes for a specific day and you'll save time and hassles.

Best

Politico Sightings

#67–69: New York has its financial "it" people, L.A. has its movie stars, and D.C. has its politicians. Though power players come and go, these establishments consistently cater to a who's who of D.C. politicos. Keep your eyes peeled and your ears open, and you'll get a taste of what makes the city tick.

Café Milano*
3251 Prospect St. NW, Georgetown, 202-333-6183 • Chic

The Draw: This is *the* place to see and be seen in D.C. Bill Clinton loves Milano. Ambassadors, diplomats, and congressional members turn up all the time, as do Hollywood actors in town to shoot a film or promote a cause.

The Scene: Regulars jostle with studly Euro males and comely women for space at the bar. Famous faces hold court at tables scattered around the room. There's really no place to hide in the window-fronted main dining room, which is the whole point. It's no wonder it was called in 2005 the "power spot of the year." *Sun-Tue 11:30am-11pm, Wed-Sat 11:30am-midnight.* $$$ B ≡

Hot Tip: The restaurant has hidden cameras capturing every move you make, no doubt at the behest of security forces protecting the VIPs who dine here.

Charlie Palmer Steak*
101 Constitution Ave. NW, Capitol Hill, 202-547-8100 • Classic

The Draw: In the shadow of the Capitol building, lobbyists, senators, and staffers conduct business over drinks or dinner at this chic steak house and bar.

The Scene: Don't expect the oppressive interior and unimaginative cuisine found at many steak houses. Charlie Palmer's airy dining room and bar serve as an excellent backdrop for the progressive American cuisine. *Sun 5-10pm, Mon-Fri 11:30am-2:30pm and 5:30-10pm, Sat 5-10:30pm.* $$$ B ⌐

Hot Tip: The crowd ebbs and flows depending on whether Congress is in session or there's an important vote going on. A glance at the news will indicate whether it will be empty as senators debate a bill or full as they celebrate a victory.

Off the Record
The Hay-Adams, One Lafayette Sq., Downtown, 202-638-6600 • Classic

The Draw: Off the Record bills itself as the place "to be seen and not heard," making it the postwork watering hole of choice for the staffers that work across the street at the White House.

The Scene: Power suits puff cigars and sip single malts on the plush red banquettes lining the walls. Longtime bartender John Boswell has served every president since Nixon. If you sit at the bar, he'll fill you in on the history. *Sun-Thu 11:30am-midnight, Fri-Sat 11:30am-12:30am.* ≡

Hot Tip: Framed political cartoons hang throughout the bar. Pay attention and you might see their subjects in the flesh.

Best

Power Lunch Spots

#70–72: Red meat, a robust bar scene, and a high-profile downtown address go a long way toward sealing a restaurant's place in the capital's deal-maker hierarchy. These three establishments offer all that, and more.

The Capital Grille
601 Pennsylvania Ave. NW, Penn Quarter, 202-737-6200 • Classic

The Draw: The capital's smoothest operators dine here to work on contracts as well as enormous slices of steak and are not averse to conducting business over an Absolut at the bar, if necessary.

The Scene: The Capital Grille is forthrightly masculine in décor, from its display of stuffed animal heads to the dark paneled walls on which the heads hang. The mostly male clientele loves it. *Sun 5-10pm, Mon-Thu 11:30am-3pm and 5-10pm, Fri-Sat 11:30am-3pm and 5-11pm.* $$$

Hot Tip: The portions are huge, so plan accordingly.

The Caucus Room*
401 Ninth St. NW, Penn Quarter, 202-393-1300 • Classic

The Draw: This bipartisan venture by politicos Tommy Boggs, Haley Barbour, and others is decorously handsome, the perfect setting for patrons who hope to extend a hand across the aisle or encourage a signature on a legislative bill.

The Scene: Weekdays when Congress is in session, the Caucus Room hums with the sounds of wheels and deals in motion. Washington's movers and shakers fill the main dining room and the bar, careful to dine, deal, and depart in time to make the evening news. *Mon-Fri 11:30am-2:30pm and 5:30-10:30pm, Sat 5:30-10:30pm.* $$$

Hot Tip: Make sure you're seated in the main dining room for the real show.

The Occidental
1475 Pennsylvania Ave. NW, Downtown, 202-783-1475 • Classic

The Draw: The black-and-white photos that blanket the walls convey some sense of the Occidental's 100-year history. If those photos could talk! For a sense of the capital's past and a seat in the middle of events in the making (bend your ear to the table behind you), the Occidental is unequaled.

The Scene: Its age and experience afford the Occidental a more relaxed and less relentlessly masculine vibe than most other Washington power dining spots. Located toward the White House end of Pennsylvania Avenue, the Occidental attracts administration and business leaders rather than Hill people. *Daily 11:30am-3pm, Sun 5-9:30pm, Mon-Thu 5-10pm, Fri-Sat 5-10:30pm.* $$

Hot Tip: The upstairs dining room isn't always open, but it's worth a visit to peek at photos of contemporary hotshots and admire the Washington Monument.

Best | Rainy Day Experiences

#73–75: No matter what the weather, these three sites are a sure-fire fun time, but if rain, snow, miserable heat, or cold does descend, it's good to know you've got a Plan B lineup to keep the party rolling.

IMAX Films and Flight Simulators
National Air and Space Museum, Independence Ave. SW,
bet. Fourth and Seventh Sts., National Mall, 202-633-1000 • Hip

The Draw: You feel as if you are walking on the moon or joyriding on the wingtip of an airplane when you attend an IMAX film and you experience the thrilling ride of a lifetime on a flight simulator at the National Air and Space Museum.

The Scene: The IMAX films are all about space exploration and aircraft wizardry, and accessible to spectators of all ages. At flight simulator central, kids and wannabes step inside machines to grab the controls and pretend to pilot a World War II fighter airplane or a modern-day jet. Best to reserve tickets in advance. *Museum daily 10am-5:30pm.* Films $, flight simulators $-

Hot Tip: Though the museum's main exhibit spaces close at 5:30pm daily, the IMAX theater usually stays open later, showing films in the evenings.

International Spy Museum
800 F St. NW, Penn Quarter, 202-393-7798 • Chic

The Draw: This is the country's only public museum solely devoted to espionage, and its collection of international spy artifacts is the world's largest on display.

The Scene: The galleries hold artifacts, photos, and interactive displays. Armchair sleuths turn out in droves to test their surveillance skills and decipher encrypted language and to watch video interviews of former intelligence officers revealing how they cracked their cases. *Mid-Aug–late-Feb daily 10am-6pm (Sat mid-Aug–late-Oct, 10am-8pm), Mar 9am-6pm, early-Apr–mid-Aug 9am-8pm.* $

Hot Tip: The museum handles crowds by posting a continually updated tour schedule outside its entrance, so you can purchase your tickets for a later tour, play somewhere else, then return.

Phillips Collection
1600 21st St. NW, Dupont Circle, 202-387-2151 • Chic

The Draw: America's first museum of modern art is the keeper of some of the world's most famous Impressionist and Modernist works.

The Scene: The Phillips exudes an air of intimacy, deriving partly from its charming 1897 mansion. The gallery's a favorite among hand-holding couples and international tourists. *Sun noon-5pm (June-Sept) and noon-7pm (Oct-May), Tue-Wed, Fri-Sat 10am-5pm, Thu 10am-8:30pm.* $-

Hot Tip: Easy to miss, but make sure you don't: the tiny Rothko Room and its four, large color-intense artworks, one of the few museum spaces dedicated solely to the work of the abstract expressionist.

THE 99 BEST OF D.C.

Best — Restaurant Lounges

#76–78: Restaurant lounges are all the rage these days, but how can you be sure that the scene won't overpower the cuisine, and that the meal won't dull the vibe? At these hot spots, the bars and restaurants are equal partners that never fail to deliver innovative dishes, decadent drinks, and a jumping scene.

IndeBleu*
707 G St. NW, Penn Quarter, 202-333-2538 • Chic

The Draw: The 50-drink cocktail list and innovative French-Indian menu cater to an adventurous palate and beautiful crowd.

The Scene: Whether in the serene formal dining room or the sensuous downstairs lounge, IndeBleu trades in indulgence. Walls glow tangerine, waterfalls gurgle from the sinks, and a regular cast of urban sophisticates adorns both tables and bars. *Daily 5:30pm-2am.* $$$

Hot Tip: If IndeBleu is your first drink stop, avoid the lounge's pricey reservation minimum. Check times on each table's cards, and you can settle in until its rightful occupants arrive (usually after midnight).

Lima*
1401 K St. NW, Downtown, 202-789-2800 • Chic

The Draw: Lima was ahead of the "supper club" trend of creating a one-stop nightlife experience. Fine dining on the top floor gives way to a cocktail bar and a subterranean lounge.

The Scene: Floors flow into one another with the aid of organic design elements like the reservoir of falling water leading guests down from the bar to the lounge. DJs spin progressive house and trance from a booth that floats above the crowd. *Mon-Thu 6-10:30pm, Fri-Sat 6-11pm.* $$$

Hot Tip: At Lima—named after the Spanish word for "lime," not the Peruvian capital—ceviche is understandably a standout. If you opt out of the formal dining room, you can still try one of four versions of the dish in the lounge.

Oya*
777 Ninth St. NW, Penn Quarter, 202-393-1400 • Chic

The Draw: This restaurant is hot in every sense of the word: it's a chic place to eat, its walls flame with inlaid fireplaces and the only thing cooling it down is the 20-foot waterfall between you and the open kitchen.

The Scene: Couples and flirty groups dine on French-Asian food in the dining room or sip sake cocktails at the scarlet crocodile bar. *Sun 5:30-10pm, Mon-Sat 5:30pm-1:30am.* $$

Hot Tip: The chef cooks up a "late-night room service" menu until 1:30am. If the sexy ambience puts you in the mood, get a Kama Sutra package to go, complete with flavored condoms.

Best Romantic Dining

#79–81: Just like love, romantic dining is all about the right chemistry. Is it too much to ask for a place that combines a perfect little niche for snuggling, an amuse-bouche whose amusement spreads to other parts, food and wine that act as aphrodisiacs, and staff with a fine sense of timing? Not at these three favorites.

Butterfield 9
600 14th St. NW, Penn Quarter, 202-289-8810 • Chic

The Draw: Butterfield 9's stylish layout, with steel-railed staircases sweeping up either side of the two-story dining room to an overlooking mezzanine, banquette-lined walls, and *Vogue*-ish 1930s and '40s black-and-white fashion photos set the stage for a singularly sophisticated kind of romance.

The Scene: It would be a little much if all the guests were cooing couples, but the scene's a bit cooler than that, with tables of business diners and friends adding to the mix. *Mon-Thu 11:30am-2:30pm and 5:30-10pm, Fri 11:30am-2:30pm and 5:30-11pm, Sat-Sun 5:30-11pm. $$*

Hot Tip: For the quietest corner, ask for table 403, off by itself, where you can observe the scene, but not be seen; for a cuddle-time booth, ask for table 123; and for a private table by the window, ask for 304.

Gerard's Place
915 15th St. NW, White House, 202-737-4445 • Classic

The Draw: Like the best small restaurants you might discover on an amble around Paris, Gerard's Place does not draw attention to itself, but simply succeeds on the strength of the chef's high standard of haute cuisine.

The Scene: The petite, 50-seat dining room is family run and has a special, charmingly intimate feel about it. *Mon-Thu 11:30am-2pm and 5:30-9pm, Fri 11:30am-2pm and 5:30-9:30pm, Sat 5:30-9:30pm. $$$*

Hot Tip: It's no secret: table 40 in the alcove has seen more than its share of marriage proposals.

1789 Restaurant
1226 36th St. NW, Georgetown, 202-965-1789 • Classic

The Draw: Splendid gentility reigns at the 1789. Cozy quarters, Currier and Ives prints, fireplaces, and decadent food make this the hands-down favorite for local romantics.

The Scene: Its traditional décor works as a perfect foil for the sophisticated food, the same way the older distinguished diners deep in conversation nicely complement the sets of younger coquettish couples holding hands across the tables. *Sun 5:30-10pm, Mon-Thu 6-10pm, Fri 6-11pm, Sat 5:30-11pm. $$$*

Hot Tip: Ask for table 7 right in front of the fireplace in the John Carroll Room (the same place that Nicole Kidman and Keith Urban dined).

THE 99 BEST OF D.C.

 Best

Romantic Trysts

#82–84: If romance were just a matter of hotel dalliances and candlelit dinners, you wouldn't be checking out this page. The trick is how to court and spark in a crowded city. The answer: remove the crowd and set the scene.

Dumbarton Oaks Gardens
R St. NW at 32nd St., Georgetown, 202-339-6400 • Chic

The Draw: Privacy and beauty combine within this stone-and-brick-walled, 10-acre garden, rife with canoodling opportunities: the wisteria-covered arbor, landscaped garden "rooms" shielded by high hedges, winding paths leading to intimate overlooks, an 1810 orangery covered in creeping fig in summer.

The Scene: The Dumbarton Oaks estate stands on a quiet residential street in upper Georgetown. Its 19th-century mansion and museum backs up to the garden. Seductive year-round, the gardens are scandalously beautiful, but also most crowded, in spring. *mid-Mar–late-Oct 2-6pm, Nov–mid-Mar 2-5pm.* $-

Hot Tip: Don't miss the real-life Lovers' Lane, which is not part of Dumbarton Oaks Gardens, but lies just outside its walls, siding its eastern border.

Rowing on the Potomac
Jack's Boathouse, 3500 K St. NW, Georgetown • Chic

The Draw: Get away from it all, but all the while enjoying views of the Washington Monument, Georgetown Harbor, the Kennedy Center, the Lincoln and Jefferson memorials, and the Capitol and Washington National Cathedral.

The Scene: Whether your starting point is Jack's Boathouse (202-337-9642) in lower Georgetown, or Thompson's Boat Center (202-333-4861) across from the Kennedy Center, the general territory is the same: the Potomac River, with views of both shores, and Theodore Roosevelt Island between the two. $

Hot Tip: Grab a jug of wine and some fancy sandwiches from Dean & Deluca or Leopold's Kafe & Konditorei (both in Georgetown) and paddle over to Theodore Roosevelt Island for a romantic picnic and some cha cha cha.

A Tour de Force
Various, 703-525-2948 • Classic

The Draw: When you hire a car and guide for a private, moonlit tour of the capital, you're having your cake and eating it, too. You get to view the capital at its most spectacular but avoid the throngs of tourists.

The Scene: Traffic subsides most evenings after 7-ish around the National Mall, removing the noise and confusion of the day. The sky darkens. Landmarks assume their memorable nighttime roles, basking in the spotlights. $$$$

Hot Tip: A number of companies offer evening tours, but A Tour de Force's ability to accommodate couples makes it best for romance. Choose the SUV for better views, since limo windows don't reveal quite as much.

Best Sexy Lounges

#85–87: Lounges often afford the most sophisticated nightlife experience, with waitstaff to save you from battling the bar crowd and setups more conducive to conversation. These spaces know how to both chill things out and heat them up with stunning spaces, a sexy clientele, and solid DJs.

18th Street Lounge
1212 18th St. NW, Dupont Circle, 202-466-3922 • Hip

The Draw: The music alone—acid jazz, trip hop, and electronica—would be enough to pack the lounge, but the space is also upscale and cozy.

The Scene: Antique couches and tables, lit by candelabras and a roaring fire, fill with stylishly hip D.C. denizens. The variable door policy is unfriendly to groups of guys. Snag some ladies to accompany you in or get there before 11pm. *Tue, Wed 9:30pm-2am, Thu 5:30pm-2am, Fri 5:30pm-3am, Sat 9:30pm-3am.* C ≡

Hot Tip: There's no sign, so look for the line next to the mattress store.

Eyebar
1716 I St. NW, Downtown, 202-785-0270 • Chic

The Draw: Nightlife heavyweights Andre Demoya and Lieven DeGeyndt created a seamless design here, including waterfalls in the bathrooms and a state-of-the-art sound system.

The Scene: Though Eyebar eschews nightclub exclusivity by nixing covers and VIP sections, the strict dress code—no flip-flops, sneakers, or baggy jeans—ensures that the clientele matches the sleek interior of the two-level Euro-style lounge. Check out Thursday's hip-hop and Saturday's house and trance night. *Tue-Thu 5pm-1am, Fri 5pm-3am, Sat 11pm-3am.* ≡

Hot Tip: You must be on the reservation list to gain entry to the red-hot Saturday parties. Email list@eyebardc.com. However, being on the list doesn't guarantee entry, so arrive before 11pm or opt for bottle service ($400-$800).

K Street Lounge
1301 K St. NW, Downtown, 202-962-3933 • Chic

The Draw: The exclusivity factor at K Street makes bottle service a priority. Reserved tables are slightly elevated above the crowd, and its inhabitants are announced on flat-screen TVs.

The Scene: The sleek, minimalist décor draws attention to the VIPs lining one whole side of the bar. A curved white wall draws the eye to the beautiful people drinking top-shelf vodkas behind velvet ropes. In between, a slightly younger crowd sips cocktails and dances to house, Latin, and remixed retro hits. *Thu 5pm-2am, Fri-Sat 10pm-3am.* C ≡

Hot Tip: If you're not reserving a table (book at least a week beforehand), get there by 10:30pm to avoid an often excruciatingly slow line.

THE 99 BEST OF D.C.

 Singles Scenes

#88–90: Sometimes you want to set out on the town for a raucous night of flirting and cocktails, with plenty of others looking for same. These bars provide just the right mix of luscious drinks and eye candy, lounge spaces and dance floors to get the party started.

Blue Gin
1206 Wisconsin Ave., Georgetown, 202-965-5555 • Chic

The Draw: Blue Gin merges the sophistication of its downtown counterparts with the spring-break energy of Georgetown.

The Scene: Clean lines and funky design details—from movie projections to shimmering chain curtains—provide the backdrop for this chic two-level club. Friendly-to-a-fault bartenders mix fresh fruit purees into delectable cocktails. *Wed-Thu 7pm-2am, Fri-Sat 7pm-3am.* C≡

Hot Tip: On Saturdays, squeeze into the second floor, where glass floor panels provide glimpses of the action below and a live percussionist bumps up DJ Frankie Fingers' hot beats.

Chloe
2473 18th St. NW, Adams Morgan, 202-265-6592 • Chic

The Draw: Stiletto marks dot the furniture because the dance floor cannot contain the masses grooving to the tunes spun from a globe above the crowd.

The Scene: Although the décor is a stylistic mishmash, the crowd sports the downtown chic uniform of designer jeans and dressy tops. The downstairs can tilt towards meet market, but always in an unthreateningly flirtatious way. *Sun 11:30am-10pm, Tue-Thu 5:30pm-1am, Fri-Sat 5:30pm-3am.* C≡

Hot Tip: Pony up for table service ($500 and up) to skip the line and ensure access to the coveted roof deck and second floor. If you opt out of table service, be prepared to wait.

MCCXXIII
1223 Connecticut Ave. NW, Dupont Circle, 202-822-1800 • Chic

The Draw: The bottle service is free-flowing, the patrons fashionable, and the dance floor packed at this swank club.

The Scene: Industrial details sass up this club's otherwise plush character. Velvet couches line the wall, and cocktails are served up at the gleaming soapstone bar. The music is a surprising mix of top 40 hits and hip-hop on the weekends. *Sun 8pm-2am, Tue 9pm-2am, Wed-Thu 6pm-2am, Fri 5pm-3am, Sat 8pm-3am.* C≡

Hot Tip: Doormen can be fickle about the dress code, but ladies should be safe with stilettos and status denim.

Trendy Tables

#91–93: Washingtonians, for better or worse, are cautious by nature. They take their time deciding on a new trend. It's the rare new restaurant that sparkles from the start, with scene-makers happily congregating there that first night and ever after. Here are three such rare birds at the top of their game.

Rasika
633 D St. NW, Penn Quarter, 202-637-1222 • Chic

The Draw: Rasika's sensuous shimmery look, exotic drinks (try the clove martini made with homemade clove syrup), new flavors of Indian cuisine, and sophisticated service prove simply irresistible.

The Scene: Well-heeled Washingtonians with a cosmopolitan air dine in the restaurant. In the adjoining lounge, handsome, smartly attired gay playboys flirt at the bar; pairs of sophisticated Indian couples chat on banquettes. *Mon-Thu 11:30am-2:30pm and 5:30-10:30pm, Fri 11:30am-2:30pm and 5:30-11pm, Sat 5:30-11pm. Lounge serves light meals all day.* $$

Hot Tip: Ask for table 8 to sit where Bill and Hill Clinton did, and try to dine around 8:30pm on a Friday or Saturday night, for best buzz and chicest vibe.

Sonoma Restaurant and Wine Bar*
223 Pennsylvania Ave. SE, Capitol Hill, 202-544-8088 • Chic

The Draw: The affable yet knowledgeable staff make tasting the more than 40 wines by the glass—preserved by Cruvinet technology behind the bar—a joy.

The Scene: The muted palette of this two-story bistro and lounge provides an ideal backdrop for a sophisticated postwork crowd sharing family-style charcuterie, handmade pastas, and so on. *Sun 5:30-9pm, Mon-Thu 11:30am-2:30pm and 5:30-10pm, Fri 11:30am-2:30pm and 5:30-11pm, Sat 5:30-11pm.* $

Hot Tip: Sonoma doesn't want diners to get locked into one wine. It has priced by-the-glass drinking to be the better deal, so explore away.

Zaytinya*
701 Ninth St. NW, Penn Quarter, 202-638-0800 • Chic

The Draw: A sleek all-white décor softened by cunning curves, a trendy Penn Quarter location, and a great swath of bar and its heady drinks all pull in the beautiful people, happy to cavort here, flirt outrageously, and make new friends.

The Scene: Lunches are tame and dinners start out that way, as the restaurant fills with locals here for a cool experience. Beyond a certain hour, though, Sex-in-the-City replaces subway-rider-from-the-suburbs, and next thing you know, someone like Bruce Springsteen's in the house. *Sun-Mon 11:30am-10pm, Tue-Thu 11:30am-11:30pm, Fri-Sat 11:30am-midnight.* $$

Hot Tip: Request tables 6 or 43 on a Friday or Saturday night to be in the thick of Washington's trendiest scene.

THE 99 BEST OF D.C.

Vegetarian Restaurants

#94–96: Though steak dinners may be the power meal of choice on Capitol Hill, D.C. diners flock to these vegetarian-friendly restaurants for their innovative cuisine and artistic ambience.

Mama Ayesha's Restaurant
1967 Calvert St. NW, Adams Morgan, 202-232-5431 • Hip

The Draw: Middle Eastern food has always been veggie friendly, but Mama's goes the extra mile with dishes like tender yellow squash stuffed with tomatoes, mint, garlic, and chickpeas.

The Scene: Journalists, diplomats, and others who could certainly afford pricier fare have been coming to Mama Ayesha's for over 50 years. The service and lovingly prepared dishes give the feel of a long meal at a beloved friend's house. *Sun-Thu noon-10pm, Fri-Sat noon-11pm.* $

Hot Tip: You'll want to linger over this meal, and *sheik*—Arabic coffee with Galliano—is the perfect excuse.

Vegetate*
1414 Ninth St. NW, U Street Corridor, 202-232-4585 • Hip

The Draw: The enticing seasonal menu draws inspiration from soul food and Caribbean spices with dishes like white bean soup with sweet potato, collard greens and cornbread, or tempeh with mango relish and coconut jerk sauce.

The Scene: Vegetate buzzes with creative energy—from the inspired vegetarian cuisine to the edgy urban art adorning the walls to records spun by owner DJ Dredd. The second-floor lounge attracts a racially diverse mix of artsy music lovers. *Sun 11am-3pm and 6-10pm, Thu 6-10pm, Fri-Sat 6-11pm.* $

Hot Tip: Save room for desserts like warm molasses cookies and milk.

Viridian
1515 14th St. NW, U Street Corridor, 202-234-1400 • Hip

The Draw: The real treats at Viridian are the little tastes that come between courses. An amuse-bouche starts off the meal, followed by breads and spreads, and the check always comes with a tiny dessert.

The Scene: The name—viridian is a green pigment—is a subtle nod to the restaurant's dual goal of serving up vegan-friendly seasonal fare and showcasing the work of local artists. A chic crowd eats up both in the large airy dining room. *Sun 10:30am-3:30pm and 4:30-11pm, Tue-Fri 11:30am-3:30pm and 5:30-11pm, Sat 10:30am-3:30pm and 5:30-11pm.* $

Hot Tip: Viridian's location along the hip 14th Street corridor means you're excellently situated for after-dinner options: catch a show at the neighboring Studio Theatre, listen to jazz at HR-57, or rock out at the Black Cat.

Best

Views of D.C.

#97-99: As vantage points go, these three are the best for showing off Washington's spectacular, landmark-studded landscape.

Old Post Office Pavilion Tower
1100 Pennsylvania Ave. NW, Penn Quarter, 202-606-8691 • Hip

The Draw: Its view may not stretch as wide, but its lower height and its location guarantee the Clock Tower certain advantages over the Washington Monument: shorter lines (usually) and fantastic views up and down Pennsylvania Avenue.

The Scene: You'll wait (if there is a wait) inside the cavernous pavilion, before taking the necessary two elevators that transport you to the summit. *Mar-Aug Sun noon-7pm, Mon-Sat 10am-8pm; Sept-Feb Sun noon-6pm, Mon-Sat 10am-7pm.*

Hot Tip: Hold out for better eats in the nearby Penn Quarter than those on offer in the Pavilion's food court.

Potomac Riverboat Company
Washington Harbour, Georgetown, 703-548-9000 • Chic

The Draw: It's a ridiculously beautiful, easy, and complete way to take in Washington's sights: hop aboard a boat out of Georgetown's harbor, settle back against your seat on the outdoor deck, and watch Washington go by.

The Scene: Local families, couples, and daytrippers tend to outnumber tourists on Potomac River excursions, like those offered by the Potomac Riverboat Company. Recorded commentary describes the passing scene on the way to Old Town Alexandria.

Hot Tip: Buy a roundtrip ticket and hop off the boat in Old Town, whose pier lies at the foot of King Street, Alexandria's main shopping district. Shop for a few hours, then re-board the boat for a return excursion back to Georgetown.

Washington National Cathedral
Massachusetts and Wisconsin Aves. NW, Upper Northwest, 202-537-6200 • Classic

The Draw: The world's sixth- and the nation's second-largest cathedral commands the highest point in Washington. Have a look at its 101 gargoyles, flying buttresses, stained glass, high towers, and spires, and the magnificent views from its seventh-floor observation gallery.

The Scene: Though it is a regular stop for tour buses, the cathedral manages to maintain a dignified presence. Its 57 acres encompass two gardens, four schools, a greenhouse, and a gift shop. *Gardens: daily to dusk; cathedral: Sun 8am-6:30pm, Mon-Fri 10am-5:30pm (7:45pm June-Sept), Sat 10am-4:40pm.*

Hot Tip: It's all downhill from here: A short walk south on Wisconsin Avenue will take you to some prime neighborhood bars and ethnic restaurants; continue further still and you're in Georgetown.

EXPERIENCE D.C.

Dive into the D.C. of your choice with one of three themed itineraries: *Chic* (p.50), *Hip* (p.82), or *Classic* (p.115). Each is designed to heighten your experience by putting you in the right place at the right time—the best restaurants, nightlife, and attractions, and even the best days to go there. While the itineraries, each followed by detailed descriptions of our top choices, reflect our very top picks, the listings include a number of additional noteworthy options. So whether you're looking to indulge in a decadent meal at one of D.C.'s top restaurants or hit the dance floor late into the night, you'll find it all right here.

Chic D.C.

Washington, D.C., has a certain image and that image is … go ahead, say it: conservative. You're seeing maybe pinstriped suits and wingtip shoes. You're thinking early to bed, early to rise. Well, there is all that, but if that's not what you're after, consider this: posses of slender women and lanky men in $250 jeans and tech jackets carrying the all-night party from a sexy Penn Quarter lounge to a dancing-on-the-furniture nightclub; fashion-forward couples slurping pomegranate martinis in the sexiest new Indian restaurant; a VIP crowd getting its groove on to the tunes of a world-class DJ.

That more like it? Then get ready to enjoy, because there's plenty more where that came from. Behind its buttoned-up cover, a fabulously chic Washington rocks on, and this chapter leads you straight to its heart.

Note: Venues in bold are described in detail in the listings that follow the itinerary. Venues followed by an * asterisk are those we recommend as both a restaurant and a destination bar.

Chic D.C.:
The Perfect Plan (3 Nights and Days)

Perfect Plan Highlights

Thursday
Breakfast	Spy City Café
Mid-morning	Int'l Spy Museum
Lunch	Zola*
Mid-afternoon	Smithsonian American Art Museum, Nat'l Portrait Gallery
Pre-dinner	Rosa Mexicano*
Dinner	CityZen
Nighttime	Pearl
Late-night	Lucky Strike

Friday
Breakfast	Bistro Bis
Mid-morning	Supreme Court
Lunch	Café Milano*
Mid-afternoon	Georgetown shopping
Pre-dinner	Mie N Yu*
Dinner	Cashion's Eat Place*
Nighttime	IndeBleu*
Late-night	K Street Lounge

Saturday
Breakfast	Four Seasons
Mid-morning	Boat Tour, Freer Gallery
Lunch	Blue Duck Tavern
Mid-afternoon	Phillips Collection, gallery-hopping in Dupont Circle
Pre-dinner	Zaytinya*
Dinner	Rasika
Nighttime	Maté
Late-night	Blue Gin

Morning After
Brunch	Café Atlantico

Hotel: **Four Seasons**

Thursday

10am Hop a cab to Ninth and F, stepping in to the Spy City Café. After fortifying yourself, enter the adjoining **International Spy Museum** for an immersion in spy mastery through the use of interactive exhibits and artifact displays; you're good for at least a couple of hours, or longer, if you succumb to the intriguing paraphernalia in the gift shop.

1pm Lunch Housed in the same building as the Spy Museum, **Zola***, with its modern American menu, is a perfect place to recover from the information overload of the morning. But if you're in the mood for something a little more exotic, consider **Zengo**'s* Asian-Latino menu one block up on Seventh Street.

3pm Across the street from both Zola and Zengo are the **Smithsonian American Art Museum** and the **National Portrait Gallery**. Step inside to admire some American originals, from portraits of U.S presidents to paintings by Edward Hopper. Stroll the art galleries and shops of the Penn Quarter afterward.

6pm Rosa Mexicano*, catty-corner from the American Art Museum and Portrait Gallery, is the place to inaugurate the cocktail hour. Toss back some killer margaritas and scoop up some guacamole, both whipped up fresh for you as you sit at the bar. Hail a taxi to the hotel, primp for the evening, and head back out for dinner.

8:30pm Dinner Dress to shine at the incomparable **CityZen**, whose tables fill nightly with visiting celebrities and local hotshots. Or try **Teatro Goldoni**, known for its high-drama atmosphere, fine Venetian fare, and beautiful faces. Slightly north of the Penn Quarter is **Acadiana**, a favorite of the local Louisiana delegation as well as other lawmakers, who come here for the flavors of New Orleans and high-spirited ambience.

11pm You'll have to be in top form to make it past the bouncers and onto the dance floor at nearby **Pearl**, where hip-hop rules. Turned away? Don't fret. Return to Georgetown to make the scene at **Degrees**, in the Ritz-Carlton. Its location in an old incinerator building means amped-up sexiness paired with Ritz-style sophistication.

12:30am To wrap up the evening on a rambunctious note, bowl a set over dirty martinis at the swank **Lucky Strike**, also in the Penn Quarter. Or hop a cab to Dupont to recline on **Gazuza**'s all-weather balcony or dance on the tables (and bar and couches) at the raucous **Play Lounge**.

Friday

9am Make your way to **Bistro Bis**, near Capitol Hill, for some French toast and excellent coffee, and your first power-broker sightings of the day.

10am From Bistro Bis, it's an invigorating walk to the **Supreme Court**, using the Capitol dome as your guide (the Court lies across the street from the eastern side of the Capitol). If the justices are hearing or delivering arguments that day, and you get here early enough, stand in line and try for admission to watch. If the court's not in session, take a tour instead, which will take you inside the courtroom.

11:30am From the Supreme Court, head down the hill to the National Mall, checking out the tremendous views of Washington landmarks on the way. Continue to the Smithsonian's **Hirshhorn Museum** to admire the fine collection of modern art; make sure to tour the Sculpture Garden.

1pm Lunch Hail a cab to Georgetown's **Café Milano***, where you're never sure who's going to turn up, even at lunch, for the Italian menu and the social scene. For a younger, more casual vibe, and lunch or just dessert, seek out **Leopold's Kafe & Konditorei**.

3pm If you've found Leopold's, then you'll already have discovered the chic furnishings, accessories, and clothing shops surrounding it called **Cady's Alley**. Linger here a while or hit Georgetown's main drags, M and Wisconsin. If you're not in the mood to shop, head over to the **Kreeger Art Museum**, which offers tours by appointment only. If you've called ahead, taxi to the Kreeger for sights of precious Impressionist and modern paintings and sculptures.

5pm Finish up the afternoon at the **SomaFit Spa** in upper Georgetown for a facial, massage, workout, or other sublime treatment that will prime you for the night ahead.

7:30pm Mie N Yu* is just getting started on a Friday night, with a young after-work crowd ready to rock the kasbah. Enjoy the Silk Road décor, all glowing tents and burnished mirrors, as you settle at the bar for a heady French Kiss.

8:30pm Dinner The Cleveland Park neighborhood beckons with the hot Indian restaurant, **Indique**. More central to later action is the Penn Quarter's contemporary **Tosca**. Guaranteed to please is **Cashion's Eat Place***, Adams Morgan's answer to sophisticates seeking a charming setting, a social scene, and sensational American food.

11pm Love may be off the beaten path, but people travel from surrounding cities every weekend for the scene at the ultraluxe club. With five floors, two decks, VIPs, and all-night action, you won't want to leave until dawn. Other options include the **IndeBleu*** lounge, where plush banquettes invite you to recline while exploring the 50 specialty cocktails on its menu. Things heating up with someone new? The lounge at **Oya*** is so sexy you may choose to end the night right there.

1am Continue the party at the exclusive **K Street Lounge**, where the beautiful people indulge in bottle service to Latin, house, and hip-hop beats. Or hop in a cab to Dupont Circle, where **Ozio Restaurant & Lounge** offers a bit of everything: dance club, lounge, and more in a see-and-be-seen setting.

Saturday

9am If the day dawns gorgeous, ask room service to pack a breakfast picnic for you, so you can hustle down to the harbor for a lovely boat ride on the Potomac with the **Potomac Riverboat Company**, past Washington's low but striking skyline, to Old Town Alexandria. The 45-minute trip allows you just enough time to enjoy your feast before dropping you at the foot of King Street, lined with shops and eateries. After exploring Alexandria, reboard the boat to make the return trip to Georgetown.

If the weather or the season aren't on task, shuffle downstairs to Seasons for a fortifying breakfast. Then head off to the National Mall to view Asian antiquities and art at the **Freer Gallery**, returning by cab to the Four Seasons.

1pm Lunch Take a leisurely stroll from Georgetown to the West End's new dining sensation, the **Blue Duck Tavern**, before continuing on to the Phillips Collection. Or head straight to the museum, whose little Vradenburg Café offers tasty soups, salads, and sandwiches.

3pm Tour the **Phillips Collection**, keeping your eyes peeled for its most famous work, Renoir's *Luncheon of the Boating Party*, and numerous other marvels. Continue your artful afternoon by visiting the many art galleries that pepper Dupont Circle's quaint side streets.

6:30pm Join the overflowing bar crowd at the Penn Quarter's flamboyant **Zaytinya***, whose cool look and party spirit will get your night off to a rousing start.

8pm Dinner The dining experience at **Zaytinya*** is worth the wait, but if you'd rather not, move on instead to the new Indian restaurant, sexy-chic **Rasika**, a few blocks east of Zaytinya. Stop in the lounge to wet your lips with a clove martini, then stay on for dinner. Alternatively, go four blocks west of Zaytinya to **Ceiba**, a restaurant that's serious about Latin cuisine and mojitos.

10:30pm For a taste of D.C.'s international scene, snag a table at Georgetown's **Maté**, where the people are as exotic as the Argentinian-inspired cocktails. The minimalist chic of Japan more your style? Head to **Dragonfly*** in Dupont Circle for sushi and saketinis. Or go Eurochic with a stop at **Eyebar** for its famed Saturday house and trance party.

12:30am As the night dances on, consider your options: hit the catwalk and the dance floor to hip-hop and top 40 at the industrial chic **MCCXXIII** in Dupont. Or opt for Georgetown's stylish **Blue Gin**, where you can party on the second floor and spy through glass floor panels on the scene below.

The Morning After

Wrap up your tour of Washington on a festive note with one last hurrah at the popular Latino dim sum brunch at **Café Atlantico**.

Chic D.C.:
The Key Neighborhoods

Dupont Circle Home to countless boutiques, bistros, and art houses, Dupont Circle draws crowds to its myriad cafes and bars, all-night bookstore, abundant shopping and people-watching opportunities, and the galleries that proliferate here.

Georgetown This is the epicenter of Chic Washington. Upscale shops are interspersed throughout this wealthy, historic neighborhood, from Cady's Alley near Georgetown University to antique stores near the Four Seasons. Fashionable shoppers in town from around the world wander up and down these streets, visiting high-end furniture emporiums, one-of-a-kind clothing boutiques and stationery stores, numerous upscale restaurants, and hot nightclubs.

Penn Quarter The 1997 opening of the massive sports stadium and concert hall the Verizon Center (originally called the MCI Center) at Seventh and F streets completely revitalized this downtown neighborhood, which continues to expand in size and scene. Its boundaries for now are, north to south, Massachusetts to Pennsylvania Avenues, and east to west, 15th to Fifth Streets. In between lie longtime "scene" restaurants like Café Atlantico, newcomers like IndeBleu, and an ever-growing crop of stores, art galleries, nightclubs—and even an upscale bowling alley.

Upper Northwest Affluent neighborhoods, like Cleveland Park and Woodley Park, are filled with gorgeous homes and lovely tree-lined streets. At one time, Irish bars provided the main social scene, but these days, upper northwest Connecticut Avenue is more and more a destination for happening restaurants like Indique and bars like Bardeo.

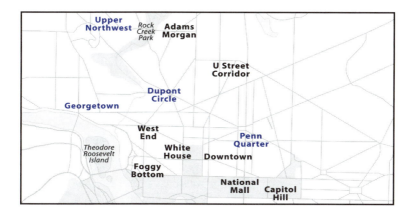

Chic D.C.:
The Shopping Blocks

Dupont

Less concentrated than Georgetown, Dupont is perfectly laid out for leisurely strolls through the stores lining Connecticut Avenue from S to M Street.

Beadazzled From seed beads to gemstones, Beadazzled helps shoppers tap into their crafty side. 1507 Connecticut Ave. NW (Dupont Cir.), 202-265-2323

Chocolate Moose Inflatable voodoo dolls, Einstein sunglass holders, pop-art kitchen spoons—Chocolate Moose has all those things you never knew you needed. 1743 L St. NW (Connecticut Ave.), 202-463-0992

The Grooming Lounge Swig a root beer and watch ESPN while this nouveau barber shop gives you a hot lather shave. You can also shop for custom razors and manly skin care products. (p.78) 1745 L St. NW (18th St.), 202-466-8900

Proper Topper You'll find whimsical gifts, quirky cufflinks, clothes by Nanette Lepore and Tracy Reese, and a treasure trove of hats from bowlers and berets to newsboys and knits. 1350 Connecticut Ave. NW (Dupont Cir.), 202-842-3055

Secondi Consignment Clothing D.C.'s working women flock to Secondi for high-end finds. 1702 Connecticut Ave. NW (Q St.), 202-667-1122

Georgetown

The 200-plus shops along D.C.'s fashion crossroads—Wisconsin Avenue and M Street NW—are enough to exhaust even the most devoted retail maven. Though the high-end chain stores are worth a look, make time for these exclusive boutiques.

Artefacto High-end Brazilian furniture is spread over 16,000 chic square feet in D.C.'s design district. (p.77) 3333 M St. NW (Banks St.), 202-338-3337

Cady's Alley This self-proclaimed "design district" has 50 high-end home furnishings retailers like Baker, Thom. Moser Cabinetmakers, and Waterworks bathroom accessories, as well as fine local shops like Gore-Dean for antiques. 3318 M St. NW (33rd St.), cadysalley.com

Hu's Shoes The well-heeled buy their Chloe and Alexandra Neel heels at Hu's. 3005 M St. NW (30th St.), 202-342-0202

Pink November Buddhist Punk tops and Trashy Diva dresses are among the funky designs sold here. (p.80) 1529 Wisconsin Ave. NW (P St.), 202-333-1121

Relish A beauty bar and flower stand are added bonuses to the high-end menswear and women's fashions from designers like Marni and Comme des Garçons. (p.80) 3312 Cady's Alley (K St.), 202-333-5343

Sugar Must-have lines from Cynthia Steffe, Mason, and Beth Bowley draw fashionistas from all over. 1633 Wisconsin Ave. NW (Reservoir Rd.), 202-333-5331

Wink The status denim and flirty tops at Wink draw a fashion-conscious youngish crowd. 3109 M St. NW (31st St.), 202-338-9465

Chic D.C.: The Hotels

Four Seasons Hotel, Washington, D.C. • Georgetown • Grand (211 rms)
   The Four Seasons is easily the chicest hotel in D.C. Its staff are smartly attentive without fawning, greet you by name, and are always thinking ahead. The concierge is the best in town. A $25 million renovation completed in November 2005 smartened up the place. Guest rooms are fewer but larger and feature burled wood and black lacquer furnishings, muted periwinkle and sage fabrics, and bathrooms closed off by pocket doors. Though the hotel backs up to the C&O Canal, the view is unlovely, unfortunately, so instead ask for a deluxe room overlooking the courtyard on the second to sixth floors. In 2005, the Mobil Travel Guide awarded the hotel five stars, D.C.'s first and only. The hotel feels like a large, incredibly gorgeous home, though one shared with guests who travel with bodyguards and personal assistants. Former owner William Louis Dreyfus' wonderful 2,000-piece art collection hangs throughout the hotel, including the guest rooms. Fresh flowers are everywhere. Beyond that, the hotel's spa, fitness center, and restaurant are first class. The Seasons social scene happens nightly in the glamorous Terrace Lounge, where strategically placed potted greenery carves out private niches. Excellent live-jazz combos or soloists perform here every evening, and Saturday nights, the room is jammed. When you see a man seated alone, an earplug in one ear, think security, not iPod, and know that a head of state or foreign dignitary is in the crowd. $$$$+ 2800 Pennsylvania Ave. NW (28th St.), 202-342-0444 / 800-332-3442, fourseasons.com

The Hotel George • Capitol Hill • Trendy (139 rms)
   Groups like the Black Eyed Peas and others headlining around town like to scoot to this boutique hotel in the shadow of the Capitol, knowing that the service is discreet, the rooms stylishly comfortable, and savvy company and savory French bistro food are only an elevator ride away. Other hotels chase after over-the-top luxury; the George pursues sleek chic. A creamy white, clean-cut décor describes the guest rooms, where punchy duvets and 300-thread-count Egyptian-cotton linens cover the beds, blue leather covers the chairs, and black granite tops the desk. Those in the know ask for room 807, whose corner perch on the top floor faces E Street, and whose extra amenities include an exercise bike and a flat-screen plasma TV with DVD player. All guest rooms provide high-speed internet service and CD players. Onsite are a complimentary 24-hour fitness center, with men's and women's steam rooms, and the fabulous Bistro Bis, gathering spot morning, noon, and night for senators and representatives, and those wanting to talk to them. Both Bis and the hotel have several entrances, including a private one that allows access out of the public eye. $$$ 15 E St. NW (North Capitol St.), 202-347-4200 / 800-576-8331, hotelgeorge.com

Hotel Palomar, Washington, D.C. • Dupont Circle • Modern (335 rms)
   The new Hotel Palomar evokes a "1930s French Moderne" look that sets "Art in Motion," buzz language that boils down to mean the décor employs geometric forms and splashes of color to maximum effect. Its arty playfulness is just right for the neighborhood, which is full of galleries, cafes, coffeehouses, and

vibrant nightlife. Too soon to tell, but the restaurant, Urbana, is poised to lure inside some of those passersby, as well as hotel guests, for a taste of its Mediterranean fare. In each guest room are an elliptical-shaped desk, an undulated, mulberry-colored chaise lounge, zebrawood furniture, and a faux alabaster nightstand, with a granite stone vanity in the bathroom. The rooms are exceptionally large, averaging 520 square feet, and come with flat-screen TV, CD player, and free WiFi internet access; room 901 is the best of the bunch, with its floor-to-ceiling windows and 9th-floor position serving up tremendous views of P Street action. Guests gather each evening for complimentary wine in the hotel's dramatic, two-story lobby and have plenty of room to get comfortable in the deep-seated lounge chairs arranged before the crimson marble–clad fireplace. $$$ 2121 P St. NW (22nd St.), 202-448-1800 / 877-866-3070, hotelpalomar-dc.com

Mandarin Oriental, Washington, D.C. • Southwest • Modern (400 rms)
The Mandarin's location, in federal government office land west of Capitol Hill, and its size, at 400 guest rooms, go against the downtown boutique hotel trend. But the Mandarin doesn't give a whit. For one thing, world leaders doing business on Capitol Hill are for the first time able to stay in a nearby, ultraluxurious hotel. For another, the hotel is minutes from the Mall and Smithsonian museums. Most important, the hotel, with its top-rated restaurant, CityZen, best-in-city spa, and winning combination of Asian philosophy and Western luxury amenities, is a chic destination in itself. A clever design positions public rooms, as well as guest rooms, to overlook landscaped gardens, the Tidal Basin and marina, and the Jefferson Memorial (no other hotel can match that), and angles guest rooms to deliver good fortune, according to the tenets of feng shui. The most fabulous rooms are the 60 and 62 series; situated in the corner of the hotel on each floor, they present guests with both city and water views—in the bathrooms, too. Furnishings include exquisite Japanese tapestries and art, sumptuous bed linens, silken fabric–covered chaise longues, and every conceivable extra, from WiFi service to aromatherapy soaps. Service is top-notch. The hotel's nightlife scene has yet to arrive. $$$$+ 1330 Maryland Ave. SW (12th St.), 202-554-8588 / 888-888-1778, mandarinoriental.com/washington

Park Hyatt, Washington, D.C. • West End • Modern (215 rms)
Park Hyatts have always positioned themselves several steps above other brands in the Hyatt family. A recent "reconcepting" has taken this property to a different planet, one with its own fragrance (created by Parisian parfumeur Blaise Mautin) and personalized design. With the help of international designer Tony Chi and $24 million, the Park Hyatt Washington reopened in spring 2006 completely revamped. Polished glass and stainless steel combine with traditional American elements, like quilt patterns and rocking chairs, for a capital-chic appeal. The large, spa-inspired bathrooms feature limestone showers and separate soaking tubs. Beloved chef Brian McBride is still in the kitchen, but that's an open room now with wood-burning oven and fireplace turning out "farm-to-table" cuisine in the Blue Duck Tavern, the new restaurant. A tea cellar, where a revolving case displays rare teas, is a venue for tea tastings. Still the same: The hotel is within walking distance of Georgetown, and its deluxe guest rooms, measuring 618 square feet, remain the city's largest. Ask for rooms ending in

numbers 10, 16, or 24, on floors four through nine, for the brightest rooms with more windows. $$$$ 1201 24th St. NW (M St.), 202-789-1234 / 888-591-1234, parkhyattwashington.com

The Ritz-Carlton, Georgetown • Georgetown • Trendy (86 rms)
The prettiest room in this hotel is its lobby, which looks like a painting, crackling fire at one end and chairs in autumn colors of Granny Smith apple green and rusty red. Guest rooms are rather more handsome than pretty, heavy on the dark wood and square furniture look. The historic building encircles an old smokestack and incorporates century-old brick walls, like those in the lobby, into its structure. Though tucked away on a Georgetown back street, this Ritz attracts an international swarm of 20- and 30-somethings and touring rock stars to its bar, Degrees, where they enjoy signature drinks like the Fahrenheit Five martini and the Georgetown Punch, as trance music plays loudly in the not-quite background. The Ritz is small but has it all: a scene, spa, restaurant, bar, and location. Cool hangouts like Maté are just around the corner on the waterfront, and chic shops are everywhere nearby. Weekday guests are usually lawyers; weekends, it's mainly couples and friends seeking getaways. The fifth (top) floor corner room is one of the hotel's few overlooking the Potomac River. $$$$+ 3100 South St. NW (31st St.), 202-912-4100 / 800-241-3333, ritzcarlton.com

Chic D.C.:
The Restaurants

Acadiana • Penn Quarter • Southern
Best American Originals Power lunchers, classy couples, and young foodies alike are no match for the Southern charms of Acadiana. The dining room's understated elegance—its muted palette lit by antique chandeliers—allows you to focus on the real star: the food. Piping-hot biscuits give way to fried green tomatoes heaped with shrimp rémoulade or blackened tuna with cheddar spoonbread. Portions are huge, but be sure to leave room for the beignets. No time for dinner? Join the after-work crowd of lawyers, lobbyists, and journalists sipping Pimms at the bar. *Mon-Thu 11:30am–2:30pm and 5:30-10:30pm, Fri 11:30am-2:30pm and 5:30-11pm, Sat 5:30-11pm.* $$ B≡ 901 New York Ave. NW (Ninth St.), 202-408-8848, acadianarestaurant.com

Agua Ardiente* • Foggy Bottom • Latin American
This seductive restaurant and lounge draws a Euro-chic clientele. *See Chic Nightlife, p.69, for details.* $$ B≡ 1250 24th St. NW (M St.), 202-833-8500, agua-ardiente.com

Al Crostino • U Street Corridor • Italian
The food here says refined, but the sassy staff adds the dose of attitude and pep that make this tiny restaurant a big favorite in the ultrahot U Street neighborhood. Though standouts like spinach ricotta gnocchi in a Gorgonzola sauce and zucchini-encrusted whitefish in prosecco and mascarpone are standouts, the real stars are the daily specials, the list of which often runs longer than the menu itself. Just interested in a small meal? Sit at the tiny bar and munch on crostini while sipping one of the more than 30 Italian wines served by the glass. *Sun-Thu 5-10pm, Fri-Sat 5-11pm.* $ B≡ 1324 U St. NW (14th St.), 202-797-0523, alcrostino.com

Bangkok Bistro • Georgetown • Thai
Even the most dedicated of shoppers will find it hard to make it up Wisconsin Avenue without at least one refueling break. Reenergize for your retail rampage with a lunch stop at Bangkok Bistro. The waiters bring out a starter salad—the peanut dressing alone is worth the trip—while you peruse the extensive list of traditional Thai offerings. The front of the restaurant opens to the street on nice days, affording diners excellent eye candy to go with their larb gai, penang curry, and mangoes with sticky rice. *Sun noon-10:30pm, Mon-Thu 11:30am-10:30pm, Fri-Sat noon-11:30pm.* $ ≡ 3251 Prospect St. NW (Potomac St.), 202-337-2424

Bistro Bis • Capitol Hill • French Bistro
Best Always-Hot Tables A favorite haunt of politicians, Bistro Bis is busiest at lunch, when "the Capitol is on." Then again, it's always busy. Come at breakfast and note the limo cooling its heels at the curb for the CEO attending a meeting inside. Friday evenings after 7pm is a scene, with booths, bar, and upstairs filled with the capital's hard workers, ready to play. Bis is Capitol Hill's best restaurant, because of the glamorous tiered glass and cherrywood dining

room, the big-name clientele, and the food, oh yes, the fabulous food, from French toast in the morning to duck confit with white beans at night. *Daily 7-10am, 11:30am-2:30pm, 5:30-10:30pm.* $$ B≡ Hotel George, 15 E St. NW (N. Capitol St.), 202-661-2700, bistrobis.com

Blue Duck Tavern • West End • New American

The tonily chic look of this new restaurant incorporates classic American elements, like Windsor benches, black walnut tables, log chairs, and white oak floors, into a 21st-century tavern setting, where large windows fill the room with lots of natural light, glass panels create smaller spaces, and an open kitchen is on view wherever you're seated in the room. That open kitchen—no bar, no partition, no nothing—is the Blue Duck's pièce de résistance. Famed local chef Brian McBride is seen conducting his orchestra of comely (male) assistants as they slow-roast, braise, or smoke foods in the wood-burning oven, churn homemade ice cream in the hand-cranked ice cream maker, and then whisk it to your table. Classic American meets modern sophistication at the Blue Duck, and it doesn't just work—it thrills. *Daily 6:30-10:30am, 11:30am-2:30pm, 5:30-10:30pm.* $$$ ≡ Park Hyatt Washington Hotel, 1201 24th St. NW (M St.), 202-419-6755, blueducktavern.com

Butterfield 9 • Penn Quarter • New American

Best Romantic Dining A cocktail crowd gathers in the narrow bar right after work and then the singles go elsewhere, the marrieds go home, the bar empties out, and the dining room fills. Butterfield 9, with its *Vogue*-ish black-and-white fashion photos from the 1930s and '40s, evokes an air of romance and sophistication. Couples come here to dine, hoping to snag one of the booths on the lower first floor. The inventive American cuisine (duo of venison with spiced pistachio gateau), the service, and the ambience all enhance each other (large parties sit upstairs, where their laughter and conversation, drifting down, sparks the atmosphere without ruining it). *Mon-Thu 11:30am-2:30pm and 5:30-10pm, Fri 11:30am-2:30pm and 5:30-11pm, Sat-Sun 5:30-11pm.* $$ B≡ 600 14th St. NW (F St.), 202-289-8810, butterfield9.com

Café Atlantico • Penn Quarter • Nuevo Latino

Best Brunches Café Atlantico is always a party in progress. People come for the Nuevo Latino cuisine, including a popular Latin dim sum brunch on weekends, and for excellent cocktails, like mojitos and mango daiquiris. Chefs have changed over the years, but certain staples stay on the menu: the guacamole made table-side and the scallops with coconut rice, crispy rice, ginger, and squid among them. Located in the Penn Quarter, the spiraling multilevel restaurant is by now a regular stop on the star circuit, with George Clooney among those spotted here. The second level's best for sights of the open kitchen and for feeling in the thick of cha-cha reveling. *Sun-Thu 11:30am-2:30pm and 5-10pm, Fri-Sat 11:30am-2:30pm and 5-11pm.* $$ B≡ 405 Eighth St. NW (D St.), 202-393-0812, cafeatlantico.com

Café Milano* • Georgetown • Italian

Best Politico Sightings Legions of the world's famous pass through Milano's doors, from former prez Bill Clinton (loves the place) to Bono. Owner Franco Nucchese orchestrates a sunny atmosphere, limelight lovers flock to it, and the buzz perpetuates itself. Watch out for locals who hog the bar as if they own it and the

maitre d' who may try to seat you upstairs (quite nice, but is that what you want? No, thank you). If the restaurant's booked, settle for a drink at the bar, hold your ground, and stay cool. If seated, try the linguine with lobster or any of the pizzas. *Sun-Tue 11:30am-11pm, Wed-Sat 11:30am-midnight (extended bar hours).* $$$
🅱≡ 3251 Prospect St. NW (Wisconsin Ave.), 202-333-6183, cafemilanodc.com

Cashion's Eat Place* • Adams Morgan • American
Best Always-Hot Tables People come here for chef/owner Ann Cashion's cooking, which has garnered her endless awards; no matter what's on the menu—New Orleans–style gumbo, a mushroom ravioli, carrot cake—it's likely to be top of the line. And the atmosphere's a winner, thanks to a comfortably sexy bar and dining room, which is curving and dimly lit, with black-and-white photos on the wall. This is a small neighborhood restaurant that draws from all neighborhoods, and when you enter, you automatically feel like you belong. Diners include Washington wonks, lots of couples, and good-looking guys with sophisticated palates here on business. Dine in the bar or in the front window, if you enjoy surveying a scene, and at the back of the room for peeps of the kitchen. *Sun 11:30am-2:30pm and 5:30-10pm, Tue 5:30-10pm, Wed-Sat 5:30-11pm.* $$
🅱≡ 1819 Columbia Rd. NW (18th St.), 202-797-1819, cashionseatplace.com

Ceiba • Penn Quarter • Latin American
With its 45 tequilas and 25 rums, and the champagne-topped mojito its signature drink, Ceiba's bar is built for serious imbibers, and attracts them right after work weeknights. Still, Friday and Saturday nights are hottest for both the dining room and bar. Couples and quartets of 20- to 40-somethings relish the modern Latin mood created by pastel paintings and murals depicting flowery, bird-populated jungles. Beyond the cool décor and fun drinks, Ceiba is about seriously good ceviche, conch chowder, and other Latin culinary treats. Insist on dining in the room to your right as you enter, and for the best table, try for the right-hand pocket. *Mon-Thu 11:30am-2:30pm and 5:30-10:30pm, Fri 11:30am-2:30pm and 5:30-11pm, Sat 5:30-11pm.* $$ 🅱≡ 701 14th St. NW (G St.), 202-393-3983, ceibarestaurant.com

CityZen • Southwest • New American (G)
Best Hot Chefs Whatever is happening in the city—Kennedy Center Honors, Congressional hearing, art exhibit grand opening, NBA playoffs, film shoot—you can be sure that at least some of the main players will be dining here that night. They'll be here for the same reason you are: chef Eric Ziebold's inspired new American cuisine, and a candlelit and columned, high-ceilinged dining room in which to enjoy it. The menu changes monthly, but recent dishes included noisettes of Atlantic monkfish tail with sauce Bordelaise, and sautéed lamb chop and braised short ribs with a spinach éclair. *Tue-Thu 6-9:30pm, Fri-Sat 5:30-9:30pm.* $$$$ 🅱≡ Mandarin Oriental Hotel, 1330 Maryland Ave. SW (12th St.), 202-787-6006, mandarinoriental.com/washington

DC Coast • White House • New American
D.C. was ripe for an unabashedly stylish place like DC Coast when chef Jeff Tunks opened it in 1998. Its two-story-high ceiling, enormous mirrors above the bar, and statuesque stone mermaid at the entrance were all designed to make a splash, and it worked. So did the menu, which was a little bit Louisiana, Pacific Rim, and the Chesapeake. The eldest in the Tunks empire that now includes

Acadiana, TenPenh, and Ceiba, DC Coast is as hot as ever, because of its K Street location and all those hungry lawyers, who can't get enough of the Chinese-style smoked lobster and the chance flirtations at the bar. *Mon-Thu 11:30am-2:30pm and 5:30-10:30pm, Fri 11:30am-2:30pm and 5:30-11pm, Sat 5:30-11pm (bar fare Mon-Fri 2:30pm until closing, Sat 5:30pm until closing).* $$ B≡ 1401 K St. NW (14th St.), 202-216-5988, dccoast.com

Dino • Upper Northwest • Italian
Nestled in the dateland that is Cleveland Park is this cozy Italian eatery and enoteca. The décor is nouveau rustic with warm copper walls, gnarled wood sculptures, and slightly funky quilt hangings. Chic young couples canoodle over dishes designed for snacking and sharing. Let the plucky staff be your guide to the meticulously crafted wine list, which introduces pinks with the warning, "Caution: may be dangerous to your preconceived notions of rose." The only whim this restaurant won't cater to is cell phone addiction. The menu warns: "Ringing cell phones will be cooked in our Girarrosto." *Sun 11:30am-2:30pm and 5-9:30pm, Mon-Thu 5:30-9:30pm, Fri 5:30-10:30pm, Sat 11:30am-2:30pm and 5-10:30pm.* $$ ▭ 3435 Connecticut Ave. NW (Ordway St.), 202-686-2966, dino-dc.com

Dragonfly* • Dupont Circle • Sushi
Enjoy a sleek scene and sushi menu accompanied by saketinis. *See Chic Nightlife, p.70, for details.* $$ B≡ 1215 Connecticut Ave. NW (Rhode Island Ave.), 202-331-1775, dragonflysushibar.com

IndeBleu* • Penn Quarter • French-Indian
Best Restaurant Lounges It's a testament to chef Vikram Garg that neither the restaurant's chic lounge nor its star clientele—from Ryan Phillippe to Ethan Hawke—outshine its stellar French-Indian cuisine. Indulge in a night at the chef's table, which rotates so diners can watch dishes like sea bass with coconut-turmeric mussels be prepared. At IndeBleu, the decadence is in the details. From the bathrooms—soft waterfalls gurgle from the sinks—to the check—tax is labeled "IRS BS" and your total "The dough you owe"—this "it" restaurant trades in serious food that doesn't take itself too seriously. Weeknights entertain business crowds. On the weekends, stylish singles are drawn to the sexy tension between the buttoned-up elegance of the dining room and the sensuous revelry of the lounge below. *Sun 5:30-10:45pm, Mon-Thu 11:30am-1:30pm and 5:30-10:45pm, Fri 11:30am-1:30pm and 5:30-11pm, Sat 5:30-11pm.* $$$ B≡ 707 G St. NW (Seventh St.), 202-333-2538, bleu.com/indebleu

Indique • Upper Northwest • Indian
Best Indian Restaurants Indian food is the "in" thing these days and this is the cuisine's "it-est" place. The two-level townhouse restaurant centers on an atrium, where customers sip un-Indian Bellinis while waiting to be seated there, in an adjoining window-fronted bar, or upstairs. That glassed-in bar juts out from the facade, so to pedestrians passing by when a full-throttle bender is under way, it can appear as if the whole packed crowd, tables and all, is about to tumble onto the sidewalk. Inside you're likely to be oblivious, if the craziness is what it should be. (Sit upstairs at a table bordering the atrium if you prefer to survey but not partake in the shenanigans.) Indique's décor is lovely, with red and golden walls, blue painted ceilings, and large windows surveying Connecticut

Avenue. By 7pm weeknights, it's jammed; Friday and Saturday nights, book ahead or expect to wait two hours for a table. Favorite dishes include vegetable samosa chaat and chicken curry. Lunch sees an embassy crowd, especially Indian and British; at dinner, it's a mix of the neighborhood and young singles swooping in. *Sun-Thu noon-3pm and 5:30-10:30pm, Fri-Sat noon-3pm and 5:30-11pm.* $ B≡ 3512-14 Connecticut Ave. NW (Ordway St.), 202-244-6600, indique.com

Komi • Dupont Circle • New American

Komi's modest dining room plays second fiddle to the real star: wunderkind chef Johnny Monis. Monis was only 24 at Komi's 2004 opening, and the restaurant's little touches—the check comes with homemade chocolate lollipops—reflect his youthful enthusiasm. A staff as hot as Monis—you may catch a view of him toiling in the open kitchen—delivers the amuse-bouche while gushing about the day's offerings. The atmosphere makes what would be foodie heaven into a hot spot for the young and the hungry. Reservations are a must any night of the week, but dress is relatively casual. *Tue-Fri 6-9:30pm, Sat 6-10pm.* $$ ≡ 1509 17th St. NW (Church St.), 202-332-9200

Lauriol Plaza • Dupont Circle • Tex-Mex

When the weather heats up, D.C.'s hot young things make a mass migration to Lauriol Plaza. The sidewalk tables and mammoth wall of windows add to the see-and-be-seen feel of this upscale Tex-Mex eatery. You'd be hard-pressed to find a weekend when the waiting crowds aren't spilling onto 18th Street with margaritas in hand. Happily, there isn't a bad seat on any one of the four floors from sidewalk to roof deck. As for the food, Mexican staples are well executed, but for a real treat, order a juicy Cuban-style steak. *Sun-Thu 11:30am-11pm, Fri-Sat 11:30am-midnight.* $ B≡ 1835 18th St. NW (Swann St.), 202-387-0035, lauriolplaza.com

Lebanese Taverna • Upper Northwest • Lebanese

The bad news is that they don't take reservations for tables after 6:30pm. The good news is that the extensive Lebanese wine list and hummus will make the wait a pleasure. Family-style servings and mezze make this D.C. institution an ideal spot for groups and couples alike. Although the courtyard-style dining room décor is subdued, a boisterous family atmosphere prevails. The jovial staff treat diners like guests in their own home and do an excellent job guiding first-timers through the extensive menu. *Sun 3-9:30pm, Mon 11:30am-2:30pm and 5:30-10pm, Tue-Thu 11:30am-2:30pm and 5:30-10:30pm, Fri-Sat 11:30am-2:30pm and 5:30-11pm.* $ B≡ 2641 Connecticut Ave. NW (24th St.), 202-265-8681, lebanesetaverna.com

LeftBank* • Adams Morgan • International

LeftBank's menu and clientele reflect its Parisian sibling's international flavor, and communal tables encourage diners to socialize over small plates and sushi. Or come for Sunday's Moët & Chandon mimosa brunches. *See Chic Nightlife, p.72, for details.* $ BO≡ 2424 18th St. NW (Columbia Rd.), 202-464-2100, leftbankdc.com

Leopold's Kafe & Konditorei • Georgetown • New American–Austrian

This place got off to a rough start in spring 2005, earning scathing reviews for service, though everyone seemed to love the food. Taking the hint, staff are more attentive now, while the preparations have never strayed from purely delicious. Available all day are Austrian classics like veal schnitzel, breakfast delectables like sugar brioche, various savories like the black olive and sweet onion tart, and many mouth-watering pastries. Darlingly modern, with glass walls, white Italian furniture, and colorful flower-petal seats at the counter, the cafe is hard to find but worth seeking out, especially when shopping in the little Cady's Alley complex, at the western end of Georgetown. *Sun 8am-9pm, Tue-Thu 8am-10pm, Fri-Sat 8am-11pm.* $ Cady's Alley, 3318 M St. NW (33rd St.), 202-965-6005, kafeleopolds.com

Lima* • Downtown • Latin American
Best Restaurant Lounges Lima offers a great bar scene downstairs and an elegant dining room upstairs. *See Chic Nightlife, p.72, for details.* $$$ 1401 K St. NW (14th St.), 202-789-2800, limarestaurant.com

Mendocino Grille and Wine Bar • Georgetown • New American
The waiter looks like a Latino George Clooney, but acts like he doesn't know it. The bar at the front overlooks M Street, and this is where the regulars gather. Back in the wooden-floored, stone-walled main dining room, George Clooney places a little bowl of warmed olives upon the table, soon to be followed by a warm spinach salad, then a bouillabaisse with a piquant rouille. The pace picks up and handsome couples mostly fill the banquettes, over which hang large mirrors. A woman looks up from her menu to see her partner checking himself out in the mirror: Leo DiCaprio, maybe? No, George Clooney. *Sun-Thu 5:30-10pm, Fri-Sat 5:30-11pm.* $$ 2917 M St. NW (29th St.), 202-333-2912, mendocinodc.com

Mie N Yu* • Georgetown • Middle Eastern
Come for the buzzing bar scene and fabulous fare in an exotic setting. *See Chic Nightlife, p.74, for details.* $$ 3125 M St. NW (31st St.), 202-333-6122, mienyu.com

Oya* • Penn Quarter • French-Asian
Best Restaurant Lounges Oya seems innocent enough with pure white lounges tucked into alcoves and a respectable French-Asian menu. But you enter past a chain curtain to reach the red crocodile bar. Fires smolder in the walls' recessed marble fireplaces. As you sip a Shochu cocktail, tilted mirrors on the walls awaken voyeuristic tendencies. Oya may be ideal for predinner drinks, but the simpering sexuality of the space may have you skipping the meal altogether and heading back to the hotel early. *Sun 5:30-10pm, Mon-Fri 11:30am-2:30pm and 5:30pm-1am, Sat 5:30pm-1am.* $$ 777 Ninth St. NW (H St.), 202-393-1400, oyadc.com

Palena • Upper Northwest • Italian–New American (G)
Best Hot Chefs Successful young sophisticates impress their parents, and older urbanites each other, by booking a table in Palena's formal dining room. Its design draws on the Italian Renaissance, with use of antique golds and deep reds, intricately designed chandeliers, heavy velvet drapes, and a 16th-century statue of Minerva. Personable waiters ply you with chef/owner Frank Ruta's elegant cuisine, prepared with fresh-from-the-market ingredients, maybe artichoke and fennel in a salad of hazelnuts, or a duo of venison loin and beef short ribs braised with quince and chestnuts. Diners always leave room for renowned pastry chef Ann Amernick's creations, like the almond-lemon pithivier. The slightly less fancy front room takes walk-ins at the cushy bar, which attracts a sportier,

younger set, especially Monday nights, when only the bar area and the cafe menu are available. *Tue-Sat 5:30-10pm. $$$* B≣ *Cafe: Mon-Sat 5:30-10pm. $-* 3529 Connecticut Ave. NW (Porter St.), 202-537-9250, palenarestaurant.com

Pesce • Dupont Circle • Seafood
Regulars arrive expecting to stand in line at Pesce, knowing that the restaurant doesn't accept reservations. It's part of the drill and part of the fun, too, since it practically requires you to eavesdrop on conversations and notice who's here and what they're eating. This neighborhood hangout is also cherished by Washington wonks, whose long hours and last-minute conference calls wreak havoc with reservation-only restaurants (look at the poor sods: still working the phone as they wait for a table). Pesce does fresh fish every which way, grilling whole snapper, sautéeing softshell crabs, pan-frying shad roe, each to perfection. The room is crowded with tables too close together, but it all adds up to a festive atmosphere. *Sun 5-9:30pm, Mon-Thu 11:30am-2:30pm and 5:30-10pm, Fri 11:30am-2:30pm and 5:30-10:30pm, Sat 5:30-10:30pm. $$* ≣ 2016 P St. NW (20th St.), 202-466-3474, pescebistro.com

Rasika • Penn Quarter • Indian
Best Trendy Tables This newcomer arrived on the scene exuding an assured and sensuous sophistication. Lounge and dining room are divided by a half-wall and a line of strung glass beads that form a curtain. Soft lighting shimmers off these glass accents, bestowing a sexy glow upon the cinnamon-and-gold-toned rooms and upon the fashionable set that gathers here. Favorite drinks are clove martinis and mango cosmopolitans; best-loved dishes are palak chaat (crispy baby spinach) and tandoori black cod. Revel in the luxurious experience of leaning back against a banquette, tilting a highball to your lips, exchanging honeyed glances with that delightful creature at the bar, and feeling your pulse race. *Mon-Thu 11:30am-2:30pm and 5:30-10:30pm, Fri 11:30am-2:30pm and 5:30-11pm, Sat 5:30-11pm. Lounge serves light meals all day. $$* B◊≣ 633 D St. NW (Seventh St.), 202-637-1222, rasikarestaurant.com

Rosa Mexicano* • Penn Quarter • Mexican
A buzzing bar scene, colorful décor, and authentic Mexican fare make this a very popular spot. *See Chic Nightlife, p.75, for details. $$* B◊≣ 575 Seventh St. NW (F St.), 202-783-5522, rosamexicano.info

Sonoma Restaurant and Wine Bar* • Capitol Hill • New American
Best Trendy Tables The words "chic" and "Capitol Hill" are seldom seen together, but this restaurant offers that rare opportunity. A 20- and 30-something crowd packs the place, especially Thursday and Friday nights. In suits and ties but also open collars and jeans, they balance on pointy-toed stilettos or in flat-footed Pumas, taking their drinks up and on a stem. Downstairs is the bistro, where the kitchen serves up pizzas, pastas, and entrées, like arctic char with sweet potato-celery root hash, using mostly organic ingredients. The big thing here, though, is to order a board of cheeses and charcuterie for sharing, with the right wine to accompany it. Upstairs is the lounge, also a scene as the night wags on. *Sun 5:30-9pm, Mon-Thu 11:30am-2:30pm and 5:30-10pm, Fri 11:30am-2:30pm and 5:30-11pm, Sat 5:30-11pm (lounge stays open later). $* B◊≣ 223 Pennsylvania Ave. SE (Second St.), 202-544-8088, sonomadc.com

Tabaq Bistro* • U Street Corridor • Middle Eastern

Tabaq Bistro has the best view in D.C., but it makes you work for it. Climb four flights of stairs past the subterranean hookah lounge and slick red room bar, and you'll be rewarded with Turkish tapas and drinks beneath a retractable roof that opens to the stars. Highlights include mini Turkish ravioli served in a light yogurt sauce and apricot-and-parsley-stuffed chicken with pomegranate dressing. Unlike the more bohemian U Street watering holes, Tabaq has a strictly enforced dress code that prohibits shorts, running shoes, and sloppy jeans. The crowd is as beautiful as the views, so dress the part. *Sun 11am-4pm and 5-11pm, Mon-Thu 5-11pm, Fri 3pm-midnight, Sat 11am-4pm and 5pm-midnight.* $ B≡ 1336 U St. NW (13th St.), 202-265-0965, tabaqdc.com

Teatro Goldoni • White House • Italian

Best Chef's Tables Nobody likes a bargain better than a reporter, so this restaurant, with its weekday $12.50 bar lunch, draws a ton of the old-school clutch, who congregate around booth 5, close to the bar, where they can smoke (until D.C.'s smoking ban goes into effect). Teatro also attracts the types of people reporters cover: Jack Valenti, Sharon Stone, Jim Kimsey—weeknights only. Come the weekend, it's the bronzed, deep-pocket crowd from the 'burbs. The dining room is spectacularly colorful and dramatic, like a carnival. The cuisine is really splendid, from frito misto to the house-made limoncello and mascarpone ice cream. *Mon-Thu 11:30am-2pm and 5-10pm, Fri 11:30am-2pm and 5-11pm, Sat 5-11pm.* $$$ B≡ 1909 K St. NW (19th St.), 202-955-9494, teatrogoldoni.com

TenPenh • Penn Quarter • Asian Fusion

A young, casually dressed crowd frequents this downtown hot spot. The main dining room is emphatically Asian, with its lacquered-wood tabletops, bronzed Buddha, and lotus-blossom light fixtures. A templelike cutout wall partly reveals the kitchen, where chef Jeff Tunks may be, if he's not presiding over one of his three other establishments. Black-attired waitstaff wearing stand-up Chinese collars carry out plates of crispy whole fish and shrimp-and-chive dumplings. Warm weather opens the restaurant's sidewalk cafe, and here you can sit on Pennsylvania Avenue, the Capitol in view ten blocks away. *Mon-Thu 11:30am-2:30pm and 5:30-10:30pm, Fri 11:30am-2:30pm and 5:30-11pm, Sat 5:30-11pm (bar fare served half-hour after kitchen closing times).* $$ B≡ 1001 Pennsylvania Ave. NW (10th St.), 202-393-4500, tenpenh.com

Tosca • Penn Quarter • Italian (G)

Best Fine Dining Tosca is an elegant restaurant, of the silently moving waiters and muted décor variety. Drama lies on the plate, on which chef Cesare Lancanfroni arranges dishes from his native Lombardy region of Italy: salad of radicchio and Bartlett pears, organic squash gnocchi dumplings with truffled fontina, and pan-seared venison chops with slow-braised green cabbage, pomegranate, and black currant sauce. Lunch diners are all business, while evening brings a mix of professionals seated at tables of four and eight, interspersed with beautiful young couples enjoying a romantic repast. *Mon-Thu 11:30am-2:30pm and 5:30-10:30pm, Fri 11:30am-2:30pm and 5:30-11pm, Sat 5:30-11pm.* $$$ B≡ 1112 F St. NW (12th St.), 202-367-1990, toscadc.com

Zaytinya* • Penn Quarter • Mediterranean

Best Trendy Tables This trendiest of D.C. restaurants is big and sits, of all places, in the first-floor side pocket of a modern office building. Its broad glass facade reveals how crowded the restaurant is, and the answer most nights after 7pm is: crowded. Different sorts turn up. Foodies adore chef Jose Andres and his small-plate interpretations of Turkish, Greek, and Lebanese cuisine. Cool, young, straight, and gay scene-makers jam the bar, spilling out either end into the main dining room. (To feel in the center of things, ask for tables 6 or 43.) The vibe is fun to the point of frantic at times, which means service isn't always what it should be. And if waiting for a table is not an option, dine at lunch or between 5pm and 6:30pm, the only times that Zaytinya accepts reservations. *Sun-Mon 11:30am-10pm, Tue-Thu 11:30am-11:30pm, Fri-Sat 11:30am-midnight.* $$ 701 Ninth St. NW (G St.), 202-638-0800, zaytinya.com

Zengo* • Penn Quarter • Asian-Latin

This new restaurant whose cuisine melds Latin and Asian tastes achieves the same sort of cultural mix in its patronage. At no other Washington restaurant are you as likely to encounter such diversity. Starting with the attractive, racially different threesome greeting you at the reception desk, Zengo is a mix of black, white, Asian, and Latino peoples in a sultry setting that features a lounge with low-slung seats and curving bar downstairs and a dining room with open kitchen and ceviche bar upstairs. The grand stone staircase that separates the two offers patrons the chance to vogue midway to lounge-dwellers below, though some are slow to catch on. Service is gracious downstairs, needs improvement upstairs; up or down, Zengo is loud and jumping. *Sun 5-10pm, Mon-Thu 11:30am-2:30pm and 5-10pm, Fri 11:30am-2:30pm and 5-11:30pm, Sat 5-11:30pm (lounge and bar stay open later).* $$ 781 Seventh St. NW (H St.), 202-393-2929, modernmexican.com/zengodc

Zola* • Penn Quarter • American

Best American Originals When work lets out, the power players take the intrigue downtown to hot spot Zola. Though it's housed next to the Spy Museum, this nouveau American eatery is no kitschy cafe. The menu—like the crowd—has a sophisticated and playfully risky take on the classics—a mac 'n' cheese appetizer gets dressed up with lobster and fontina. Pork loin is smothered in black plum molasses. Wash it all down with a shaken-not-stirred martini at a high-backed velvet booth amid glass etched with KGB code. *Sun 5-9pm, Mon-Thu 11:30am-3pm and 5-10pm, Fri 11:30am-3pm and 5-11pm, Sat 5pm-11pm.* $$ 800 F Street NW (Eighth St.), 202-654-0999, zoladc.com

Chic D.C.: The Nightlife

Agua Ardiente* • Foggy Bottom • Bar
   Best International Scenes The food and cocktails are Latin American, but this restaurant lounge attracts expats from every continent, especially Europe. The unofficial dress code is black, black, and more black, which is just as well, considering the seductive palette of Agua's restaurant and lounge. Burnished gold and deep red walls glow by the light of innumerable candles. Take full advantage of the space by reserving a table in the VIP room. It provides a welcome respite when DJs pack the dance floor with Latin and Arabic beats. *Mon-Wed 5:30-10:30pm, Thu-Fri 5:30-11pm, Sat 6-11pm.* 1250 24th St. NW (M St.), 202-833-8500, agua-ardiente.com

Bardeo • Upper Northwest • Bar
   Much like the animals on Noah's Ark, drinkers and diners in Cleveland Park come in twos—first-date twos, anniversary-celebrating twos, and occasionally double-date twos. In Couples-land, the Bardeo wine bar would play the part of the honeymoon period. The intimacy of the space, the passion of the fiery-red walls and full-bodied merlots, and the flirtatiousness of shared small plates smack of the dizzy days of a new relationship. The weekend crowds can make navigating the small space difficult, so be sure to snag seats in a cozy booth or at the long marble bar. *Sun-Thu 5-11pm, Fri-Sat 5pm-1am.* 3311 Connecticut Ave. NW (Macomb & Porter Sts.), 202-244-6550, bardeo.com

Blue Gin • Georgetown • Lounge
   Best Singles Scenes Owen Wilson and Vince Vaughn partied here while filming *Wedding Crashers*, and it's not hard to figure out why. Blue Gin, tucked down an alley off Wisconsin Avenue in Georgetown, provides just the right mix of upmarket exclusivity and rowdy fun. Although the young and stylish spend hundreds to reserve tables in the sleek upstairs lounge, Saturdays find a high-energy percussionist pulling girls up to dance on the bar. The bartenders are serious about cocktails—mixing designer liquors with fresh fruit purees—but playful with patrons. The second level, where glass floor panels provide glimpses of the action below and movies are projected onto a recessed brick wall, is the place to be. *Wed-Thu 7pm-2am, Fri-Sat 7pm-3am.* 1206 Wisconsin Ave. (M St.), 202-965-5555, bluegindc.com

Café Milano* • Georgetown • Restaurant Bar
   Come to enjoy the power-player scene at this stylish bar. *See Chic Restaurants, p.61, for details.* 3251 Prospect St. NW (Wisconsin Ave.), 202-333-6183, cafemilanodc.com

Cashion's Eat Place* • Adams Morgan • Restaurant Bar
   The bar's unstuffy sophistication draws an eclectic crowd, from artists to lobbyists. *See Chic Restaurants, p.62, for details.* 1819 Columbia Rd. NW (Biltmore St.), 202-797-1819, cashionseatplace.com

Chloe • Adams Morgan • Bar

Best Singles Scenes The small sign marking Chloe is easy to overlook, but the line snaking down 18th Street every weekend certainly isn't. The crowds don't seem to mind the club's grab-bag décor of glowing glass panels, exposed brick, and color-blind furniture pairings. Perhaps it's because the furniture is obscured by the writhing masses of scantily clad girls dancing on top of it. Pony up for table service to skip the line and ensure access to the coveted roof deck and second floor where DJs spin house and hip-hop in a suspended metal globe. If you opt out of table service, be prepared to wait. *Sun 11:30am-10pm, Tue-Thu 5:30pm-1am, Fri-Sat 5:30pm-3am.* 2473 18th St. NW (Columbia Rd.), 202-265-6592, chloedc.com

Cobalt • Dupont Circle • Gay Bar

Best Gay Bars Located in what is affectionately known as the "gay-berhood" on 17th Street, Cobalt offers two clubs in one: a classy cocktail lounge and a raucous dance club. The unmarked entrance above Food Bar D.C. feeds into the smoke-free 30 Degrees Lounge, where men sip cocktails amid a décor of dark-wood floors and cozy couches. Just upstairs, a young crowd dances to thumping house and retro remixes. Though the second floor looks the worse for wear, the Thursday and Friday night crowds pack the dance floor until the lights come on. *Sun 6pm-1:30am, Mon 5pm-1:30am, Tue-Thu 5pm-2am, Fri-Sat 5pm-3am.* 1639 R St. NW (17th St.), 202-462-6569, cobaltdc.com

Degrees • Georgetown • Hotel Bar

Best Hotel Bars Built in an old incinerator building, this is not your parents' Ritz Carlton. The leather club chairs remain—but they sit beneath vibrant abstract paintings and subtle industrial touches. The moneyed clientele remains, but it has traded Chanel suits for designer jeans. This classic-modern mix makes the hotel's lobby and bar an ideal place to bookend dinner. Looking for a romantic pre-meal drink? Opt for the lobby lounge, where plush sofas ring a towering jet-black fireplace, and a grand piano muffles cooing couples. Just starting the night off? Heat things up at Degrees, where some of D.C.'s top bartenders mix up first-rate cocktails like the Georgetown Punch. The bar tends to empty by midnight as patrons head to nearby hot spots like Maté and Blue Gin. *Sun-Thu 2:30pm-midnight, Fri-Sat 2:30pm-2am.* Ritz-Carlton, Georgetown, 3100 South St. NW (31st St.), 202-912-4100, ritzcarlton.com/hotels/georgetown

Dragonfly* • Dupont Circle • Restaurant/Club

It's midnight, and you need the two s's to keep the night moving: sushi and saketinis. Look no further than Dragonfly, the über-chic restaurant and club in the buzzing Dupont club district. Frosted glass obscures the space-pod barstools and sleek white interior from those on the street. The lines are mercifully fast on the weekends, so you're likely to make it inside quickly. Dining? Opt for a table downstairs where anime flicks light the stark walls. Head upstairs afterward to dance to progressive house and hip-hop. *Sun 7pm-2am, Mon-Thu 5:30pm-2am, Fri 5:30pm-3am, Sat 7pm-3am.* 1215 Connecticut Ave. NW (Rhode Island Ave.), 202-331-1775, dragonflysushibar.com

Eyebar • Downtown • Bar

Best Sexy Lounges Though the name refers to the two-level bar's location on I— aka Eye—Street, it also references a thematic element of the sleek Euro lounge's décor: seen and not seen. Dark mirrors are revealed to be two-way when images emerge from flat-panel TVs hidden behind them. A shared sink between bathrooms affords glimpses of hands washed in the adjacent room. The popularity of Saturday's house and trance night means you'll have to be on the list to gain entry. Though you can call or email list@eyebardc.com, the best way to skip the line is to reserve a table for bottle service. *Tue-Thu 5pm-1am, Fri 5pm-3am, Sat 11pm-3am.* 1716 I St. NW (17th St.), 202-785-0270, eyebardc.com

Felix • Adams Morgan • Bar

Felix packs a punch despite its relatively small space. The drink menu boasts more than 20 top-flight specialty cocktails. The kitchen serves up Mediterranean-inspired small plates. The nouveau Art Deco décor matches the stylish yet unpretentious patrons. Top-notch combos lay down jazz and funk grooves to fill the small dance floor. The music can sometimes inhibit mingling, so Felix offers the adjoining Spy Lounge for chatting and the upstairs Zipper Lounge for more dancing. *Sun-Thu 5pm-2am, Fri-Sat 5pm-3am.* 2406 18th St. NW (Columbia Rd.), 202-483-3549, thefelix.com

Fly Lounge • Dupont Circle • Lounge

The pet project of the famous DJ Dirty Hands, Fly is one of the most exclusive tickets on the D.C. scene. The long thin lounge looks much like a private jet cabin, complete with curved aluminum walls, flat-screen plane windows, and scantily clad stewardesses serving up peanuts along with pricey bottle service. Fly attracts a first-class crowd, so dress the part or you'll be left at the gate— that means no flip-flops, no hats, and definitely no pleated khakis. Tables will run you $600 on the weekends, but that may be the only way to get in on a Saturday. *Tue-Thu 9pm-2am, Fri-Sat 9pm-3am.* 1802 Jefferson Pl. NW (18th St.), 202-828-4333, flyloungedc.com

Gazuza • Dupont Circle • Lounge

Best Outdoor Drinking Those lucky enough to snag spots on the balcony recline on bedlike lounges as Hitchcock flicks are projected on the brick walls of neighboring buildings. Gazuza is Spanish for hunger, but the crowds come for the seating as much as the food. Fridays host up-tempo hip-hop and house while Saturdays mix in bhangra and Arabic beats. Although heaters and an over-hanging roof ensure that the balcony is a year-round hot spot, it's easy to be seduced by the inside bar where groups share hookahs under candles that seem to float on the walls. The crowd is diverse—gay, straight, black, white, and everything in between—but is united by a sense of style and international flair. *Daily 5pm-last call (generally around 2:30am on weekends).* 1629 Connecticut Ave. NW (Q St.), 202-667-5500, latinconcepts.com/gazuza

Halo • U Street Corridor • Gay Bar

Best Gay Bars Halo eschews the D.C. gay bars' penchant for Madonna, kitschy specials, and shirtless dance parties. Instead, well-heeled gay men lounge on sleek white and orange leather couches. Glowing glass pillars double as tables, bar bottles are backlit by mod-orange panels, and the whole space has the feel of a boutique hotel bar. The health-conscious set appreciate the low-carb and alcohol-free drink offerings, but most opt for the seasonal cocktail menu. Expect lines for Thursday and Friday postwork hours and most of the night Saturday. The downtempo lounge music stays low enough to encourage conversation and discourage dancing all night. *Sun-Thu 5pm-1:30am, Fri-Sat 5pm-2:30am.* 1435 P St. NW (14th St.), 202-797-9730, halodc.com

IndeBleu* • Penn Quarter • Restaurant Lounge
Don't be fooled by the generic entrance bar to this superchic French-Indian restaurant lounge. Squeeze past the DJ booth and recline along with other sleekly clad young things on buttery banquettes cushioned by richly embroidered pillows. Settle in, because it may take you a while to choose one of the bar's exotic cocktails. Thankfully, the mixologists can guide you through the decision with a menu styled on D.C.'s metro map. Start on the blue—sorry, Bleu—line, with a house cocktail, change lines with a champagne drink, or throw back a white chocolate shot. The bathrooms are a must-see: Flat-screen TVs replace mirrors as cameras catch you fixing your hair. *Daily 5:30pm-2am.* 707 G St. NW (Seventh St.), 202-333-2538, bleu.com/indebleu

K Street Lounge • Downtown • Lounge
Best Sexy Lounges With blocks of expense-account law offices and lobbying firms lining K Street, it was only a matter of time before K Street Lounge hit the scene. Reserve a table at least a week in advance to skip the long lines of urbanistas that form on the weekends. Inside, stunning waitresses ferry bottles of top-shelf liquor alight with sparklers from the white-on-white bar that lines one wall to the velvet-roped VIP section that lines the other. Despite the exclusivity, the lounge has an energetic, youthful feel. Fridays cater to an international clientele, while the retro dance mixes make for a younger Saturday crowd. *Thu 5pm-2am, Fri-Sat 10pm-3am.* 1301 K St. NW (14th St.), 202-962-3933, kstreetdc.com

LeftBank* • Adams Morgan • Lounge
The glowing orbs and mod-orange booths of this restaurant lounge would not be out of place on *la vraie rive gauche*. Don designer denim and sky-high heels and join the Euro-chic crowd sipping signature champagne cocktails. LeftBank's menu and clientele reflect its Parisian sibling's international flavor, and communal tables encourage diners to socialize over small plates and sushi. After dinner, sip martinis by the fire in the glass-enclosed back lounge. Can't get enough? Peruse European design magazines over Sunday's Moët & Chandon mimosa brunches. *Sun 10am-4:30pm and 5-11:30pm, Mon-Thu 5-11:30pm, Fri 5pm-1am, Sat 10am-4pm and 5pm-1am.* 2424 18th St. NW (Columbia Rd.), 202-464-2100, leftbankdc.com

Lima* • Downtown • Restaurant Lounge
Lima—named after the Spanish word for "lime," not the Peruvian capital—boasts clean modern lines softened with organic touches like reservoirs of water, floors of rock, and flames ... coming from the tops of Grey Goose bottles. Though the third-floor dining room attracts D.C.'s moneyed elite, the real fun happens in the subterranean lounge, where DJs spin in a suspended booth and the international set reclines on buttery leather sofas. However, one design element might pose problems later in the night: Avoid the transparent staircase if you've had one too many caipirinhas. *Mon-Thu 6-10:30pm, Fri-Sat 6-11pm.* 1401 K St. NW (14th St.), 202-789-2800, limarestaurant.com

CHIC • NIGHTLIFE

Local 16 • U Street Corridor • Bar
Best Outdoor Drinking It's hard to pull yourself away from the baroque drama of this bar's merlot-colored walls, draped fabrics, and crystal chandeliers. But do so and you'll be rewarded with the best rooftop bar in D.C. Open to the stars but obscured by manicured greenery, this is where hot young professionals come to mingle into the wee hours over pricey cocktails. DJs spin everything from Brazilian beats to old-school soul. But the music takes a back seat to the mingling. Lines can be unbearable on beautiful nights, and there's no guest list. Book a table for dinner or be prepared to wait. *Sun-Thu 5:30pm-2am, Fri-Sat 5:30pm-3am.* 1604 U St. NW (16th St.), 202-265-2828, localsixteen.com

Love • Northeast • Club
Best Dance Clubs In life, love may be a high-stakes, volatile investment, but at the D.C. club bearing its name, if you're willing to front the cash, you're guaranteed to enjoy impressive returns. From the mahogany concierge desk to the penthouse VIP area, Love caters to a high-rolling nightlife clientele. It's been the setting for performances by Beyoncé and the Roots, and for Cam'Ron's video "Hey Ma." Love's five levels mean there's something for every nightlife taste, from lounging to dancing to hip-hop, Latin, trance, house, and international beats. Waits can be upwards of an hour on popular nights, but you can choose one of two ways to expedite the process: bottle service—which runs from $400 into the thousands depending on where you'd like to sit—or the cut line—where you can pay $40 and up for instant entrance. It's in a rough neighborhood on the outskirts of the city, so take a cab or park in a secured lot ($20-$30 per night). *Thu 9pm-3am, Fri-Sat 9pm-4am.* 1350 Okie St. NE (Kendall St.), 202-636-9030, lovetheclub.com

Lucky Strike • Penn Quarter • Bowling Alley/Lounge
Gone are the bowling alley days of bad polyester and even worse beer. Now you can trade your Jimmy Choos for bowling shoes while sipping a dirty martini. At Lucky Strike, flat-screen TVs project contemporary art, and the deep-red walls are hung with vintage movie posters and skater-chic prints. Call ahead to score a private lane with VIP bottle service. Or skip the sport altogether to sip cocktails at the 50-foot bar. But Lucky Strike isn't all luxe—order a Budweiser. Your sexy server will deliver it in a bowling-pin-shaped bottle. Call at least a few days ahead of time to reserve a lane ($75 an hour). *Daily 11am-2am.* 701 Seventh St. NW (G St.), 202-347-1021, bowlluckystrike.com

Maté • Georgetown • Lounge
Best International Scenes Surrounded by embassies and the ultrachic design district, Maté (MAH-teh) fuses international flavor with a fluid, futuristic aesthetic. The Pantone-inspired interior's twisted light fixtures, silver and red pod chairs, and aluminum bar provide a fitting backdrop for the sophisticated international crowd and visiting celebrities (recent sightings include Mick Jagger and Nicole Kidman). Model-chic waitresses in retro wear serve up Latin-inspired sushi and energy-rush cocktails made from Argentinian yerba mate tea. The kitchen is open until 1:30am on the weekends, but the crowds hang on much later. Doormen make sure you dress the part. *Sun-Thu 5pm-2am, Fri-Sat 5pm-3am.* 3101 K St. NW (31st St.), 202-333-2006, matelounge.com

MCCXXIII • Dupont Circle • Lounge
Best Singles Scenes See-and-be-seen is the name of the game at 1223. An illuminated catwalk suspended over the crowd facilitates the process for VIPs and high rollers. The club juxtaposes opulent crystal chandeliers and plush lounges with industrial-chic design. Though there is a dedicated dance floor, the grooving tends to spill over to the bar (and onto couches and banquettes). For the swank feel of the place, the music tends to be a surprisingly unassuming mix of top 40 crowd pleasers and hip-hop hits on the weekends. Lines loom after 11:30, and the only way to expedite the process is to get on the online guest list or call ahead to reserve a table. *Sun 8pm-2am, Tue 9pm-2am, Wed-Thu 6pm-2am, Fri 5pm-3am, Sat 8pm-3am.* 1223 Connecticut Ave. NW (Rhode Island Ave.), 202-822-1800, 1223dc.com

Mie N Yu* • Georgetown • Restaurant Bar
Seduced by the souks of North Africa, the mountains of Tibet, the colonial intrigue of old Hong Kong? Indulge your Marco Polo fantasies by getting lost in the sensory decadence of Mie N Yu. Dine and drink beneath glowing tents in a Moroccan bazaar or among burnished mirrors in the Venetian Bar. Rise above the crowd by booking the wrought-iron birdcage table. Suspended between the first and second floor, you can feast on a specially prepared tasting menu while spying on the exotic crowd below. World music pulses into the early morning as belly dancers slink between drinkers and diners. *Sun-Thu 4pm-2am, Fri-Sat 4pm-3am.* 3125 M St. NW (31st St.), 202-333-6122, mienyu.com

Modern • Georgetown • Lounge
Want big club amenities without the big club hassles? Try Modern's sleek circular bar, sunken dance floor, and chic but sweet staff. Don't bother getting a table because the DJs spin such infectious grooves, you'll have a hard time sitting still. Breakdancers kick things off for Thursday's hip-hop night while Saturdays mix in reggae and house. Whatever the music, the vibe is always a welcome break from the sometimes buttoned-up feel of Georgetown's M Street. The club attracts chicks in hot kicks (especially on Sunday's Sneaker Pimp night) and stilettos alike. The only requirement is that you be prepared to dance. *Wed-Thu 9pm-2am, Fri-Sat 9pm-3am.* 3287 M St. NW (33rd St.), 202-338-7027, primacycompanies.com

Oya* • Penn Quarter • Restaurant Lounge
This is quite possibly D.C.'s sexiest restaurant lounge. *See Chic Restaurants, p.65, for details.* 777 Ninth St. NW (H St.), 202-393-1400, oyadc.com

Ozio Restaurant & Lounge • Dupont Circle • Restaurant Bar
It makes sense that Ozio's walls feature paintings of Hollywood starlets; this four-story club is a see-and-be-seen place that's prepared to take on any number of roles. Want to puff cigars with the power players? Visit the walk-in humidor during postwork hours. Looking to dance among the District's pretty young things? Don stilettos and head upstairs to the dance floor. Need a private space for your entourage? Get bottle service in a VIP lounge. Unlike those of the other clubs in the neighborhood, the weekend lines tend to be on the shorter side. If you're looking to dress the part, opt for biz-casual early in the evening and urban chic as the night goes on. *Mon-Thu 5pm-2am, Fri 5pm-3am, Sat 6pm-3am.* 1813 M St. NW (18th St.), 202-822-6000, oziodc.com

CHIC • NIGHTLIFE

Pearl • Penn Quarter • Bar
Inspired by the opalescence of its namesake, Pearl's bars glow with a shifting spectrum of colored lights—which in turn glint off the jewelry of its well-heeled clientele. Big-name hip-hop DJs draw crowds of largely African American urban professionals. The only way to skip the weekends' long lines is to spring for bottle service at one of the orange and white lounges that line the walls. It'll run you $500 and up depending on where you'd like to sit. But no amount of money will get you in the door if you're not dressed the part. *Wed-Sat 6pm-1:30am.* 901 Ninth St. NW (I St.), 202-371-0681, dcpearl.com

Play Lounge • Dupont Circle • Lounge
Billed as a playground for adults, this lounge brings the upscale debauchery of Sin City to D.C. The walls, couches, and tables are tarted up in bright citrus hues. There is not a single area where people can't dance, and the hip-hop, '80s, and top 40 tunes have girls up on the bar, on top of tables, and on the pole behind the DJ booth from 11:30pm until closing time. Expect a postcollege party crowd, and dress to dance. *Tue-Wed 10pm-2am, Thu 5pm-2am, Fri 5pm-3am, Sat 10pm-3am.* 1219 Connecticut Ave. NW (Jefferson Pl.), 202-466-7529, playloungedc.com

Republic Gardens • U Street Corridor • Bar
An institution since the 1920s, Republic Gardens has hosted African American icons from Pearl Bailey to Puff Daddy. Although it made its name on performances by jazz greats like Duke Ellington and Charlie Parker, DJs now stick to hip-hop and R&B to get the largely black urban professional crowd moving. Although the original club closed in 1960, the latest incarnation enjoys just as illustrious a reputation. Expect to spend $500-plus to drink with the D.C. sports stars or visiting hip-hop moguls in the exclusive first-floor lounge. *Sun 8pm-2am, Thu 6pm-2am, Fri 6pm-3am, Sat 9:30pm-3:30am.* 1355 U St. NW (14th St.), 202-232-2710, republicgardens.com

Rosa Mexicano* • Penn Quarter • Restaurant Bar
The massive Rosa Mexicano pulses with color—from the wall of water washing down indigo-hued tiles to chairs woven from pink and orange seatbelts. The crowd is as lively as the décor. Urban sophisticates sidle up to the tequila bar to sample the more than 80 varieties on offer. With guacamole made fresh barside and Rosa's signature pomegranate margaritas, guests often have so much fun waiting for their tables they opt not to sit down when called. If you do manage to pry yourself away from the bar, don't expect to find your typical burrito-and-fajita fare. Rosa focuses on authentic Mexican food. *Sun noon-3pm and 5-10:30pm, Mon-Thu 11:30am-3pm and 5-10:30pm, Fri 11:30am-3pm and 5-11:30pm, Sat noon-3pm and 5-11:30pm.* 575 Seventh St. NW (F St.), 202-783-5522, rosamexicano.info

Sequoia • Georgetown • Bar
Best Outdoor Drinking The giddy onset of spring brings the crowds rushing back to the waterfront bars of Georgetown. As the sun sets on balmy afternoons, a breeze floats off the Potomac River and lights go on in the trees around the sprawling four-level patio at Sequoia. The socialite set dock their boats for early evening martinis and stunning views of the Kennedy Center and Roosevelt Island. Preppy Georgetown denizens mix with the Euro-chic set over margaritas

and Coronas. If you need a break from the crowds, have a drink inside—the towering glass-front structure doesn't skimp on views. *Sun 10:30am-12:30am, Mon-Thu 11:30am-12:30am, Fri-Sat 11:30am-1:30am.* ≡ 3000 K St. NW (30th St.), 202-944-4200, arkrestaurants.com

Sonoma Restaurant and Wine Bar* • Capitol Hill • Wine Bar
Nightlife options around Capital Hill skew toward dingy pubs overrun with young Congressional staffers and the men that prey on them. Enter Sonoma, the perfect antidote to the meet market scene. The first floor serves up California cuisine and 40 wines by the glass in the bustling bistro and wine bar. In the upstairs lounge, suede couches are arranged for mingling under the soft light of candles and a crackling fire. Sonoma's wine list encourages exploration with 3-ounce tasting sizes. The lounge is at its best after 6pm on Thursday and Friday when the postwork crowds loosen their ties and drink to bills passed and scandals averted. *Sun 5:30-9pm, Mon-Thu 11:30am-2:30pm and 5:30-10pm, Fri 11:30am-2:30pm and 5:30-11pm, Sat 5:30-11pm.* ≡ 223 Pennsylvania Ave. SE (Second St.), 202-544-8088, sonomadc.com

Spank • Dupont Circle • Lounge
An investor in the famed Miami club B.E.D. decided D.C. needed naughtier nightlife options, so he opened Spank. The egregious name choice hasn't stopped the crowds from lining up behind velvet ropes each weekend to gain entry to this ultrachic lounge. Located on the top floor of MCCXXIII, model-caliber waitstaff serve strong cocktails to sophisticates reclining on white-vinyl beds. The underlit dance floor casts a mysterious glow on the sexy heels and bare legs grooving to house and Latin beats. Gaining entrance can be tricky on the weekends, but opting for bottle service should speed things up. *Fri-Sat 10pm-3am.* ©≡ 1223 Connecticut Ave. NW (M St.), 202-822-1800

Tabaq Bistro* • U Street Corridor • Lounge
Best Drinks with a View Locals flock here for fabulous drinks with a view of the stars through the retractable roof. *See Chic Restaurants, p.67, for details.* ≡1336 U St. NW (13th St.), 202-265-0965, tabaqbistro.com

Zaytinya* • Penn Quarter • Restaurant Bar
One of the city's trendiest restaurants also draws crowds at the bar. *See Chic Restaurants, p.68, for details.* ≡ 701 Ninth St. NW (G St.), 202-638-0800, zaytinya.com

Zengo* • Penn Quarter • Restaurant Bar
The lounge with low-slung seats and curving bar downstairs has a dining room with open kitchen and ceviche bar. *See Chic Restaurants, p.68, for details.* ≡ 781 Seventh St. NW (H St.), 202-393-2929, modernmexican.com/zengodc

Zola* • Penn Quarter • Restaurant Bar
Join the exuberant crowd of singles at the bar and enjoy a shaken-not-stirred martini at a high-backed velvet booth amid glass etched with KGB code. *See Chic Restaurants, p.68, for details.* ≡ 800 F St. NW (Eighth St.), 202-654-0999, zoladc.com

Chic D.C.: The Attractions

Artefacto • Georgetown • Store
Brazil and Italy are in a dead-heat competition to claim the title of world's chicest furniture designers. With the opening of stores like Artefacto, Brazil may find itself in the lead. The 16,000-square-foot store serves shoppers espresso and champagne as they peruse the clean lines and impeccable craftsmanship of pieces like the handwoven steel and Malacca wicker chairs. Fall in love with a sleek platform bed? Artefacto can ship it anywhere in the world. Artefacto is just one of the 50 home furnishing stores in the burgeoning D.C. design district centered on Cady's Alley off Wisconsin. *Mon-Sat 10am-7pm, Sun noon-6pm.* 3333 M St. NW (Bank St.), 202-338-3337, artefacto.com

Dumbarton Oaks Gardens • Georgetown • Garden
Best Romantic Trysts Trysting lovers who seek out the Lovers' Lane here quickly discover two things. First, the Lane, though secluded, lies just outside the private garden, adjoining a public park. Second, these 10 acres of walled formal gardens are in fact so enchantingly beautiful, they might be considered one big fat Lovers' Maze. Behind the large Georgetown mansion that houses a museum (closed for renovation) lies this year-round, terraced park with masses of roses, a Mexican tile–bordered pebble garden, a wisteria-covered arbor, cherry tree groves, overlooks, and lots of romantic winding paths. *Mid-Mar–late-Oct 2-6pm, Nov–mid-Mar 2-5pm.* $- R St. NW (32nd St), 202-339-6400, doaks.org

Dupont Circle Art Galleries • Dupont Circle • Galleries
Best Insider D.C. Experiences Art galleries are nearly as copious as embassies in the Dupont Circle neighborhood. R Street alone has 10, just within a single two-block stretch between Florida and Connecticut Avenues. It's easy to laze away a Saturday afternoon, wandering these tree-lined streets, popping in and out of the charming old townhouses that hold the showrooms. The art ranges widely, from Inuit sculpture and graphics at Burdick Gallery (2114 R St.), to fine traditional arts of Africa at Affrica (2010 R St.), to the contemporary fine art on show at Anton Gallery (2108 R St.). Finish with a stroll along Connecticut Avenue, stopping to browse for good reads at KramerBooks (1517 Connecticut Ave.), a Washington institution, and certainly for a pick-me-up at any bistro or bar along the way. Intersection of Massachusetts, Connecticut, and New Hampshire Aves.

Freer Gallery of Art • National Mall • Art Museum
The Freer is the Smithsonian's museum for Asian art, but it's the Peacock Room that is the real draw: a dining room completely covered in thickly painted patterns of peacock feathers, as rendered by American artist James McNeill Whistler. Long story, but fascinating. The Freer happens to possess the greatest collection of art by Whistler and rotates his works in special exhibits—for example, of his Paris or London paintings. Throughout the rest of the handsome museum are Asian masterpieces, including Japanese screens, Chinese ceramics, and Iranian manuscripts. *Daily 10am-5:30pm.* Jefferson Dr. SW (12th St.), 202-633-4880, asia.si.edu

The Grooming Lounge • Downtown • Barber Shop
Cocktails, dark wood, and ESPN put the manly in manicure at the Grooming Lounge. D.C. power players swear by the nouveau barber shop's Hot Lather Shave, a 30-minute indulgence that involves seven steamed towels, three applications of lather, and a silicon-enhanced postshave solution. The Lounge sells the custom razor designed for the shave, as well as a variety of skin and haircare products aimed at men. *Sun 11am-4pm, Mon-Fri 9am-7pm, Sat 9am-6pm.* 1745 L St. NW (Connecticut Ave.), 202-466-8900, groominglounge.com

Hirshhorn Museum and Sculpture Garden • National Mall • Art Museum
Best Art Museums Until the National Museum of the American Indian debuted in 2004, the Hirshhorn was the Smithsonian's most unusual-looking building. Called "the drum," "the doughnut," and "just plain ugly," the Hirshhorn displays contemporary art that's just plain cool, about 600 works at any given time, by international modern artists like Roy Lichtenstein, Willem de Kooning, and Louise Bourgeois. The museum wraps around a central fountain; the third floor includes a large lounge overlooking the Mall. Don't miss the museum's plaza and Sculpture Garden to study sculptures by Auguste Rodin, Henry Moore, and other greats. *Daily, museum 10am-5:30pm, Sculpture Garden 7:30am-dusk.* Independence Ave. SW (Seventh St.), 202-633-1000, hirshhorn.si.edu

International Spy Museum • Penn Quarter • Museum
Best Rainy Day Experiences D.C. has more spies than any other city in the world. So claims the Spy Museum in its *Briefing* film. Your mission here is to infiltrate three levels of international spymania facts and fun. Interactive exhibits allow you to test your powers of observation and pretend to be a spy. The history section establishes that spies through the ages have included everyone from Moses to Julia Child. Artifacts abound. Most fascinating are the videos and recordings of former spies telling their own stories. *Mid-Aug–late-Feb, daily, 10am-6pm (Sat mid-Aug–late-Oct, 10am-8pm), Mar 9am-6pm, Apr–mid-Aug 9am-8pm.* $ 800 F St. NW (Eighth St.), 866-779-6873, spymuseum.org

International Spy Museum Gift Shop • Penn Quarter • Store
You crawled through ceiling ducts and decoded communiqués at the International Spy Museum, and now you're inspired to get your Bond on. Instead of just sipping a (shaken-not-stirred) martini, stop in the gift shop. From nightscopes to invisible ink, KGB flasks to recorder pens, the shop will equip you with the accoutrements needed to launch your international espionage career—or at least to ensure that you come home with some killer (no pun intended) souvenirs. *Mid-Aug–late-Feb, daily, 10am-6pm (Sat mid-Aug–late-Oct, 10am-8pm), Mar 9am-6pm, Apr–mid-Aug 9am-8pm.* 800 F St. NW (Eighth St.), 202-654-0950, spymuseum.org

Kreeger Art Museum • West of Georgetown • Art Museum
Just a mile or so west of Georgetown, on a winding road dotted with architecturally interesting houses, is one such designed by Phillip Johnson that has served as a private museum since 1994. Its great hall, rear terrace, and other harmonious spaces show off 180 stellar works by Pierre Bonnard, Frank Stella, Felix Ziem, Aristide Maillol, Eduard Munch, Auguste Renoir, and Pablo Picasso, including an extraordinary one painted when Picasso was 17. And if the exhibit of African masks on the lower level doesn't seem to fit here, listen to a docent

CHIC • ATTRACTIONS

explain otherwise. Worth a cab ride for sure, the museum will call you a taxi when you're ready to leave. *Sat 10am-4pm, Tue-Fri by appointment only.* $- 2401 Foxhall Rd. NW (Reservoir Rd.), 202-338-3552, kreegermuseum.org

Meridian International Center • Upper Northwest • Art House
Sixteenth Street slopes upward from the White House, passing many a fine embassy and century-old mansion as it rises. On a side street near the summit is Meridian International Center, which occupies two interesting buildings. Open to the public is the White-Meyer House, whose first-floor galleries host art exhibits related to Meridian's purpose of promoting international understanding. High ceilings, paneled walls, parquet floors, and beautiful fireplaces are some of the features that remind visitors that this house was once a home, lived in first by diplomat Henry White and then by *Washington Post* owner Eugene Meyer. *Wed-Sun 2-5pm.* 1630 Crescent Pl. NW (16th St.), 202-667-6800, meridian.org

National Building Museum • Penn Quarter • Museum
This place is so big it could practically host the next Super Bowl: its Great Hall measures 316 feet by 116 feet, and 159 feet at its tallest point. Built in 1887 to house government offices. the structure was reborn as the National Building Museum in 1980. Its size and majesty guarantee its use as an inaugural ball location every four years, and make it worth stepping inside to gape. Architecture exhibits include one noteworthy for its illustrated history of the city, covering both neighborhood and federal government development. The sleeper here is the museum shop, which sells some truly imaginative gifts, like the array of housewares cleverly crafted by famous architects and designers. Those Eva Zeisel salt and pepper shakers, for example, are a great find. *Sun 11am-5pm, Mon-Sat 10am-5pm.* 401 F St. NW (Fourth St.), 202-272-2448, nbm.org

National Geographic Museum • Dupont Circle • Museum
A list of current and recent exhibits mounted in this hall reads like a table of contents in a social studies textbook: Mongolia: Traditions Reborn, Archipelago: Portraits of Life in the Northwestern Hawaiian Islands, and Maya: Portraits of a People. Only somehow, the subjects are way more interesting than they were in school. Could it be you've grown up? Naaaaaah. It's all in the presentation, and at National Geo, masterful photography always gets your attention, and then, well, you're hooked. *Sun 10am-5pm, Mon-Sat 9am-5pm.* 17th St. NW (M St.), 202-857-7588, nationalgeographic.com/museum

National World War II Memorial • National Mall • Site
Say what you will about this memorial—and people have said plenty—its purpose is on point, to honor those who served in World War II. This latest of National Mall memorials debuted on Memorial Day, 2004. Whether or not the memorial suits its setting or rightly marks the war as well as a museum would have is now irrelevant. The open-plan, 7.5-acre design includes sculpted bas relief panels depicting scenes from the Pacific and Atlantic Theaters and fountains commemorating important battles. 17th St. NW (Constitution Ave.), 202-619-7222, wwiimemorial.com

Phillips Collection • Dupont Circle • Art Museum
Best Rainy Day Experiences It was always founder Duncan Phillips's intention that visitors should feel at home in his museum of modern art, which was easy in 1921, because the mansion was a home—his. Since then, the collection of

79

French, American, and post-Impressionist art, as well as modernist art, has grown to 2,500 works, and the museum has sprouted wings, but a tour of these rooms still provokes a sense of intimacy. Look for Renoir's *Luncheon of the Boating Party,* the many Bonnards, and whatever special exhibit is on. *Sun noon-7pm (Oct-May), noon-5pm (June-Sept), Tue-Wed, Fri-Sat 10am-5pm, Thu 10am-8:30pm.* Admission to permanent collection is free weekdays; paid admission to permanent collection weekends and to special exhibits any time: $- 1600 21st St. NW (Q St.), 202-387-2151, phillipscollection.org

Pink November • Georgetown • Store

The boutique's bright pink and black exterior has more sass than most Georgetown boutiques combined. Inside you'll find clothes that aren't afraid to make a statement. Pink November specializes in dresses like boldly patterned Trashy Diva pieces that update kimonos and 1940s silhouettes. The soul soundtrack will get you in the groove, and owner Shelly McNair will help you sustain it with advice about the pieces you need to complete your look. *Sun noon-6pm, Tue-Sat noon-8pm.* 1529 Wisconsin Ave. NW (Volta Pl.), 202-333-1121

Potomac Riverboat Company • Georgetown • Boat Tour

Best Views of D.C. From the deck of a boat rolling on the Potomac River, one thing's clear: Washington was meant to be viewed from the water. Oddly enough, few boats offer tours. Best are the Potomac Riverboat Company's two vessels each holding up to 149 passengers; the *Matthew Hayes* is open-air, the *Miss Mallory* has both open-air and enclosed decks. The boats depart from Georgetown and cruise past the memorials as far as Old Town Alexandria, as a recording narrates the passing scene. Passengers debark to tour Old Town or stay aboard for the return trip, 90 minutes, round trip. Time your passage right and you'll catch the sunset. *Apr-Oct: tour schedule varies by month and day.* $$ Washington Harbour (31st St.), 703-548-9000, potomacriverboatco.com

Relish • Georgetown • Store

From the fresh flower station at the entrance to the French doors that open onto Cady's Alley, Relish is designed for shoppers who want to luxuriate in the shopping experience. The huge industrial space is softened by blond-wood shelves and sunlight. Sophisticated menswear offerings range from hot Japanese designer Junya Watanabe to prestigious Italian label Marni. Womenswear offerings include Zac Posen and Narciso Rodriguez. After shopping, head over for pastries at Leopold's Kafe and Konditorei. *Mon-Wed, Fri-Sat 10am-6pm, Thu 10am-7pm.* 3312 Cady's Alley NW (34th St.), 202-333-5343, relishdc.com

Rowing on the Potomac • Georgetown Waterfront • Sport

Best Romantic Trysts Do like the locals do and paddle your own way along the Potomac. Summer is the optimum season, and the Fourth of July the prime date, to rent a kayak or canoe from Jack's Boathouse at the bottom of Georgetown, and skim to Theodore Roosevelt Island to watch fireworks explode in the night sky over the Washington Monument. But it's a great excursion on any fine day: Head downstream to view the monuments, or upstream to find Three Sisters' Islands and the C&O Canal, observing wild herons, cormorants, and turtles along the way. Boat rental includes flotation device and paddle. Jack's Boathouse operates spring through fall. *Mon-Fri 10am-sunset, Sat-Sun 8am-sunset.* $ 3500 K St. NW (35th St.), 202-337-9642, jacksboathouse.com

Smithsonian American Art Museum and National Portrait Gallery •
Penn Quarter • Art Museums

Best Patriotic Adventures It's a wrap—finally. The historic Greek Revival structure that Walt Whitman once called "the noblest of Washington buildings," and the two museums that lie within, the American Art Museum and the National Portrait Gallery, finally reopened in July 2006, after a six-year renovation. The museums reenter a society that's come to snappy life in the intervening years, as the museums themselves have been transformed. The Verizon Center and sleek hotels, restaurants, and clubs have grown up around this Smithsonian, which is now way cooler than it ever was before. Visitors can view conservation work under way in glass-walled labs, 3,200 works on display, performances in the theater, and the building's original architectural features. The two museums alternate by floor and wing, but the transition is seamless to the visitor. Look for Edward Hoppers, Georgia O'Keeffes, and Gilbert Stuarts. *Daily 11:30am-7pm.* F St. NW (Eighth St.), 202-275-1500, americanart.si.edu, npg.si.edu

SomaFit Spa and Fitness Center • Georgetown • Spa/Health Club

Best Luxury Spas Its strange name seems to phase no one. SomaFit has created quite the buzz since it debuted in late 2004. Architects Adamstein and Demetriou, famous for trendy restaurant creations like Zaytinya, designed the center's clean, white, spare look. It's a health club, but you don't have to be a member to take any of the Pilates classes, personal training, yoga, or nutrition counseling on offer. The spa gets pretty booked up, dispensing massages, facials, waxing, and pedicures to Washington's most upscale customers, but it will take walk-ins for a 10-minute pick-me-up massage. ("Soma" is the Greek word for body, by the way.) *Sun 10am-6pm, Mon-Fri 6am-9pm, Sat 8am-6pm.* $$$$ 2121 Wisconsin Ave. NW (35th St.), 202-965-2121, somafit.com

Spa at the Mandarin Oriental • National Mall/Southwest • Spa

Best Luxury Spas Eastern philosophy meets "because I'm worth it" sensibility at this spa, where so much attention is paid that you might just be convinced that your body is a temple and you are God. Every spa experience is seen as a "personal journey designed to engage each of the five senses," beginning with a consultation, fruit- or herb-infused water, steam-room aromatherapy, and jet-pulsing whirlpooling, and going on from there. Most decadent? The two-hour, two-therapist Oriental Harmony massage. *Sun 9am-7pm, Mon-Sat 9am-9pm.* $$$$ Mandarin Oriental, 1330 Maryland Ave. SW (12th St.), 202-787-6100, mandarinoriental.com/washington

Supreme Court • Capitol Hill • Site

Take your place in line: That's the best way—the only way, really—to see the Supremes. Nine people, nine votes, and the world can shift. You've got several options here. On days when the court is not in session, you can tour the building and attend a lecture about court procedure in the Supreme Court chamber; cool, few hassles, no Supremes. You can attend an argument for three to five minutes; cooler, long line outdoors, seating at the back of the chamber so limited view of Supremes. You can try to attend a full, hourlong argument or a delivery of opinions; coolest, long line outdoors, sometimes for hours, great view of Supremes and proceedings. Information is key; call ahead. *Mon-Fri 9am-4:30pm.* One First St. NE (E. Capitol St.), 202-479-3000, supremecourtus.gov

Hip D.C.

Given a choice of staying in a hotel named after a president or one named after a color, go for the color. If you're thinking, hmm, martinis in Georgetown or Oreo-tinis and disco at a U Street lounge bar, it's the Oreo-tinis. Memorials touring on the Mall? Great, but first kick-start the day by riding the flight simulators in the National Air and Space Museum. If brunch options vary from eggs Benedict served by drag queens in an Adams Morgan eatery, to a sumptuous buffet politely consumed in the dining room of an elegant hotel, choose the drag brunch. And finally this: If you're lining up a night's entertainment and trying to decide between spoken word at Busboys and Poets, down-and-dirty blues at Madam's Organ, underground hip-hop at Capital City Records, hookahs and house at Chi Cha Lounge, or the live alternative sounds blaring at the Black Cat, do it all, man, do it all.

*Note: Venues in bold are described in detail in the listings that follow the itinerary. Venues followed by an * asterisk are those we recommend as both a restaurant and a destination bar.*

Hip D.C.: The Perfect Plan (3 Nights and Days)

Perfect Plan Highlights

Thursday
Breakfast	Poste
Mid-morning	Nat. Air and Space, American Indian Museum
Lunch	Mitsitam
Mid-afternoon	Art Museum of the Americas
Pre-dinner	Café Saint-Ex
Dinner	Rice
Nighttime	Busboys and Poets
Late-night	Ben's Chili Bowl

Friday
Breakfast	Teaism
Mid-morning	Bike the Sites
Lunch	Matchbox*
Mid-afternoon	Nat. Museum of Women in the Arts
Pre-dinner	Helix Lounge*
Dinner	Vegetate*
Nighttime	Capital City Records
Late-night	Wonderland Ballrm.

Saturday
Breakfast	Market Lunch
Mid-morning	Shakespeare Library, Eastern Market
Lunch	Belga Café
Mid-afternoon	Textile Museum
Pre-dinner	Firefly
Dinner	Minibar
Nighttime	18th Street Lounge
Late-night	Five

Morning After
Brunch	Perrys

Hotel: Hotel Monaco

Thursday

9am Look to **Poste**, right in the hotel, for a fine brioche start to the day.

10am Then mosey down Seventh Street to the **National Air and Space Museum** on the Mall, and it's all systems go as you strap yourself inside a **flight simulator** and aim for the sky. Catch an **IMAX** flick if time allows.

Noon Go next door to the **National Museum of the American Indian** to look at pottery, masks, and other artifacts, and learn about Indian culture and history.

1pm Lunch Mitsitam, the Indian Museum's eatery, is the exception to the rule about poor dining options at sightseeing attractions. Get in line to sample the varied tastes of Native American cuisines, ranging from salmon cakes to fry bread with cinnamon and honey.

2:30pm Hop a subway or walk down the Mall to the precious little **Art Museum of the Americas**: a charming gallery with colorful contemporary paintings. Just across the street is the **U.S. Department of the Interior Museum**, a funky exhibit space full of old photographs, art, and artifacts chronicling

America's westward expansion, and the not-to-be-missed **Indian Crafts shop**, whose art and jewelry are exquisite, one-of-a-kind gems. From here, it's a short walk to 22nd Street to view the sculpture of pacificist, scientist, and humanitarian **Albert Einstein**. Afterward, cross the avenue to pay your respects at the **Vietnam Veterans Memorial**.

5pm If you have the energy and the inclination, and the weather's in your favor, try to squeeze in **pedalboating on the Tidal Basin**.

6:30pm Soak in the neighborhood color of U Street's hipster haven from the comfort of a sidewalk table or bar stool at **Café Saint-Ex**. Or opt for a beer at neighborhood hangout **Logan Tavern**.

8pm Dinner Head to nearby **Rice** for excellent Thai food in a minimalist setting, or switch neighborhoods and cuisines to scoop up spicy Ethiopian stews at **Meskerem** in Adams Morgan. Always a good option is Dupont Circle's **Bistrot du Coin**, whose boisterous owner always makes sure your glass is full and your mussels cooked to perfection.

11pm The night's your oyster, and the pearls include **Busboys and Poets**, the hub of the D.C. activist scene and center stage for spoken word artists; Adams Morgan's rowdy **Madam's Organ**, where live music plays nightly; and Dupont Circle's laid-back **Brickskeller Saloon**, where 1,000 beers are available from every corner of the world.

1am Wrap up the night on U Street at D.C. institution **Ben's Chili Bowl** for a taste of its famous half-smokes, cheese fries, and milkshakes. In Adams Morgan? Head to **Bedrock Billiards** for a round of pool or Chutes and Ladders, or mellow out on the couches at coffeeshop and bar **Tryst***.

2am Still not ready to call it a night? Head to **The Diner**, long-time refuge of night owls.

Friday

9am Get the day going at the Japanese-influenced **Teaism**, a few steps from the Monaco.

10am Ride the elevators to the top of the Clock Tower in the **Old Post Office Pavilion** for a sweeping view of Pennsylvania Avenue, the Capitol, and the surrounds of the city. Exit the building at 12th Street and look for the **Bike the Sites** kiosk. It's time to cover the capital—by bike—on this three-hour guided tour that pedals past the memorials, the White House, and other sites.

1pm Lunch Climb off your wheeled horse and satiate that worked-up appetite at **Matchbox*** in Chinatown, with crispy pizza cooked in a wood-burning oven. For excellent Chinese fare, go to nearby **Chinatown Express** to slurp up fresh dumplings and Cantonese specialties.

2:30pm Just a couple of blocks west of Chinatown is the **National Museum of Women in the Arts**, where women's art from the 16th century to the present is on view. Or hop the Metro's Red line to the Union Station stop to tour the **National Postal Museum**'s love letter of an exhibit on postal history and the importance of written correspondence. On your way back to the hotel, pop in to the **National Building Museum** for a little local history and a stellar shopping op at the gift shop.

6pm Nothing is quite like happy hour at kitsch-tastic **Helix Lounge***, where stools light up when you sit down and burgers and beers are half-price until 7pm.

8pm Dinner For artsy urban atmosphere and a vegetarian menu, try **Vegetate***, but be sure to drink up before you come, because the restaurant's liquor license is still in the works. Alternatively, head to **Viridian**, an art gallery cum dining room serving vegan offerings. **Café Asia*** will satiate you with spicy pan-Asian tastes.

11pm Start your night at a store, **Capital City Records**, where emcees spit rhymes among the record racks. Continue on to **DC9**, which showcases live and DJ music, including the indie rock spun at Friday's Liberation Dance Party; or to the **Science Club**, for breakbeat sounds, a clever crowd, and hot bartenders.

1am Feeling energetic? Hop a cab and squeeze onto the dance floor at the **Wonderland Ballroom** for classic soul, old-school hip-hop, and funk. Or have a Ms. Pac-Man tournament while bopping to the Ramones in the downstairs bar. Time to calm down? Toke on a hookah and sip the popular Andean cocktails at **Chi-Cha Lounge**.

3am If you're in need of a late-night snack, bookstore and cafe **Afterwords** stays up all night serving everything from filet mignon to Dysfunctional Family sundaes.

Saturday

9am Blue-line it from the subway's Metro Center station to **Eastern Market** to participate in the blueberry-pancakes-on-Saturday-morning-at-**Market Lunch** ritual that is so near and dear to Capitol Hillers' hearts. Or buy something delicious from the bakery vendor at the other end of the hall. In any case, you'll want to make like a local and browse, barter, and people-watch your way past the food and arts and crafts stands.

11am Once you get your fill, amble to the nearby **Folger Shakespeare Library** to tour the Great Hall, theater, and Elizabethan garden. Arrive by 11am and you'll be in time for the free, docent-led tour.

Noon Retrace your steps toward Eastern Market, following Pennsylvania Avenue away from the Capitol, until you reach the stretch of Eighth Street known as Barrack's Row. Posted signs throughout this neighborhood lead one on a heritage trail past Lilliputian townhouses and historic structures.

1pm Lunch Back on Eighth Street, recharge your batteries with Belgian frites and a hefeweizen at the **Belga Café**. For cafe fare, try nearby **Bread and Chocolate**.

3pm Say so long to Capitol Hill and make your way to Georgetown for a vigorous fine-tuning of your karma, in an all-levels yoga class at **Down Dog Yoga**. If yoga's not for you, consider a sublime "me" moment and hurry to the eco-friendly spa **Nusta**, for a pick-me-up facial, pedicure, or massage. On the other hand, Dupont Circle's **Textile Museum** might be just the ticket. The Textile Museum's exhibits are charmers, revealing textiles as both works of art and historical artifacts. And from there, you're only a brief walk from …

5:30pm … the cozy restaurant **Firefly**, where a glass of wine at the bar should strike just the right note before you head back to your hotel.

8pm Dinner If the idea of foie gras cotton candy intrigues rather than repulses, indulge your adventurous palate at **Minibar**. Come hungry and curious, as two chefs will guide you through a two-hour culinary odyssey of 30 funky new-wave dishes. For Lebanese comfort food, dine at **Mama Ayesha's Restaurant**, a long-time D.C. establishment at the entrance to Adams Morgan. American comfort food—from mac 'n' cheese to ice cream sandwiches—and a low-key ambience are the draws at **Tonic***, in Mount Pleasant, near Adams Morgan.

11pm It's your last night in D.C., so you want to do it up right. First stop is **18th Street Lounge**. Thievery Corporation got their start here, so the music—whether DJ on the first floor or live on the second—is always good. Sexy samba or Latin reggae more your vibe? Check out the bands at Adams Morgan's **Bossa**.

1am The Converse-shod masses sip their Pabst and bop to Brit pop and indie rock at the **Black Cat**. Saturdays alternate between buzz bands and DJ nights.

3am When every place else has closed, come to **Five** and stay until dawn, moving to house, hip-hop, drum and bass, or lazing in a rooftop hammock.

> **The Morning After**
>
> If you stayed up all night, stay up a bit longer to take in the drag brunch at **Perrys**, a hoot to send you on your merry way.

Hip D.C.:
The Key Neighborhoods

Adams Morgan Before it was called Adams Morgan, this neighborhood was called 18th Street and Columbia, named for the main roads that still anchor it. Today it's best known for its buzzing bar scene and the 20- and 30-somethings who arrive in droves after work and on weekends to drink, dance, and listen to live music. Come closing time, the crowds pour onto the streets in search of jumbo-slice pizza, empanadas, and falafel.

Capitol Hill Young government workers and Hill staffers collect after hours in creaky bars like the Hawk and Dove and the Tune Inn, located along Pennsylvania Avenue, southeast of the Capitol. A few blocks further along is Eighth Street, south of Pennsylvania, which hipsters are turning into another popular destination.

Dupont Circle Perennially hip, Dupont Circle's art galleries, lounges, gay bars, boutiques, and thriving nightlife draw fun seekers day and night along Connecticut Avenue and side streets. It's not especially cutting-edge, but sophisticated and casually pleasant, with carousing packs, strolling lovers, the fashion-conscious, and the unconventional.

U Street Corridor This section of town is hipster mecca in the city, where rough and ready meet head on and discover they get along, in lounges like Chi Cha, restaurants like Bistro Tabaq, casual coffee bars like Sparky's, clubs like the Black Cat, and theaters like Studio. It's taken a while to get here, but you'll believe it when you see it, or rather feel it—a hip scene has finally taken hold in Washington.

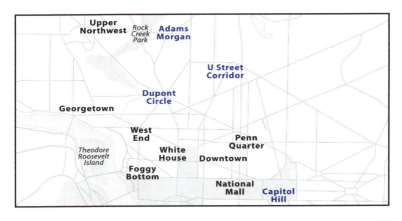

Hip D.C.: The Shopping Blocks

Adams Morgan

From Ethiopian record stores to British clothing boutiques, Adams Morgan's shopping opportunities give visitors a taste of D.C.'s international flavor.

Botanica Yemaya-Chango Practitioners of Santeria and voodoo will find their candles, herbs, and statues here. 2441 18th St. NW (Belmont Rd.), 202-462-1803

Crooked Beat Records You'll find hard-to-find LPs, posters, local music, imports, and independent labels. 2318 18th St. NW (Belmont Rd.), 202-483-2328

The District Line Fred Perry, Lionsdale, and English Laundry bring the looks of England to D.C. 2118 18th St. NW (California St.), 202-558-5508

Miss Pixie's Furnishings and Whatnot From vintage postcards to retro furnishings, Pixie has a great mix. (p.111) 2473 18th St. NW (Columbia Rd.), 202-232-8171

Oya's Mini Bazaar Come for carved African masks, ethnic jewelry, woven goods, and other little oddities. 2420 18th St. NW (Belmont Rd.), 202-667-9853

Penn Quarter

The rapid gentrification of the Penn Quarter neighborhood brought in a slew of retail chains like Urban Outfitters (737 Seventh St. NW, 202-737-0259), Aveda (713 Seventh St. NW, 202-824-1610), H&M (1025 F St. NW, 202-347-3306), and American Apparel (555 11th St. NW, 202-628-0438).

U Street Corridor

These quirky boutiques carry vintage threads, retro furniture, and local designs.

Carbon This shoe store professes a desire to change D.C. from federal to funky, one sole at a time. 1203 U St. NW (12th St.), 202-986-2679

Go Mama Go This is the place to come for gifts, glassware, and art from around the world. 1809 14th St. NW (S St.), 202-299-0850

Meeps Vintage Fashionette You'll find everything from the ridiculous—sequin bubble dresses—to the cool—perfect cowboy boots. (p.111) 1520 U St. NW (15th St.), 202-265-6546

Millennium Decorative Arts Come for retro furniture, housewares, and accessories from the 1950s, '60s, and '70s. 1528 U St. NW (16th St.), 202-483-1218

Muléh Antik denim, Development dresses, and Jungal coats are sold alongside Asian-inspired furniture. (p.111) 1831 14th St. NW (T St.), 202-667-3440

Nana You'll find vintage finds and fresh lines like House of Spy, Wrangler 47, and Hobo International bags. (p.111) 1528 U St. NW (16th St.), 202-667-6955

Pulp This shop carries goofy and edgy cards, mullet magnets, sex report cards, and "Wash Away Your Sins" soap. 1803 14th St. NW (S St.), 202-462-7857

Hip D.C.:
The Hotels

Hotel Helix • Dupont Circle • Trendy (178 rms)
This could easily be considered D.C.'s trendiest hotel. It's got swishing curtains in the lobby, where a nightly bubbly hour treats guests to complimentary champagne. It's got bright reds and blues, lime greens, and stripes in the whimsical and youthful guest rooms. It's got high-tech toys, like Nintendo on the flat-screen TV, complimentary WiFi-internet access in guest rooms and throughout the hotel, CD players in each room, and a 24-hour on-site fitness room. Ask for room 1018 for the best views, of old architecture and the trendy neighborhood. Eighteen suites offer more room, and the 12 specialty rooms feature more fun, like bunk beds, plasma-screen TVs and lava lamps, or a papaya and lime-green kitchenette. Come cocktail hour, the Helix Lounge fills with singles downing whatever's on special offer that night: if it's Thursday, it must be Oreo-tinis; Saturday, it's electric lemonades; and Monday through Friday, half-price beer and burgers. The Helix is just around the corner from hip 14th Street, where more bars and clubs await. $$ 1430 Rhode Island Ave. NW (14th St.), 202-462-9001 / 800-706-1202, hotelhelix.com

Hotel Madera • Dupont Circle • Trendy (82 rms)
This sweet little hotel has a great location within walking distance of Dupont Circle, Georgetown, Foggy Bottom, and even parts of downtown. And because of its slightly elevated position, the Madera's highest floors, six to ten, proffer a range of views, from the Dupont neighborhood on the New Hampshire side (rooms 803 and 903 are best), to distant sightings of Rock Creek Park and Georgetown on the back of the house (ask for rooms 905 or 1005). Guest rooms are surprisingly large and cleverly furnished in animal prints, elegant hues of gold and green, and sunburst mirrors. Every room has a CD player and complimentary high-speed internet service. The Madera attracts a casually hip clientele, who are pleased to find they need look no further than the hotel's own Firefly restaurant and lounge for delicious food and an easy nightlife scene. It's cozy, crowded, and a bit noisy, and it does the trick for couples who've just this moment checked in, for those seeking a before-or-after drink, and for those who need some comfort food before they go out on the town. $$ 1310 New Hampshire Ave. NW (N St.), 202-296-7600 / 800-430-1202, hotelmadera.com

Hotel Monaco • Penn Quarter • Trendy (182 rms)
At the restored 1866 landmark Monaco, D.C.'s history is whimsically on display. A bust of Thomas Jefferson perches on top of your armoire; bed linens are done in (fire engine) red, (eggshell) white, and (periwinkle) blue; and the restaurant is called Poste, a reference to the building's post office beginnings. Its all-marble, columned facade is classically elegant, but the hotel's interior design turns high vaulted ceilings and star-studded fabrics into the latest greatest thing. Historic preservation rules preclude closets, so armoires hold all, a tight fit for some. Guest rooms are on all four floors; ask for rooms on the second and third, facing Seventh or E streets, for terrific city views and privacy; and ask for corner rooms 201, 301, and 401 for brightest chambers and more prime city

sights. Interior rooms overlook the hotel's enclosed courtyard, noisy sometimes in summer, since this is the restaurant's outdoor terrace. The Monaco lies in the heart of the Penn Quarter and its guests are often sports and concert stars playing across the street at the Verizon Center. Look for them in Poste, where the modern American cuisine soars and the happy hour jumps. On your way to Poste, stop first in the gorgeous lobby's salon, where hotel guests gather in front of the fireplace for complimentary wine served every evening from 5:30 to 6:30pm. $$$ 700 F St. NW (Seventh St.), 202-628-7177 / 800-649-1202, monaco-dc.com

Hotel Rouge • Dupont Circle • Trendy (137 rms)

Red is racy. Red is not shy. Red is flashy. That's the idea behind this boutique hotel, located due east of Dupont Circle, halfway between the White House and U Street. Indeed, everything is a shade of red, from the hallways and elevator walls on the way to your room, to the drapes, bed headboards and platforms, and minibar items (Red Bull) in your room. Rooms 909 and 1009 are especially spacious and feature excellent city views. Specialty rooms are a thing here and the hotel has 15 of them, five for each of three themes: chat rooms come with a flat-screen computer and DVD player; chill rooms offer a Sony Playstation2 and two flat-screen TVs; and chow rooms have a kitchenette. The Rouge hosts a free red wine and beer hour weeknights 5-6pm and Bloody Mary tastings weekends 10-11am in the lobby, which is too tiny to handle this much fun. Complimentary internet access is in all rooms, WiFi in the lobby, and there's a fitness center on site. The Bar Rouge is mainly a convenient place to start or end the night. $$ 1315 16th St. NW (Massachusetts Ave.), 202-232-8000 / 800-738-1202, rougehotel.com

Tabard Inn • Dupont Circle • Timeless (40 rms)

Its guests are the jeans-clad student with disheveled hair sprawled on a chair in the small lobby and the goateed man dashing through the dining room, taking the back stairs to his guest room. The place is a little funky, you might say, and the guests a bit unbuffed. But there are all kinds of hip in the world and the ones who wash up here are artsy and unconventional, which rather describes the Tabard. The townhouse hotel's 40 rooms are individually decorated with antiques and original art, and painted in unusual hues: azure, ruby red, lupine. Thirteen of the 40 rooms share a bath. The funkiest is the penthouse: one very large skylit room painted a chartreusey green, with its own kitchen and living room area. The Tabard is partly unplugged, since rooms lack televisions but each has a telephone and WiFi access is available in public rooms throughout the hotel. Guests receive free passes to the massive YMCA just around the corner and benefit from the Tabard's excellent location off Connecticut Avenue. The hotel's popular restaurant is a sure thing for free continental breakfast, and later for great food and neighborhood atmosphere at lunch and dinner. $$ 1739 N St. NW (17th St.), 202-785-1277, tabardinn.com

Topaz Hotel • Dupont Circle • Trendy (99 rms)

Like most of D.C.'s hip hotels, the Topaz belongs to the Kimpton group, a company that takes whimsy to new decorative heights. Here, that means guest rooms with polka-dotted bed headboards, paisley comforters at the foot; red-striped drapes and green- and yellow-striped walls, and gold-star–embossed red armchairs. "Wellness and relaxation" are the overall themes, so guests find a daily horoscope and two totems (smooth stones of "energy and empowerment") placed upon the pillow. Its best room is 1006, which is airy and spacious and includes a nook with a stairclimber. All rooms provide free wireless internet access and CD players. Like the Tabard next door, the Topaz lies within walking distance of the 18th Street Lounge and many other nightclubs on and off Connecticut Avenue, and is surrounded by embassies, whose international visitors account for much of the hotel's clientele. The Topaz does have its own bar off the lobby, but the scene is elsewhere; try a heady concoction like the Blue Nirvana to get you going, and then ... get going. $$ 1733 N St. NW (17th St.), 202-393-3000 / 800-775-1202, topazhotel.com

Hip D.C.:
The Restaurants

Afterwords Cafe • Dupont Circle • Bookstore-Cafe
Attached to the landmark Kramerbooks, this bustling cafe has been serving lattes to the literati since 1976. Cultured cliques talk Proust over single malt and sea bass. Early risers read the *Washington Post* over wild-berry waffles. And the postclub crowd gets Freudian takes on dessert with the Dysfunctional Family sundae. With live music (Wed-Sun) and even livelier discussions, this is a high-energy salon for D.C.'s social smarties. Oh, and it's the only place to get a 4am filet mignon on weekends. *Sun-Thu 7:30am-1am, 24 hours Fri and Sat.* $ ▤ 1517 Connecticut Ave. NW (Dupont Cir.), 202-387-1462, kramers.com

Bardia's New Orleans Café • Adams Morgan • Southern
Nothing cures a hangover like a cup of chicory coffee and a steaming plate of fresh beignets. Bardia's serves up both in its tiny ten-table dining room. Though the po' boy sandwiches and jambalaya turn up the heat, the real treat is brunch, when neighborhood denizens linger over the *Washington Post* and Eggs New Orleans with fried oysters, crab meat, and hollandaise sauce. The service is far from snappy, but what respectable person rushes through brunch anyway? *Sun 10am-10pm, Tue-Thu 11am-9:30pm, Fri-Sat 11am-10pm.* $- ▤ 2412 18th St. NW (Mintwood Pl.), 202-234-0420

Belga Café • Capitol Hill • Belgian
In an area typically reserved for steak and single malts sits this stylish Euro-fusion café. Airy lavender curtains welcome you into a sleek dining room of cream walls and dark wood. Congressional staffers escape buttoned-up offices for pots of Hoegaarden mussels and Belgian frites with Flemish mayonnaise. Brunch is a standout with goat-cheese–stuffed waffles and poached eggs with smoked salmon, asparagus and hollandaise. Clad in black and every bit as beautiful as the cuisine, the staff will ably guide you through the wine list and 40 beers. Suits dominate the lunch crowd, while young politicos and attractive Hill denizens have custody of nights and weekends. *Sun 11:30am-3pm and 5-9pm, Mon-Thu 11:30am-3pm and 5:30-10pm, Fri-Sat 11:30am-3pm and 5:30-11pm.* $ ℬ▤ 514 Eighth St. SE (E St.), 202-544-0100, belgacafe.com

Ben's Chili Bowl • U Street Corridor • Diner
Only-in-D.C. Restaurants This greasy spoon fed the likes of Duke Ellington, Miles Davis, and Martin Luther King, Jr., back when the neighborhood was known as "Black Broadway." The classic chili half smoke—a favorite of Bill Cosby—made the joint a D.C. institution, and its recipe hasn't changed since 1958. These days, "the Bowl" packs in a rowdy crowd after the music venues, jazz clubs, and bars let out. Nothing like chili cheese fries served to the groove of Al Green to feed your late-night munchies. *Sun noon-8pm, Mon-Thu 6am-2am, Fri-Sat 6am-4am.* $- ℬⓄ▤ 1213 U St. NW (13th St.), 202-667-0909, benschilibowl.com

Bistrot du Coin • Dupont Circle • French Bistro
D.C.'s French contingent finds a home away from home here. From the pale yellow walls to the steaming pots of mussels, this is the real deal. The owner wan-

ders between tables, shirt barely buttoned, puffing on a cigar and flirting with ladies and gentlemen alike. With the best bistro fare this far west of the Seine, it's hard to order wrong, but standouts include the steak frites, bouchée à la reine, and moules marinières. *Sun-Wed 11:30am-11pm, Thu-Sat 11:30am-1am.* $ 1738 Connecticut Ave. NW (Florida Ave.), 202-234-6969, bistrotducoin.com

Bread and Chocolate • Capitol Hill • Cafe

The real estate market for tables here on the weekend is more prime than that of 1600 Pennsylvania Avenue. That's because the patio's position at the entrance to Eastern Market makes it ideal for people-watching. There's no better way to fuel up for a day of shopping than over café au lait and chocolate-stuffed brioche French toast. The cafe's popularity can translate into waits and slow service at brunch. If you're on the move, grab an espresso and pastry to go. $- *Sun 7am-6pm, Mon-Sat 7am-7pm.* 666 Pennsylvania Ave. SE (Seventh St.), 202-547-2875

Cafe Asia* • Downtown • Asian

Cafe Asia captures the ever-popular minimalist Asian aesthetic—white on white, glowing light panels—but manages to avoid the cold, antiseptic feel of other bars. Here, low white tables shift like puzzle pieces to accommodate lively groups of postwork revelers, couples on dates, and friends making their first stop on a night out. Although the sushi happy hours are legendary, you can't choose wrong from the expansive menu of pan-Asian cuisine. For a (slightly) quieter seat, head upstairs, where tables overlook the bustling main room below. *Sun noon-11pm, Mon-Thu 11:30am-11pm, Fri 11:30am-midnight, Sat noon-midnight.* $ 1720 I St. NW (17th St.), 202-659-2696, cafeasia.com

Café Bonaparte • Georgetown • European

"It is not enough to conquer. One must know how to seduce," Voltaire once said. In a town of power players, Bonaparte has taken that credo to heart. This tiny cafe plies first dates, gossiping girlfriends, and married couples alike with generously poured glasses of wine amid pressed tin ceilings and striking photos of European cityscapes. It does not play favorites: the crepe menu pays homage to all manner of European cuisine from Lisbon to Santorini. And it closes the deal with lusty desserts and potent espressos tempered with Nutella and vanilla. *Sun 9am-10pm, Mon-Thu 10am-11pm, Fri-Sat 10am-1am.* $ 1522 Wisconsin Ave. NW (P St.), 202-333-8830, cafebonaparte.com

Café Saint-Ex* • U Street Corridor • American

This bustling cafe and bar is one of the top people-watching spots in the district, and you'll find excellent bistro fare. *See Hip Nightlife, p.102, for details.* $ 1847 14th St. NW (T St.), 202-265-7839, saint-ex.com

Chinatown Express • Penn Quarter • Chinese

The general rule with Chinatown goes: The more divey the restaurant, the better the food. Chinatown Express is no exception. This humble dining room's only adornment is hanging ducks and fluorescent paper advertising traditional fare like pig intestine. But a peek in the window reveals a packed room of hip couples and Chinese families focused on the real star: lai mein, noodles magically stretched from large balls of dough and served stir-fried or in bowls of soup. Or share a hot pot in which diners season and cook veggies and meat in steaming broth. *Daily 11am-11pm.* $- 746 Sixth St. NW (H St.), 202-638-0424

Creme Cafe • U Street Corridor • Southern
Diversity rules at this new hangout on U Street. Packing the slender, 50-seat Creme on a typical night are blacks, whites, young and not-so, couples, girlfriends, male friends, boyfriends, even a family or two from the neighborhood. Creme doesn't take reservations so come early if your focus is eating, and order topsellers shrimp and grits or pork and beans, Southern comfort food taken uptown. Arrive after 9pm on a Saturday for the full-fledged lively scene of fellow fun seekers, but expect to wait in line for a table. Be sure to order a slice of coconut cake, then hit U Street for a night of clubbing. *Sun 11am-4pm, Mon-Thu 6-10:30pm, Fri 6-11:30pm, Sat 11am-3pm and 6-11:30pm.* $ ≡ 1322 U St. NW (13th St.), 202-234-1884

The Diner • Adams Morgan • Diner
Avoid Adams Morgan's ubiquitous jumbo-slice pizza joints and opt for postclub grub at the Diner. As the inebriated masses pour out of 18th Street bars, they squeeze into the Diner's red booths and grab seats at the chrome counter. Round up your new best friends for classic greasy-spoon options from steak and eggs to burgers and malts. Always open, the Diner's greasy goodness satisfies early birds, night owls, and everyone in between. Late-night tables aren't a problem, but seats are at a premium for weekend breakfasts. Pop over to neighboring Tryst for a cup of coffee while you wait. *24/7.* $ ⓑ ≡ 2453 18th St. NW (Columbia Rd.), 202-232-8800, trystdc.com/diner

Domku Bar & Café • Upper Northwest • Eastern European
Cozy up with friends on the mismatched couches of this warm Eastern European eatery. The airy neighborhood feel makes this the perfect place to share a hearty meal of carrot and ginger soup and Kielbasa kanapki (open sandwich) or sweet pea and vanilla soup followed by Swedish meatballs. Share a three-shot flight of aquavits—vodkas infused with everything from cardamom to vanilla to rose petals. Then move on to a Polish Zywiec beer sweetened with black currant syrup. The kitchen closes at 10 sharp. *Sun 10am-3pm, Tue-Wed 11am-11pm, Thu-Sat 8am-midnight.* $ ⓑ ≡ 821 Upshur St. NW (Eighth St.), 202-722-7475

Firefly • Dupont Circle • American
An amber glow presides over the intimate dining room of this cozy spot. Lanterns hang from a tree that branches out across the ceiling. Freshly baked bread comes in copper pails. And the check is tucked into the firefly-catching jars of your childhood. These touches might seem contrived were they not accompanied by a nearly flawless menu of American fare and a lovingly selected wine list. Chef and oenophile John Wabeck often walks the dining room chatting up patrons and pouring tastes of vintages selected on his tasting trips. The bustling atmosphere makes Firefly ideal for the young and in love. *Daily 7-10am, Sun 11am-2:30pm, and 5-10:30pm, Mon-Thu 11:30am-2:30pm, and 5-30-10pm, Fri 11:30am-2:30pm and 5:30-10:30pm, Sat 5-10:30pm.* $$ ⓑ≡ 1310 New Hampshire Ave. NW (20th St.), 202-861-1310, firefly-dc.com

Hank's Oyster Bar • Dupont Circle • Oyster Bar
A genial staff. A blackboard listing the day's specials. Sunny sidewalk seating. Everything about Hank's says "Welcome to the neighborhood." Chef Jamie Leeds takes care of diners with stick-to-your-ribs seafood like fried calamari wrapped in bright red paper and served in shiny silver pails. She takes care of the environ-

ment by using seasonal produce from a local co-op. Diners ride the friendly vibe, getting acquainted between tables in the snug dining room. In keeping with the laid-back feel, the restaurant doesn't accept reservations, but if you call ahead, they'll be happy to put your name on the list while you're en route. *Sun 11am-3pm, Sun-Tue 5:30-10pm, Wed-Fri 5:30-11pm, Sat 11am-3pm and 5:30-11pm.* $ B= 1624 Q St. NW (17th St.), 202-462-4265, hanksdc.com

Helix Lounge* • Dupont Circle • Bar Food
This place is busy from happy hour to closing with hipsters drinking and eating the night away. *See Hip Nightlife, p.104, for details.* $- B= Helix Hotel, 1430 Rhode Island Ave. NW (14th St.), 202-462-9001, hotelhelix.com/heldini

Jaleo • Penn Quarter • Tapas
Named after John Singer Sargent's passionately dynamic flamenco painting, Jaleo offers an organically choreographed exploration of Spanish cuisine. The more than 60 different tapas on the menu come out sporadically as they're ready, and diners are encouraged to order in spurts. Though run by *Bon Appetit* Chef of the Year Jose Andres, the restaurant lacks any hint of pretension and truly embodies the "uproarious merry-making" term after which it's named. On Wednesday nights the wall's flamenco murals come to life when tables are pushed back to make room for live shows. *Sun 11:30am-10pm, Mon 11:30am-10pm, Tue-Thu 11:30am-11:30pm, Fri-Sat 11:30am-midnight.* $ B= 480 Seventh St. NW (E St.), 202-628-7949, jaleo.com

Johnny's Half Shell • Capitol Hill • Seafood
Best American Originals Step right in and leave your worries behind. The food, the mood, and the service so easily please, and it's exactly because Johnny's doesn't try to be all the rage, that it always is. Crab cakes and crab imperial are authentic versions of Chesapeake Bay cuisine, while the po' boys and seafood gumbo speak highly of New Orleans. Johnny's moved in 2006 from Dupont Circle to this location, but thanks largely to the winning presence of the owner himself, and to essential features, like the enormous aquarium behind the bar and the tile-floored fishhouse look, this Johnny's, like the old Johnny's, feels every bit the neighborhood haunt. *Mon-Thu 11:30am-10:30pm, Fri-Sat 11:30am-11pm.* $$ B= 2002 P St. NW (20th St.), 202-296-2021, johnnyshalfshell.net

L'Enfant Café • Adams Morgan • French
Belgian beer happy hours and wine and wig nights (customers donning fake hair are treated to half-price bottles) keep L'Enfant busy until late into the night, but the best time to check it out is at brunch. In the great European cafe tradition, a meal at L'Enfant is a leisurely event. Sit beneath an umbrella on the coveted patio sipping your espresso. Munch on croissants or one of the chef's sweet crepes. The good-looking waitstaff will oblige your leisurely pace as they serve up mimosas and bellinis. Positioned at the meeting point of the city's hottest neighborhoods—U Street and Adams Morgan—the cafe draws a lively mix of gay couples, chatty girlfriends, and friendly regulars. *Sun 10am-midnight, Mon-Thu 6pm-midnight, Fri-Sat 10am-1am.* $- B= 2000 18th St. NW (Florida Ave.), 202-319-1800, lenfantcafe.com

Logan Tavern* • U Street • American
Logan Tavern, like any good tavern, is a meeting place: a meeting of friends, of old-school fare with a modern aesthetic, and of the neighborhood's past as

Victorian status address and present as ground zero for D.C. gentrification. The décor mimics this nouveau tap house feel in the antique clock hanging over the dark black bar and the massive black-and-white photos of neighborhood spots. Expect a diverse mix of hip D.C. denizens to appear for every meal from its hearty brunch—and its famous Bloody Mary bar—to lively dinners. *Mon-Fri noon-close, Sat-Sun 11am-4pm and 5pm-close.* $$ 1423 P St. NW (15th St.), 202-332-3710, logantavern.com

Love Café • U Street • Bakery/Cafe
Great loves last a lifetime, and D.C. sweet tooths have found their soulmate in Love Café. The affair sparked in 2000 when the luscious Warren Brown left a successful law career to open a bakery. Everyone from Oprah to the Food Channel (which gave him his own TV show, *Sugar Rush*) is glad he did. The sit-down arm of Brown's CakeLove bakery gives the sugar-starved immediate gratification for their wildest dessert fantasies (not to mention a look at their creator). Chocoholic? Indulge in molten cocoa cake. Jealous? Keep the mini-pound cakes all to yourself. Lovelorn? Find comfort in coffee-flavored cream puffs. Though the cozy coffee shop serves up sandwiches and soups, don't kid yourself. You know what you came for. *Sun 10am-10pm, Mon-Fri 8am-11pm, Sat 9am-11pm.* $- 1501 U St. NW (15th St.), 202-265-9800, cakelove.com

Mama Ayesha's Restaurant • Adams Morgan • Middle Eastern
Best Vegetarian Restaurants Stepping through the intricate wrought-iron gates of Mama Ayesha's transports you into the heady sensuality of prewar Beirut. Deep red and navy walls glow by the light of punched metal lanterns. Water trickles lightly from burnished copper fountains. Let the affable staff guide you through its selection of Middle Eastern fare and list of Lebanese wines. The intimate entrance room is a great casual date spot, while the adjoining room caters to lively groups of nonprofit and writer types. *Sun-Thu noon-10pm, Fri-Sat noon-11pm.* $ 1967 Calvert St. NW (20th St.), 202-232-5431, mamaayeshas.com

Market Lunch • Capitol Hill • Diner
The lines on the weekends snake far out the door for the blueberry buckwheat pancakes, crab cakes, and fried fish sandwiches at this old-school lunch counter. But don't worry, it moves fast due to posted rules: Know what you want when you get to the counter, no saving seats, and no reading the paper. Though the staff tends to customers with straight-up Southern hospitality, the message is clear: Clean your plate and make way for the next wave of people. With all the activity of Eastern Market whirling around you, you'll be ready to scarf down the greasy goodness and peruse the market's other offerings. *Sun 11am-3:30pm, Tue-Sat 7:30am-3pm.* $- 225 Seventh St. SE (C St.), 202-547-8444

Marrakesh • Penn Quarter • Moroccan
You could easily miss the small Arabic letters identifying this building. But once you step through its doors, your every sensory desire is catered to. After being ushered to plush seats laden with pillows, waiters wash your hands with fragrant water before bringing out the first of six courses. Get drunk on the indulgence of exotic spices and the swaying hips of belly dancers purling to the strains of Moroccan music. The communal nature of Moroccan dining makes it an intimate experience for groups and couples alike. Reservations a must. *Mon-Fri 6-11pm, Sat-Sun 5-11pm.* $$$ 617 New York Ave. NW (Sixth St.), 202-393-9393, marrakesh.us

HIP • RESTAURANTS

Matchbox* • Penn Quarter • Pizzeria
Matchbox squeezes quite a bit into its skinny 15-foot-wide space. The first floor houses an always-packed bar overlooking a brick oven where smoldering hickory, oak, and cherry wood crisps New York–style pizzas. The second and third floors play host to slightly calmer dining rooms whose booths are inlaid with matchboxes from around the world. The cozy, bustling restaurant is the embodiment of casual chic, serving straightforward modern food to a friendly jeans-and-Converse crowd. It doesn't take reservations, so be prepared for a half-hour wait on the weekends. *Mon-Thu 11am-10pm, Fri 11am-11pm, Sat noon-11pm.* $ B≡ 713 H St. NW (Seventh St.), 202-289-4441, matchboxdc.com

Merkado • U Street • Asian-Latin
Fusion has reached frenzied heights, and the marriage of the moment is Latin and Asian. This urban cantina gets the blend just right as paper lanterns cast a soft glow on photographic murals painted in relief on cheery yellow walls. The food is a similarly happy union of East-West spices: the chile relleno is fried tempura-style; wonton skins heaped with gingered beef, cheddar, and wasabi cream replace traditional nachos. Even the drinks play cultural exchange: Mojitos are made with Korean Soju liquor and rumtinis get a kick of ginger syrup. Situated near the 14th Street galleries and theaters, Merkado draws a cultured but casual crowd for dinner. *Mon-Fri 5-11pm, Sat-Sun 11am-3pm and 5-11pm.* $$ B≡ 1443 P St. NW (14th St.), 202-299-0018, merkadodc.com

Meskerem • Adams Morgan • Ethiopian
D.C. boasts more Ethiopian restaurants than any other North American city. From the packed eateries of Little Ethiopia (along U Street) to the upscale options in Georgetown, the cuisine—served communally in bread-lined baskets—is a perfect fit for close friends and couples. New to the experience? The welcoming atmosphere of Meskerem makes for an excellent introduction. Carafes of tej (honey wine) complement the spicy stews, which are scooped up by hand with tangy injera bread. Don't be surprised if you see diners feeding each other. The practice—known as *gursha*—is the ultimate expression of loyalty and friendship. Opt for a table on the loft overlooking the dining room, and avoid the impersonal basement seating. *Sun noon-11pm, Mon-Thu noon-midnight, Fri-Sat noon-3am.* $ ≡ 2434 18th St. NW (Columbia Rd.), 202-462-4100, meskeremonline.com

Minibar at Café Atlantico • Penn Quarter • American (G)
Best Chef's Tables It may look just like any sleek downtown bar, but the six-seat Minibar is art in motion, created with the idea that food should be experienced through all of the senses. Two chefs will guide you through more than 30 new wave dishes—from foie gras cotton candy to saffron gumdrops. Minibar will stimulate not only your palate but your mind. You may have considered the notes in a glass of white wine, but how would those flavors play out on a plate? You'll find out when you taste the "Deconstructed Glass of White Wine." Reservations are a must: Call at 9am one month before you'd like to eat. *Tue-Sat seatings at 6 and 8:30pm.* $$$$ B≡ 405 Eighth St. NW (D St.), 202-393-0812, cafeatlantico.com

Mitsitam • National Mall • Native American
Best Indian Restaurants Remember when your third grade teacher taught you fractions with a pizza pie? Or probability with M&Ms? Well, the Smithsonian took a lesson from your teacher: Few can resist learning when there's food involved. So

when it opened the National Museum of the American Indian in 2004, it included the Mitsitam Cafe, a bite-by-bite lesson on cuisines indigenous to the Americas. It's a subject you should be eager to study with mouthwatering units like cedar-planked fire-roasted juniper salmon and fry bread with cinnamon and honey. But don't be tardy—the full menu is served between 11am and 3pm with stragglers getting only a limited taste. *Daily 10am-5:15pm.* $- Independence Ave. SW (Fourth St.), 202-633-1000, nmai.si.edu

Palette • Downtown • American

This restaurant and lounge mimics the artist's tool after which it is named. Frosted glass, muted tones, and sleek tables serve as a backdrop to Palette's foci: food and art. The restaurant's design makes the outside world a work of art when viewed through clear frames set into the otherwise sandblasted glass front. Works of local artists are suspended in other glass walls that break up the space. Colorful nouveau American fare is artfully presented on white plates. The front lounge attracts a diverse crew of young artsy types, while the prices of the dining room skew it toward a hip older crowd. Both types of crowds pack Palette as nearby offices let out on Fridays. *Sun 6-10:30pm, Mon-Thu 11:30am-2:30pm and 6-10:30pm, Fri 11:30am-2:30pm and 6-11pm, Sat 6-11pm.* $$ Madison Hotel, 1155 15th St. NW (M St.), 202-587-2700, palettedc.com

Perrys • Adams Morgan • Asian-American

Best Brunches By night, Perrys serves up sake, sushi, and seasonal fare to D.C.'s hippest on its twinkling rooftop and at white-linen–covered tables. Come Sunday morning, campy cross-dressers caper about the loftily dramatic dining room as diners sip (alcohol-infused) coffee. The drag brunch is a D.C. institution where you're as likely to see partiers who just got out of the clubs as postchurch service politicians' families. Get there by 10:15am to get a table, or wait until after the morning crush. If you have to wait, load up on mimosas at the bar as Marilyn, Madonna and Aretha shamelessly flirt on their path to performance. *Sun 10:30am-2:30pm, Sun-Thu 5:30-10:30pm, Fri-Sat 5:30-11:30pm.* $$ 1811 Columbia Rd. NW (Biltmore St.), 202-234-6218, perrysadamsmorgan.com

Poste • Penn Quarter • New American

With its jumping happy hour and key location, Poste welcomes celebs like Usher, but also a hungry after-work crowd. Sometimes the party stays here, sometimes it moves on. No matter, the food's great. Sit in the skylit main dining room, in a comfy booth across from the open kitchen, and enjoy gourmet comfort food, like crispy-skin wild-striped bass or beef bourguignon. *Sun 9am-4pm and 5-9pm, Mon-Thu 7-10am, 11:30am-2:30pm, and 5-10pm, Fri 7-10am, 11:30am-2:30pm, and 5-10:30pm, Sat 9am-4pm and 5-10:30pm.* $$ Hotel Monaco, 555 Eighth St. NW (F St.), 202-783-6060, postebrasserie.com

Rice • U Street • Thai

Minimalist chic and Asian fare have long been a match, but Rice makes it a happy marriage. The restaurant's otherwise spare décor draws the eye to exquisite details like the delicate orchids on the tables, the funky crowds around you, and the nouveau Thai cuisine on your plate. The Zen feel of the place can be broken by the noise levels, but it's hard to eat food this good without some kind of buzz. Order a Singha and be prepared for dishes that can test your threshold for spice. *Sun 11am-10:30pm, Mon-Thu 11am-2:30pm, 5-10:30pm, Fri-Sat 11am-11pm.* $ ≡ 1608 14th St. NW (Q St.), 202-234-2400, ricerestaurant.com

Teaism • Penn Quarter • Cafe
Heading down to the culinary wasteland that is the National Mall? Avoid the hot dog stands by stopping into Teaism for upscale picnic fare. Pick up one of its signature teriyaki salmon bento boxes or tuna tataki. While the simple Pan-Asian dishes are great on the go, the serene tea room tempts you to stay with exhibitions by local artists and potters. Need an extra dose of Zen? Sip on chai, ginger limeade, or any of the 26 varieties of tea. *Mon-Fri 7:30am-10pm, Sat-Sun 9:30am-9pm.* $- ⓘ≡ 400 Eighth St. NW (D St.), 202-638-6010, teaism.com

Tonic* • Mount Pleasant • American
Tough day of walking the monuments? Politics got you down? Never fear, Tonic is here to cure what ails you. This cute neighborhood spot serves up comfort food from cold meatloaf sandwiches to mac 'n' cheese the way Mom made it (with breadcrumbs on top!) to the come-as-you-are crowd. White paper and crayons encourage predinner playfulness, as does the dessert menu—a Good Humor ice cream poster. The bartenders have been known to ask, "What's your sign?" and serve up zodiac-themed cocktails. Taurus—the sensualist—is a blend of Stoli peach, cherry vodka, sour mix, and champagne. Skip the downstairs bar in favor of the sunny second-floor dining room. *Sun 10am-3pm, Sun-Thu 5pm-2am, Fri 5pm-3am, Sat 10am-3pm and 5pm-3am.* $- ⓑ≡ 3155 Mt. Pleasant St. NW (Kilbourne Pl.), 202-986-7661, tonicrestaurant.com

Tryst* • Adams Morgan • Cafe
This popular neighborhood hangout is serious about coffee and alcohol, but whimsical with its menu. *See Hip Nightlife, p.107, for details.* $- ⓑ≡ 2459 18th St. NW (Columbia Rd.), 202-232-5500, trystdc.com

Vegetate* • U Street Corridor • Vegetarian
Best Vegetarian Restaurants Owned by hip-hop DJ Dredd, this restaurant and bar makes you want to do anything but vegetate. Slick urban art sets off the apple-green walls. Hot beats underscore a sophisticated menu that will appeal to veggies and nonveggies alike. Spread over three floors of a row house in the up-and-coming Shaw neighborhood, Vegetate draws an eclectic mix of artists, hipsters, and neighborhood locals. *Sun 11am-3pm and 6-10pm, Thu 6-10pm, Fri-Sat 6-11pm.* $ ⓑ≡ 1414 Ninth St. NW (O St.), 202-232-4585, vegetatedc.com

Viridian • U Street Corridor • American
Best Vegetarian Restaurants The warmly minimalist décor of the dining room puts the focus on the local artwork exhibited on the walls. Beneath glowing fixtures sits a still-life–worthy bowl of local produce, a nod to the kitchen's commitment to seasonal fare. All of the nonmeat offerings are vegan—yes, that means no butter. However, you'd never know it from the creamy mashed potatoes and flaky apple turnovers. The standout food and subtle décor draw a sophisticated crowd of artists and gallery-goers. *Sun 10:30am-3:30pm and 4:30-11pm, Tue-Fri 11:30am-3:30pm and 5:30-11pm, Sat 10:30am-3:30pm and 5:30-11pm.* $ ⓑ≡ 1515 14th St. NW (P St.), 202-234-1400, viridianrestaurant.com

Hip D.C.:
The Nightlife

Avenue • Penn Quarter • Bar
The lines—long—and the dress code—strict—mimic those of other D.C. clubs, but it's less a function of exclusivity than of the necessity to maintain the friendly, chill vibe of this four-level club. The building retains architectural details from its past as a lumber company—the DJ booth is housed in an old elevator shaft and the weathered bricks from 1865 remain. You can always expect a mix of old school and current hip-hop. Fridays mix in reggae, and Saturdays draw a slightly more eclectic crowd by mixing in salsa and merengue. Waits can be long—be sure to get on the list at avedc.com to speed things up. *Sun 7pm-2am, Mon-Thu 4pm-2am, Fri-Sat 4pm-3am.* 649 New York Ave. NW (Sixth St.), 202-347-8100, avedc.com

Bar Nun • U Street Corridor • Bar
Bar Nun caters to an eclectic U Street clientele: from the cerebral—Mondays host D.C.'s top spoken-word poets—to the hedonistic—lingerie-clad women dance in a cage at Saturday's swingers night. In between, regulars sip after-work drinks and late-night crowds groove to hip-hop and house. The range of offerings is a testament to the versatility of the space. The bar manages to be both spacious with dancing on two levels and intimate with gauzily veiled alcoves for trysting. Expect lines and a $10 cover for Friday's hip-hop night. Saturday's swingers party admits couples for $40 and single women for $20, but bars single men. *Sun 7pm-3am, Mon-Thu 4pm-2am, Fri-Sat 4pm-3am.* 1326 U St. NW (14th St.), 202-667-6680, dcbarnun.com

Bar Pilar • U Street Corridor • Bar
An offshoot of neighbor Saint-Ex, this smaller, Hemingway-themed bar features stellar mojitos, Icelandic Viking beer, and killer tater tots. The writer's spare prose is reflected in the menu's straightforward take on global comfort foods from chicken-fried steak to lomo saltado. Named after his fishing boat, the place has a vintage nautical décor that reflects Hemingway's peripatetic lifestyle in Paris, the Florida Keys, and Spain. Hipsters get lit up on lager and lit-talk, and capture the fun in the bar's vintage photo booth. *Sun-Thu 5pm-2am, Fri-Sat 5pm-3am.* 1833 14th St. NW (T St.), 202-265-1751, barpilar.com

Bedrock Billiards • Adams Morgan • Pool Hall
Pool halls in D.C. tend to be decidedly dingy or overcrowded behemoths. Thankfully, there's Adams Morgan's Bedrock Billiards. Mismatched '70s couches, Dali-esque pool murals, and an amoeba-shaped bar lend this place the right mixture of grit and glitter. Though the wait for a table can be 45 minutes or more on the weekends (shorter during summer months), the stellar jukebox, wry wit of the bartenders, and collection of vintage board games will keep you more than occupied. $10 for one person per hour up to $20 per hour for a table where four people are playing. *Sun 1pm-2am, Mon-Thu 4pm-2am, Fri 4pm-3am, Sat 1pm-3am.* 1841 Columbia Rd. NW (Mintwood Pl.), 202-667-7665, bedrockbilliards.com

HIP • NIGHTLIFE

The Big Hunt • Dupont Circle • Dive Bar
Booths shaped into safari tents, Guinness ice cream, and the catchphrase "happy hunting ground ... for mates, food, and drink." In any other bar (outside Orlando) this would be an odious combination. But Big Hunt manages to play on the kitsch factor to create a laid-back alternative to the nearby prestige bars. Perhaps it's the excellent selection of foreign beers and microbrews, the indie rock juke box, or the cozy back deck. Whatever the reason, the Big Hunt is the perfect place to play pool, get rowdy, and chat up the friendly locals from happy hour until last call. *Sun 5pm-2am, Mon-Thu 4pm-2am, Fri-Sat 5pm-3am.* 1345 Connecticut Ave. NW (Dupont Cir.), 202-785-2333

The Black Cat • U Street Corridor • Bar
Best Live Music Ground zero for hipster D.C., the Black Cat is a nationally known music venue and bar with an impressive pedigree—Foo Fighter Dave Grohl is one of the main investors. Opened in 1993, the Cat has played host to a veritable who's-who list of musicians from Jeff Buckley to Pavement, Modest Mouse to the White Stripes. The upstairs doubles as a concert venue and dance club—try to catch Mousetrap, the club's legendary Brit-pop dance nights. In the downstairs Red Room Bar, the vintage-clad masses sip Pabst and play pinball, Pac-Man, or pool to tunes from the district's best jukebox. *Sun-Thu 8pm-2am, Fri-Sat 7pm-3am.* 1811 14th St. NW (S St.), 202-667-7960, blackcatdc.com

Bohemian Caverns • U Street Corridor • Jazz Club
This legendary jazz joint has hosted performers from Coltrane to Calloway, Dizzy to Davis and everyone in between. The subterranean supper club lives up to its name with candlelit cavelike walls and recessed grottoes. Though the music is still stellar—especially for Wednesday's open mic night and Saturday's jams—the owners decided to up the ante by opening a dance club dubbed Liv upstairs. Thursday's Uncle Q's Loft is the top hip-hop night in the city, with old-school jams and a casual crowd. Sunday 4-10pm hosts Daylight, a chill come-as-you-are event, where Big Tony serves up heaping plates of Caribbean and soul food to friendly neighborhood crowds. *Daily, performance times vary.* 2003 11th St. NW (U St.), 202-299-0801, bohemiancaverns.com

Bossa • Adams Morgan • Bar
Seductive strains of samba draw couples to the sexy first floor of Bossa. Under the soft light of candles, couples tease one another on the dance floor and cuddle on buttery leather lounges. The unattached find a more raucous party upstairs, where live bands play more energetic fare from salsa to latin reggae. If the dance floor gets too hot, take a break to peruse the rotating art-shows or grab a seat upstairs near the front wall of windows to get a bird's-eye view of 18th Street. *Mon-Thu 6pm-1am, Fri-Sat 6pm-2am.* 2463 18th St. NW (Columbia Rd.), 202-667-0088, bossa-dc.com

The Brickskeller Saloon • Dupont Circle • Bar
Best Local Favorites Take one down, pass it around—'cause there are 1,000-plus varieties of beer at this bar. "The Brick" will please everyone from frat friends to cultured clients. The atmosphere is laid back, but the offerings are sophisticated—the expansive beer collection garnered it a spot in the *Guinness Book of World Records.* So pull up a barrel seat and peruse the beer menu, er, book. Try a brew from every continent, spend the whole night sipping Belgians, or ask for

recommendations from the suds-savvy staff. *Sun 6pm-2am, Mon-Thu 11:30am-2am, Fri 11:30am-3am, Sat 6pm-3am.* ≡ 1523 22nd St. NW (P St.), 202-293-1885, thebrickskeller.com

Busboys and Poets • U Street Corridor • Bookstore/Lounge
Named after legendary D.C. poet Langston Hughes, this restaurant, bookstore, and lounge is a lesson in D.C.'s past and present. Activists, writers, and artsy neighborhood types congregate for readings, spoken word, or to just chat over drinks. Both the spirit and the setup—rooms flow into one another and communal tables and couches encourage mingling—reflect a desire to bring together all walks of D.C. life. Tuesday's spoken-word nights are standing-room only, but drop in any given night and you'll find a vibrant cross-section of political and artistic movers and shakers. *Sun-Thu 9am-midnight, Fri-Sat 10am-2am.* ◨≡ 2021 14th St. NW (V St.), 202-387-7638, busboysandpoets.com

Cafe Asia* • Downtown • Restaurant Bar
Low white tables shift like puzzle pieces to accommodate lively groups of post-work revelers, couples on dates, and friends. Their sushi happy hours are legendary. *See Hip Restaurants, p.93, for details.* ≡ 1720 I St. NW (17th St.), 202-659-2696, cafeasia.com

Café Citron • Dupont Circle • Caribbean
"Dancing on the bar is not only allowed, it's encouraged," Citron's menu says. And it's a good thing because live salsa bands make it hard to keep hips from swaying, and Citron's tiny rooms leave little space for the groove they encourage. Enthusiastic dancers find room between tables, on couches and, yes, on the bar, to samba, salsa (on Fridays), belly dance (early evening on Saturdays) and otherwise shake while sipping caipirinhas and Guarana—an aphrodisiac. For a less-crowded option, get there early and nosh on Caribbean and South American food. *Mon-Thu 11:30am-2am, Fri 11:30am-3am, Sat 4pm-3am.* ≡ Fri-Sat ◯ 1343 Connecticut Ave. NW (Dupont Cir.), 202-530-8844, cafecitrondc.com

Café Saint-Ex* • U Street Corridor • Bar
Best Local Favorites At this bar, located in the heart of the super-hip U Street 'hood, hipsters mix with yo-pros at this Parisian bistro and bar. From the breezy sidewalk cafe to the vintage aviation-themed décor, this is the place to go for lively conversation over a bottle of merlot or a crisp Chimay. On the weekends, the stiletto set grooves to hip-hop at the dark downstairs bar. During the week, it's all Converse and cigarettes, as DJs spin indie rock and Brit pop. If you're lucky, you'll catch a surprise set by rockers dropping in after shows at the nearby Black Cat. *Sun 11am-1:30am, Mon 5pm-1:30am, Tue-Thu 11am-1:30am, Fri-Sat 11am-2:30am.* ≡ 1847 14th St. NW (T St.), 202-265-7839, saint-ex.com

Capital City Records • U Street Corridor • Dive Bar
It's a testament to the intensity of D.C.'s hip-hop scene that this booze-less open-mic night packs in more Friday crowds than most bars. Located on the same street that made Duke Ellington famous, this is where today's most promising D.C. musicians gather to spit rhymes, show off beats, and forge their own kind of musical history. Record store racks are cleared away to make room for dancing, and the freewheeling nature of the night tends to take on a house-party feel. Expect an open vibe ... and record giveaways. *Sun noon-6pm, Mon-Thu*

11am-9pm, Fri 11am-11pm, Sat 11am-10pm. 1020 U St. NW (10th St.), 202-518-2444, capitalcityrecords.com

Capitol Lounge • Capitol Hill • Dive Bar
Although it underwent extensive renovations after a blaze destroyed much of the bar, the Capitol Lounge managed to maintain all the history and dive bar character that made it a D.C. institution. Catering to the Hill's younger denizens, the lounge is your best bet for bipartisan boozing. The décor gives nods to Republicans and Democrats alike: Political memorabilia ranges from an LBJ board game to a Last Supper poster with Nixon as Jesus. The downstairs Golden Fez martini and cigar lounge is not the class affair you'd expect. Decorated like a Shriner's Hall complete with fez lighting fixtures, the basement fills with the jeans-and-sneakers set playing pool or watching soccer matches on TVs. Busiest on Thursday and Friday. *Sun 10am-2am, Mon-Thu 4pm-2am, Fri 4pm-3am, Sat 10am-3am.* 231 Pennsylvania Ave. SE (Independence Ave.), 202-547-2098

Chi-Cha Lounge • U Street Corridor • Lounge
Think lounge has to mean overpriced bottle service, exorbitant cover charges, and stark minimalist décor? Think again. Chi-Cha embodies the true meaning of the word *lounge* with antique couches grouped family-room–style underneath glowing lanterns. An eclectic crowd shares hookahs, Nuevo Latino tapas, and carafes of chi-cha, an Andean drink reminiscent of spiced sangria. Expect crowds and loud hip-hop and house on the weekends, so you'll have to get up close and personal to chat with the people around you, which, considering the hotness of the crowd and aphrodisiac qualities of the chi-cha, could be just what you're looking for. A hint for the gentlemen: Though the dress code is flexible, the owner has a strong aversion to men in hats. Leave the lid at home. *Sun-Thu 5:30pm-1:30am, Fri-Sat 5:30pm-2:30am.* 1624 U St. NW (16th St.), 202-234-8400, latinconcepts.com/chicha

Chief Ike's Mambo Room • Adams Morgan • Dance Club
Dwight Eisenhower cut off relations with Cuba in 1961, but never fear, the kitschy Chief Ike's Mambo Room is here to restore décor-ous diplomacy. OK, maybe not. Though the rainbow beach murals and tiki totem poles of this dive bar loosely reflect its Ike-Havana theme, everyone's attention is focused on the cheap booze and packed dance floor. Check it out on Fridays, when crowd-pleasing cheese dominates the downstairs bar, while Jimmy the Truth keeps the hipsters happy by bringing the rock to the upstairs Cosmos lounge. *Daily 8pm-2am.* 1725 Columbia Rd. NW (17th St.), 202-332-2211, chiefikes.com

D.C. Improv • Dupont Circle • Comedy Club
Although there's little room for funny business in politics, D.C. is rife with unintentional humor. However, if you're not getting your giggles from presidential malapropisms, D.C. Improv will most certainly do the trick. Nationally known acts sell out the small but prestigious club most nights, and the humor is a welcome departure from "How many senators does it take to screw in a lightbulb?" jokes. Tables are packed in, so be prepared to get up close and personal with your neighbors. There is a two-item minimum, but it's not hard to find something to suit your fancy from the menu of bar fare and burritos. *Daily 8pm-2am.* 1140 Connecticut Ave. NW (M St.), 202-296-7008, dcimprov.com

DC9 • U Street Corridor • Bar
Musicians, scenesters, and nonprofit types head to DC9 for intimate performances by top local bands, or to grab a Sparks on their way to concerts at the nearby 9:30 Club. The downstairs jukebox bar may be the place to talk records. But the upstairs is where you can go to actually dance to them. The District's top indie-rock DJs spin at the weekly Friday Liberation Dance Party and the monthly Tease parties. Sundays often play host to Taint, an alterna-queer dance party whose electro pop, fashion shows, and drag performances draw gay, straight, and everything in between. *Sun 8pm-2am, Mon-Thu 5pm-2am, Fri 5pm-3am, Sat 7pm-3am.* C≣ 1940 Ninth St. NW (U St.), 202-483-5000, dcnine.com

Duplex Diner • Adams Morgan • Gay Bar
Best Gay Bars Though the old-school neon sign out front screams "diner," don't expect hairnetted waitresses or chrome countertops. Duplex serves up standard greasy-spoon fare, but the real draw of this see-and-be-seen place is its jumping bar. Drawing predominantly gay men, Duplex packs in a fashionable but laid-back crowd nearly every night of the week. Though the cozy environment may make a lone visitor feel uncomfortable earlier in the evening, the friendly vibe makes it easy to meet people as the night progresses. *Sun-Mon 6-11pm, Tue-Wed 6pm-12:30am, Thu 6pm-1am, Fri-Sat 6pm-1:30am.* ≣ 2004 18th St. NW (Florida Ave.), 202-265-7828, duplexdiner.com

18th Street Lounge • Dupont Circle • Lounge
Best Sexy Lounges From the outside, 18th Street Lounge is all about exclusivity. There's no sign. The lines are long. And you're not getting in unless you look the part. (Men: Trade the khakis for status denim. Ladies, channel your inner Sienna Miller.) But once you get in, be prepared to check your pretensions at the door and make yourself at home. Lit by ornate candelabras and fireplaces, jet-setters and neo-hipsters sip cocktails on plush antique couches in the three large lounges. Because it's home base for red-hot DJs Thievery Corporation, expect your conversations to be underscored by a chill mix of acid jazz, trip-hop, and Brazilian beats. The ideal night: Catch the sunset on the back deck, hear a live jazz combo upstairs, and then groove with new friends on the small dance floor. *Tue-Wed 9:30pm-2am, Thu 5:30pm-2am, Fri 5:30pm-3am, Sat 9:30pm-3am.* C≣ 1212 18th St. NW (Jefferson Pl.), 202-466-3922, eslmusic.com

Five • Dupont Circle • Bar
Best Dance Clubs Because of the limited number of after-hours clubs in D.C., Five's dance floor mixes patrons of punk clubs and cocktail bars alike. Drum and bass, house, and hip-hop keep the crowds moving until breakfast time. Survey the action from a catwalk overlooking the dance floor and its retro-funky disco ball chandelier. Energy flagging? Take a nap in the hammocks at the open-air reggae-on-the-roof bar. The line and cover charge increase exponentially at 2am, so get there before 1am. *Sun 9pm-3am, Wed 9pm-3am, Thu 10pm-2am, Fri-Sat 9pm-5am.* C≣ 1214B 18th St. NW (Jefferson Pl.), 202-331-7123, fivedc.com

Helix Lounge* • Dupont Circle • Hotel Lounge
Best Hotel Bars Kooky kitsch governs the Helix Hotel's lounge: White stools light up when you sit down. Warhol and Lichtenstein preside over pop culture fiends sipping cocktails with names like Tom-Kat Collins. Busy from happy hour to closing

time, Helix makes it easy to move from munchies at the long communal dining table to alcoves partitioned with gauzy curtains or to the outdoor patio's boldly striped cabanas and plump cushions. Aside from Thursday's Disco and Oreos night, the music bounces from Sergeant Pepper to Salt-N-Pepa, and though there's no dance floor, the playful atmosphere often inspires spontaneous dance-offs. *Sun-Thu 5-11:30pm, Fri-Sat 5pm-1:30am.* Helix Hotel, 1430 Rhode Island Ave. NW (14th St.), 202-462-9001, hotelhelix.com/heldini

Home • Penn Quarter • Lounge
Though the club includes subtle nods to its name—the massive second-floor window seat is modeled on a bed—this moniker is more of a tribute to the club's laid-back brand of house party fun. The décor owes more to its past as a turn-of-the-century bank—safe deposit boxes peek from behind colored panels of glass and the palette of the VIP lounge tends toward the precious metals it once guarded. The downstairs crowd occasionally skews cheesy, so sweet-talk your way to the classier debauchery of the fourth-floor penthouse. Waits shouldn't be much longer than 20 minutes, but as always, opting for bottle service will expedite the process. *Daily 9pm-3:30am.* 911 F St. NW (Ninth St.), 202-638-4663, homenightclub.net

HR-57 • U Street Corridor • Cabaret
Named for the Congressional resolution that designated jazz "a rare and valuable national American treasure," HR-57 is the real deal. Don't expect the slick décor of other supper clubs. HR-57 resembles your neighborhood coffee shop with mismatched old couches, tables, and chairs set under cozy candlelight. Home to the Center for the Preservation of Jazz & Blues, the club's walls highlight D.C.'s rich musical history, and the affable owners will school you on everything from Miles to Marsalis. Patrons take the music seriously, so be prepared for shushing if you chat too much in the main performance room. For more social seating, opt for the front entrance room, which still affords excellent views of the stage. *Wed-Thu 8pm-midnight, Fri-Sun 9pm-1am.* 1610 14th St. NW (Q St.), 202-667-3700, hr57.org

Logan Tavern* • U Street Corridor • Restaurant Bar
This place is famous for its Bloody Mary bar. See Hip Restaurants, p.95, for details. 1423 P St. NW (15th St.), 202-332-3710, logantavern.com

Madam's Organ • Adams Morgan • Bar
Best Live Music The busty madam's mural lures 18th Street revelers from blocks away. Once named one of *Playboy*'s top 25 U.S. bars, Madam's Organ claims to be the place "where the beautiful people come to get ugly." That may be the case, but it belies the fact that this raucous club attracts some of the top blues, jazz, and bluegrass acts in the country. From the lofted mezzanine, music lovers eat stick-to-your-ribs soul food and drink jam jars of beer next to a roaring fire. The second floor plays host to free pool and Big Daddy's Love Lounge & Pick-Up Joint. Cover runs a mere $3-$5, and redheads always get half-price beer. *Sun-Thu 5pm-2am, Fri-Sat 5pm-3am.* 2461 18th St. NW (Columbia Rd.), 202-667-5370, madamsorgan.com

Mantis • Adams Morgan • Lounge
The Asian vibe at Mantis plays out in the complementary opposites of the upstairs and downstairs bars, creating a sort of yin-yang nightlife experience. A

bronze Buddha sculpture presides over a sleek white lounge where hipsters sip cocktails and munch on Asian tapas. Downstairs, candles light an all-black room where DJs spin insistent hip-hop and house for the dancing crowds. A late-night menu, summer patio, and laid-back line and cover-free entry policy combine to make Mantis a one-stop nightlife experience. *Mon-Sat 6pm-2am.* 1847 Columbia Rd. NW (Mintwood Pl.), 202-667-2400

Matchbox* • Penn Quarter • Restaurant Bar

The first floor of this casual restaurant houses an always-packed bar overlooking a brick oven where smoldering hickory, oak, and cherry wood crisps New York–style pizzas. *See Hip Restaurants, p.97, for details.* 713 H St. NW (Seventh St.), 202-289-4441, matchboxdc.com

Saki • Adams Morgan • Lounge

Don't bother to wait for a seat in the long, thin dining room. Although the cozy banquettes and creative sushi menu are tempting, the real fun is the downstairs bar where colored panels cast a glow on the otherwise all-white interior. By 11, the floor is packed with pretty young things dancing to hip-hop, retro tunes, and crowd-friendly house. The carefree, laid-back feel attracts a fun-loving younger set. The dress code on the weekends is at the bouncer's discretion, but designer denim and nice shoes should get you through the door without a problem. *Mon-Thu 6pm-2am, Fri-Sat 6pm-3am. Sushi served until midnight.* 2477 18th St. NW (Columbia Rd.), 202-232-5005, sakidc.com

Science Club • Downtown • Lounge

The following observations may lead one to conclude that the name Science Club aptly encapsulates this downtown bar:
1. It's tall and skinny like that physics nerd in high school.
2. Lab stools, an equation-laden blackboard, and biology filmstrip boxes are scattered throughout.
3. DJs perform Nobel-worthy experiments on the turntables in the fields of breakbeat, downtempo, and drum and bass.
However, further research reveals a hip crowd, hot bartenders, and a sleek interior. In addition, the turn-of-the-century stone building brings to mind Darwin-era intellectual salons more than your friendly high-school geek-and-greet. Final conclusions? The Science Club is a pretension-free hot spot for the brainy and beautiful. *Mon-Thu 5pm-2am, Fri-Sat 6pm-3am.* 1136 19th St. NW (L St.), 202-775-0747, scienceclubdc.com

Tapatinis • Capitol Hill • Bar

In D.C., power equals status, but not necessarily a fat paycheck. Therefore it's not hard to understand the raging popularity of happy hours at Capitol Hill watering holes. Tapatinis has mastered the art with nightly specials that pack its funky cocktail bar with Congressional staffers and nonprofit types. Free cocktails on Thursday and all-you-can-drink specials on Friday mean standing-room only from five onward. Get there at quitting time to snag one of the large curved booths amid a cheery palette of blue, yellow, and green walls. *Tue-Thu 5pm-midnight, Fri 5pm-2am, Sat 7pm-2am. Sushi served until midnight.* 711 Eighth St. SE (G St.), 202-546-8272, tapatinis.com

Tonic* • Mount Pleasant • Restaurant Bar

This cute neighborhood spot caters to a relaxed, come-as-you-are crowd. The bartenders have been known to ask, "What's your sign?" and serve up zodiac-themed cocktails. See Hip Restaurants, p.99, for details. 3155 Mt. Pleasant St. NW (Kilbourne Pl.), 202-986-7661, tonicrestaurant.com

Trio's Fox and Hound • Dupont Circle • Dive Bar
Order a rum and coke at Fox and Hound, and the waitress plunks down a glass of liquor with a bottle of coke. This is the place to go if you like your drink strong and your music loud. The hipster crowd camps out inside and in warm weather spills out onto the sidewalk tables. The old-school diner attached to the bar serves up chocolate shakes and fries until late into the night. *Sun-Thu 11am-2am, Fri 11am-3am, Sat 10am-3am.* 1537 17th St. NW (Church St.), 202-232-6307

Tryst* • Adams Morgan • Cafe
Neighborhood types consider the spacious Tryst their second living room. Hot hipsters serve stiff drinks from morning until passing-out time. Come for a hangover-curing breakfast of caramel apple waffles drizzled in hazelnut chocolate, or chat late into the night as conversation is spiced up by booze-caffeine combos and underscored with live jazz or hip-hop. Though the menu and mood are whimsical, Tryst is serious about caffeination. It serves only one blend of coffee in order to control its quality. It offers twenty teas; Cuban, Spanish, and Italian treatments of coffee drinks; and all manner of alcoholic blends. *Sun 7am-2am, Mon-Thu 6:30am-2am, Fri-Sat 6:30am-3am.* 2459 18th St. NW (Columbia Rd.), 202-232-5500, trystdc.com

Vegetate* • U Street Corridor • Restaurant Bar
The sophisticated menu in a funky setting will appeal to veggies and nonveggies alike. See Hip Restaurants, p.99, for details. 1414 Ninth St. NW (O St.), 202-232-4585, vegetatedc.com

Warehouse • Penn Quarter • Bar/Theater
Housed in an old hardware store, this arts complex retains the former structure's weathered concrete, ancient wood floors, and storefront windows. Warehouse plays host to more shows a year than any space in D.C. aside from the Kennedy Center. On a given night, visitors can see an edgy new play in one of two theaters, catch a flick in its screening room, browse exhibits at its art gallery, or catch a rock show in its music venue. Try to make it to one of the venue's Art Romps, an open show of local artists that devolves into a raucous party. Find out about this and other events online. *Sun noon-6pm, Mon-Fri 5pm-11pm, Sat 10am-midnight. Show, gallery, and concert hours vary.* 1021 Seventh St. NW (New York Ave.), 202-783-3933, warehousetheater.com

The Wonderland Ballroom • Upper Northwest • Dive Bar
Best Local Favorites Wonderland is a dive bar in the best sense of the term. The bar—decorated with vintage album covers and furnished with a Pac-Man table and bench seats from a minivan—is host to one of D.C.'s best jukeboxes (with a note reminding patrons that after 11 selections must please the funk in your soul). Beer is cheap, but the selections are sophisticated—from Chimay to Delirium Tremens. On weekends, DJs pack the upstairs dance floor, spinning funk, hip-hop, and soul with some breakbeat and indie rock. The streets around the bar aren't always well lit, so take a cab and keep a phone number handy to call one for your ride home. *Sun-Thu 5pm-2am, Fri-Sat 5pm-3am.* 1101 Kenyon St. NW (11th St.), 202-232-5263, thewonderlandballroom.com

Hip D.C.: The Attractions

African American Civil War Museum and Memorial • U Street Corridor • Museum/Site
The Spirit of Freedom sculpture is the first thing you see as you approach or exit the Metro station at U and Vermont streets. In a semicircle around the sculpture are a series of plaques engraved with the names of the 209,145 African Americans mustered into military service during the Civil War. Two blocks west is the museum, a tiny storefront gallery that resides in the same building where Duke Ellington once played and Joe Lewis once trained as a boxer. The museum's illustrations and exhibits reveal the history of slavery and of the African American experience in the Civil War. The key here is to ask the staff person on duty to take you through it. All in all, it's a 30-minute history lesson. Memorial: at the entrance to the U St./African American Civil War Memorial/Cardozo Metro station. *Museum: Mon-Fri 10am-5pm, Sat 10am-2pm.* 1200 U St. NW (12th St.), 202-667-2667, afroamcivilwar.org

Albert Einstein Memorial • National Mall • Site
It's clear that this famous mathematician and scientist, pacifist and philosopher was a hipster in disguise. "The most beautiful thing we can experience is the mysterious," Einstein once said. While in the neighborhood of the Vietnam Veterans and Lincoln memorials, cross Constitution Avenue at 22nd St. and wander back to a grove of elm trees to find this 12-foot statue of Einstein, slouched on a granite bench, celestial map at his feet. Lean up against him and absorb his vibe. Constitution Ave. NW (22nd St.)

Art Museum of the Americas • National Mall • Art Museum
Welcome to Little Latin America. A tiny triangle of land off Constitution Avenue displays a very large sculpture representing "liberator" Simon Bolivar on horseback; a statue of Jose Artigus, "Father of the Independence of Uruguay"; and behind Artigus, the pretty Spanish colonial–style building that houses this museum. Through its blue door are two floors of brightly painted galleries exhibiting 20th-century paintings by mostly Latin American and Caribbean artists. You'll be on your own touring, which takes 30 minutes tops. A beautiful blue-tiled loggia at the back leads to a terrace and the museum's garden, which separates the museum from the Organization of American States headquarters. *Tue-Sun 10am-5pm.* 201 18th St. NW (Constitution Ave.), 202-458-6016, museum.oas.org

The Bead Museum • Penn Quarter • Museum
Beads are ancient. Beads are beautiful. Every civilization has used them. The first bead was probably a snail shell with a hole in it. Scholars now study beads to learn about past peoples and cultures. Who would have thought? Step right into this one-room museum surrounded by trendy restaurants in the Penn Quarter to admire the beautiful colors and designs of beads, which are displayed in a timeline, from 70,000 BC to today, each bead identified by geographic origin and age. It's all much more fascinating than you'd think it would be. And

you're in and out in 20 minutes. *Sun 1-4pm, Wed-Sat 11am-4pm.* 400 Seventh St. NW (D St.), 202-624-4500, beadmuseumdc.org

Bike the Sites • Penn Quarter • Sport/Tour
Avoid the crowds, but still see D.C.'s most famous landmarks by bike-touring at night. The three-hour tour travels the National Mall and the Tidal Basin, stopping at the memorials, with a guide narrating and leading the way. This is just one of the tours Bike the Sites offers, with others held during the day and covering other sites. The outfit provides bikes, helmets, water bottles, and, at night, reflective vests and safety lights; you'll be part of a group that never exceeds 15 people and often is smaller. *Night tours start at 6:30pm. Tours are offered year-round, but by appointment only December through February. For rides during Cherry Blossom season, call way ahead.* $$$$ Old Post Office Pavilion, Rear Plaza, 1100 Pennsylvania Ave. NW (12th St.), 202-842-2453, bikethesites.com

DownDog Yoga • Georgetown • Sport
Not your mama's yoga studio in a church basement, this one's a glorious space with 14-foot-high ceilings, tall windows, and views of the C&O Canal. The version taught here is Baptiste power Vinyasa yoga, which is vigorous, athletic, and guaranteed to make you sweat—basically, it's yoga with attitude. Never done yoga before? Doesn't matter. All-levels and walk-ins are welcome, though on weekends you might want to reserve a space in advance. Classes are 90 minutes long, $17 per class; towels and mats are available to rent. *Check website for times.* $ 1046 Potomac St. NW (M St.), 202-965-9642, downdogyoga.com

East Potomac Golf Course at Hains Point • Southwest • Sport
East Potomac's real draw is its spectacular setting: it's a peninsula extending into the Potomac River, the Washington Monument in full view. Of course, its windy prominence can be a challenge, but it's worth it. Hains Point is at the tip of East Potomac Park and in addition to golf offers miniature golf, tennis, and a swimming pool. The club doesn't rent shoes (soft spikes required), but offers everything else, and there's a snack bar that's open to everyone, golfers or otherwise. From the memorials along Independence Avenue, cut through the park and follow the path along the river for a 20-minute walk or so. *Driving range: Mon, Wed-Sun 7am-8pm, Tue 10am-9pm (other concessions operate seasonally).* $$ East Potomac Golf Course, 972 Ohio Dr. SW, 202-554-7660, golfdc.com

Eastern Market • Capitol Hill • Market
Insider D.C. Experiences In continuous operation since 1873, Eastern Market feels a bit like the famous French neighborhood markets. This is a community farmers and flea market, and you'll see residents walking through the streets and alleys from their homes, headed to market to buy fresh chickens, produce, cheeses, flowers, baked goods, and sundry other foods that have been grown or prepared regionally. Food vendor booths, including Market Lunch, serving crab cakes and blueberry pancakes (there's a counter and stools at that end), line the walls of the South Hall, and arts vendors occupy the North Hall. Aim for visiting Saturday, when the market's a rollicking hubbub as market-goers greet each other and vendors like old friends, parents try to keep track of wandering kids, and neighbors catch up on gossip as they look over the merchandise. Outside vendors sell more of the same daily, as well as flea market items, everything

from pashminas to wooden bowls, on Sundays. *Indoor market: Sun 9am-4pm, Tue-Sat 7am-6pm; outdoor market: Sat-Sun 7am-4pm (farmers market) and Sun 9am-6pm (flea market).* Seventh St. SE (North Carolina Ave.), 202-544-0083, easternmarketdc.com

Flight Simulators • National Mall • Sport

Best Rainy Day Experiences Inside the National Air and Space Museum, the most popular Smithsonian (read: often a 30-minute wait just to get in the door in spring and summer), are some amazing exhibits of airplane and spacecrafts, good for hours of wide-eyed looks. And then there are the simulators, 14 of them in the northwest pocket, first level of the museum. You choose: wild or mild ride, an F18 Hornet (modern-day jet) or a P51 Mustang (World War II fighter), interactive or autopilot, fly solo or with a partner. You're enclosed in a machine turning upside down and all around, and just like the real thing, you control the motion. $7.50 gets you two minutes to train and three minutes to fly; pay a bunch of money and you're good for a while. Tip: you can reserve one or more in advance. *Daily 10am-5:30pm.* $- National Air and Space Museum, Independence Ave. SW (Seventh St.), 202-633-1000, nasm.si.edu

Folger Shakespeare Library • Capitol Hill • Site/Garden

Behind the enormous buildings housing the Library of Congress is this more modest-sized library, whose collection of works about Shakespeare numbers 250,000. You can't see those (scholars only). Open to the general public are the Elizabethan theater, the Elizabethan garden, whose plants replicate those of the times, and the lofty Great Hall and its constantly changing exhibits chronicling, for example, English music of the late 16th century. Arrive in time for the 11am free docent's tour and you'll get a peek into the Reading Room and in-depth information about Elizabethan times and the man himself. On your own or with a docent, a tour takes about 45 minutes. The Folger hosts many acclaimed theater, music, and literary performances. *Mon-Sat 10am-4pm.* 201 E. Capitol St. SE (Second St.), 202-544-4600, folger.edu

IMAX Films • National Mall • Museum/Entertainment

Best Rainy Day Experiences Well, you just have not flown until you've perched on the wing of a plane as it flies, which is exactly how it feels when you watch the IMAX film *To Fly*. Your other options at the National Air and Space Museum include walking on the moon, exploring the surface of Mars, or becoming a fighter pilot. Across the Mall at the National Museum of Natural History, IMAX films put you in the picture with elephants, rhinos, and leopards on an African safari, or have you swimming with sharks and sea lions in the depths of the sea. These three-dimensional films take your breath away—and perhaps call for a drink to settle your nerves. Friday evenings at the Natural History museum you can follow up a film with a cocktail and listen to a little jazz, too, in the museum's "jazz cafe." Film times vary; best to reserve tickets in advance. *Museum daily 10am-5:30pm, theaters stay open later.* $ National Air and Space Museum, Independence Ave. SW (Seventh St.), 202-633-4629, nasm.si.edu; National Museum of Natural History, Constitution Ave. NW (10th St.), 202-633-4629, mnh.si.edu

Indian Craft Shop • National Mall • Store
In the same Interior Department building that houses the U.S. Interior Department Museum, but across the hall, is the Indian Craft Shop, well stocked with gorgeous kachina dolls, sculptures, jewelry, and other art, all handcrafted by Native Americans, each work authenticated. Unbeknownst to most locals even, both the museum and shop have been here since 1938. The shop has been working with the same Indian tribes for generations and sells art that you will not find at the better-known Smithsonian National Museum of the American Indian. Crafts lovers might happily while away an hour here, but others will finish perusing sooner, for the shop is small. Photo ID and metal detector clearance required to enter the building. *Mon-Fri 8:30am-4:30pm and third Sat each month 10am-4pm.* 1849 C St. NW (18th St.), 202-208-4056, indiancraftshop.com

Meeps Vintage Fashionette • U Street Corridor • Store
Although Meeps sells a small collection of local designer wares like Manatee and Chocolate City Designs, the real focus is on its mind-boggling selection of vintage wares. An expansive collection of sleek '70s cocktail dresses, aged leather jackets, and funky enamel jewelry sits alongside polyester jumpsuits, patent leather go-go boots, and other costume-worthy creations. And the sensory overload doesn't stop at the clothes: forest murals, faux-crackling fireplaces, and crystal chandeliers compete for attention on the store's two floors. *Sun noon-5pm, Tue-Sat noon-7pm.* 1520 U St. NW (15th St.), 202-265-6546, meepsonu.com

Miss Pixie's Furnishings and Whatnot • Adams Morgan • Store
Miss Pixie Windsor herself often presides over the furnishings and whatnot at this whimsical Adams Morgan shop. Bright pink walls are lined with vintage prints, shabby chic dressers, retro barstools, and, you guessed it, whatnot. Miss Pixie clearly selects pieces with urban dwellers in mind. Most pieces are well suited to small spaces. If you're not in the market for furniture, check out the colorful barware, vintage magazines, and other bric-a-brac displayed throughout. Since Miss Pixie's loads in new furniture every Wednesday night, Thursdays are the best time to stop in and get dibs on your favorite pieces. *Thu noon-9pm, Fri-Sun noon-7pm.* 2473 18th St. (Columbia Rd.), 202-232-8171, misspixies.com

Muléh • U Street Corridor • Store
Muléh means "to come home to" in Javanese, and Christopher Reiter created the store upon his return from four years in Southeast Asia. The furniture is inspired by the minimalism and harmony of some Asian design, and includes organic elements like reeds, teak, and rattan. Amid the furniture, shoppers find racks of womenswear like 3.1 by Philip Lim, Black Halo, and Development, and menswear by 4YOU and Parameter. D.C. isn't the only city impressed with Muléh's aesthetic: hot spots like New York's Nobu 57 and Las Vegas' Whiskey Sky Bar contain custom Muléh pieces. *Tue-Sat 11am-7pm, Sun noon-5pm.* 1831 14th St. NW (T St.), 202-667-3440, muleh.com

Nana • U Street Corridor • Store
The owners of the quirkiest stores along U Street—from Meep's to CakeLove—all cut their teeth among the cubicle farms of D.C. before branching into retail. Nana's owner Jackie Flanagan is no exception. Her past as a marketing worker bee means that the clothes at her cozy boutique are distinctive yet versatile wardrobe pieces that translate well from the office to the coffee shop to the bar.

Nana carries youthful, funky lines like House of Spy, OK 47, and Hobo International, as well as select vintage pieces. The friendly staff gives excellent advice about how to wear new pieces. Stop in on the first Thursday of every month for Shopper Socials, when Nana serves up free wine and generous discounts. *Sun noon-5pm, Mon-Sat noon-7pm.* 1528 U St. NW (16th St.), 202-667-6955, nanadc.com

National Museum of the American Indian • National Mall • Museum
The building's a looker, its five-story, rippled limestone architecture an audaciously different structure from others on the Mall. Inside is a large atrium, where, if you're lucky, Native Americans are boat-building or performing a ceremonial dance. On the third and fourth levels are multimedia presentations through which Indians share their varied stories. These two levels also display hundreds of artifacts, old and contemporary, from headdresses to intricate carvings, in glass cases; computer kiosks allow visitors to zero in on objects, to view them more clearly and find out what they are. The museum is more a show-and-tell than a chronological history, and depending on how that suits you, you might stay anywhere from 30 minutes to two hours here. *Daily 10am-5:30pm.* National Mall, Independence Ave. SW (Fourth St.), 202-633-1000, americanindian.si.edu

National Museum of Women in the Arts • Penn Quarter • Art Museum
If it weren't for this museum, few but art historians would know about Clara Peeters, a 16th-century Flemish master of still-life paintings, or Russian artist Sonia Delaunay, who created murals, theater sets, and ceramics, and was the first living female artist to have a retrospective exhibit at the Louvre (1964). Certainly no one would have had the chance to view such magnificent works, from a collection of 3,000, covering the 16th century to the present, mostly American and European artists. The building was once a Masonic temple and looks it, it's so white marble. The museum does not display as much art as the building's awesome size would seem to indicate—you might ramble through in 45 minutes or so. *Sun noon-5pm, Mon-Sat 10am-5pm.* $- 1250 New York Ave. NW (H St.), 202-738-5000, nmwa.org

National Postal Museum • Capitol Hill • Museum
Email, IM, and text messaging have their place, but nothing beats a special letter that arrives by U.S. mail. It's always been this way, that's the message that hits home here as one peruses letters written during colonial times, wartime, the Depression, on the frontier, and overseas, as well as personally compelling letters in everyday exchanges between family members, lovers, and friends. The museum also explores the history of the postal system, in a way that illuminates the inherent danger and devotion attendant to mail delivery. *Daily 10am-5:30pm.* 2 Massachusetts Ave. NE (N. Capitol St.), 202-633-5555, postalmuseum.si.edu

Nusta Spa • Dupont Circle • Spa
Beauty comes at a price here, but at no cost to the environment. Nuesta is the only spa to have won U.S. Green Building Council certification, and its eco-friendly design uses recycled and energy-efficient parts, a pollution-screening air-filtration system, and products made from botanical ingredients harvested sustainably from South American rain forests. Enviros love all that, but are equally crazy about the highly trained staff, hydrating mud wraps, interpretive touch massages, seaweed facials, and pure pedicures. Leave your oats and

HIP • ATTRACTIONS

groats at the door, for this spa is ultrahip with décor to match: ethereal whites, modern furniture, and light wood floors. *Sun 11am-5pm, Mon-Fri 10am-8pm, Sat 9am-6pm.* 1129 20th St. NW (M St.), 202-530-5700, nustaspa.com

Old Post Office Pavilion Tower • Penn Quarter • Site
Best Views of D.C. It's the panoramic view, from the Capitol to the National Cathedral, that'll bring you here. Half the height of the Washington Monument, and differently situated, it offers a perspective that's less wide, but still tremendous, and there are compensations: a grand look up and down Pennsylvania Avenue and, if there's a line, at least you'll be waiting inside this 1899 building. Word is out, so in spring and summer, there usually is a line. You switch elevators at the 9th floor to reach the 12th, and the elevators only hold ten people, little wrinkles that account for much of the wait. *Mar-Aug Sun noon-7pm, Mon-Sat 10am-8pm; Sep-Feb Sun noon-6pm, Mon-Sat 10am-7pm.* 1100 Pennsylvania Ave. NW (12th St.), 202-289-4224, oldpostofficedc.com

Pedal Boats • Southwest • Sport
Best Outdoor Activities Indulge your inner child. Take a break from touring on foot and rent a pedal boat to skim the surface of the Tidal Basin for an hour. You'll still be sightseeing, as you pedal away, in full view of the Washington Monument standing tall on the Mall, and of the colossal Jefferson Memorial at the south end of the Tidal Basin. If you're able to snag a boat during the famous cherry blossom season, you're in for a rare treat: the spectacular cherry blossom trees, which encircle the Tidal Basin, bloom for only about ten days in late March to early April. *Daily mid-Mar–Labor Day, Wed-Sun Labor Day–Columbus Day weekend, 10am-6pm, weather permitting.* $- Raoul Wallenberg Pl./15th St. SW (Independence Ave.), 202-479-2426, tidalbasinpeddleboats.com

Textile Museum • Dupont Circle • Museum
One of those quintessential Dupont Circle side streets, lined with embassies and even the post–White House residence of a president (Woodrow Wilson), is the backdrop for this treasure. Inside the handsome 1913 building are several galleries whose rotating exhibits highlight different themes—splendid attire of mid–19th century central Asia, ceremonial textiles from 7th and 8th century Peru—and objects from the 17,000-piece collection, spanning 5,000 years. Prepare to be surprised. Allow an hour and be sure not to miss a stroll in the garden and a visit to the museum shop, which is full of cool presents, like pretty beaded handbags from India and jewelry from Turkey. *Sun 1-5pm, Mon-Sat 10am-5pm.* 2320 S St. NW (24th St.), 202-667-0441, textilemuseum.org

U.S. Department of the Interior Museum • National Mall • Museum
Inside a ponderous Interior Department building is this museum that's often deserted, no sign of a curator or attendant. A series of double glass doors open and shut on silent cue. Exhibits cover the histories of national parks and public lands, and the country's environmental and conservation agencies and efforts, from 1849 to the present, using a minute fraction of the 150 million artifacts, photographs, maps, and other objects in the department's collection. This is a must for greenies. Elsewhere in the building are old murals by Native Americans and New Deal artists; reservations are required for those. Combine a visit here with a trip across the hall to the Indian Crafts Shop, and you might spend an hour all in all. Photo ID and metal detector clearance required to enter the

building. *Mon-Fri 8:30am-4:30pm and third Sat each month.* 1849 C St. NW (18th St.), 202-208-4743, doi.gov/museum

Vietnam Veterans Memorial • National Mall • Site
The power of this memorial lies in seeing rows upon rows of the names of the war's dead and missing etched into the black granite slabs that start small at each end and gradually rise to a height over your head, the two angled sections dovetailing at the vertex, so that the whole sculpture forms a gentle V for Vietnam, for Veteran. This memorial sneaks up on you if you're approaching from the Constitution Avenue side, eyes looking ahead to the Lincoln Memorial. Visitors leave mementos below the names of loved ones, and National Park Service rangers come by at the end of the day to collect them and place them with others in a repository. Constitution Ave. NW (21st St.), 202-426-6841, nps.gov/vive

Classic D.C.

Like no other city in the world, the nation's capital represents the "magnificent intentions" of democracy (to borrow Charles Dickens' term), but in true democratic fashion, its symbols are living and breathing institutions that are open to the public. You can attend a session of Congress, listen to a Supreme Court argument, tour the exterior of the White House, and visit the free Smithsonian museums. And you should.

That's Washington, the federal city. But D.C. has all kinds of other time-honored traditions. Be sure to sip a mint julep in the Willard Hotel's Round Robin bar, where statesman Henry Clay introduced the drink to the city in 1850. Dine where senators dine, seek out the perfect crab cake, and listen to jazz in the same neighborhood where Duke Ellington once played.

Note: Venues in bold are described in detail in the listings that follow the itinerary. Venues followed by an * asterisk are those we recommend as both a restaurant and a destination bar.

Classic D.C.: The Perfect Plan (3 Nights and Days)

Perfect Plan Highlights

Thursday
Breakfast	Willard Room
Mid-morning	National Archives
Lunch	Occidental Grill
Mid-afternoon	White House, Corcoran
Pre-dinner	Sky Terrace
Dinner	Laboratorio del Galileo
Nighttime	Round Robin
Late-night	Habana Village

Friday
Breakfast	Library of Congress Cafeteria
Mid-morning	Capitol
Lunch	The Monocle
Mid-afternoon	National Gallery of Art
Pre-dinner	The Caucus Room*
Dinner	1789 Restaurant
Nighttime	Private tour of monuments
Late-night	Old Glory BBQ*

Saturday
Breakfast	Old Ebbitt Grill*
Mid-morning	Lincoln Memorial
Lunch	Café MoZU
Mid-afternoon	Holocaust Museum
Pre-dinner	Kinkead's*
Dinner	Citronelle
Nighttime	Blues Alley
Late-night	U-topia

Morning After
Brunch	Hay-Adams Hotel

Hotel: Willard InterContinental Washington Hotel

Thursday

9:30am Stun yourself awake in the splendid **Willard Room**, trying not to stare at distinguished guests in other pockets of the restaurant as you consume your eggs Benedict.

10:30am Gear up for a most American of days, starting with a visit to the **National Archives** to have a look at the original Declaration of Independence, Constitution, and Bill of Rights, alongside interactive, multimedia displays tracing the creation and influence of those documents.

1pm Lunch Stop at the **Occidental Grill** (next door to the Willard) for a crab cake lunch. Another fine option is **The Bombay Club**, across Lafayette Square from the White House. This oasis of civility and delicious Indian food draws White House staff and newspaper reporters.

3pm Time for a stroll around the **White House**, which is all you'll be allowed to do, unless you've arranged for a tour by contacting your senator's or representative's office ahead of time. Continue on to the **Renwick Gallery**, which displays exquisite decorative art, and further to the **Corcoran Gallery of Art** for American paint-

CLASSIC · ITINERARY

ings and sometimes a provocative contemporary show (the gallery stays open until 9pm on Thursdays, so you could opt to linger here awhile). If you'd prefer to relax, go to the other extreme and book a couple's spa experience at the **Willard's I Spa**.

6pm Drinks are in order, and there's one standout choice: the **Sky Terrace at the Hotel Washington**, just around the corner from the Willard. Open April through October, the hotel's 11th-floor outdoor verandah proffers spectacular views of the Washington Monument and the White House. Off season, try **Off the Record**, the subterranean bar in the Hay-Adams Hotel; what it lacks in view it more than makes up for in character.

8pm Dinner Roberto Donna presides in his chef's kitchen/dining room, **Laboratorio del Galileo**, preparing perfect Piedmontese tastes that win him worldwide praise. Seats are slightly easier to reserve at Donna's main restaurant, **Galileo**, which serves extraordinary Italian fare. Another star is **Gerard's Place**, near the White House, where Gerard Pangaud uses culinary poetic license on classic French cuisine.

11pm Head to the legendary **Round Robin** bar, where Jim Hewes or another expert barkeep will fix you a clever cocktail and regale you with the history of drinkers' past. For a more intimate drink, head to the lush **Le Bar**, in the Hotel Sofitel, which is popular with the upscale European set.

12:30am Cab it to **Russia House**, where silk damask walls and roaring fireplaces provide a regal backdrop for the crowds sipping vodka and eating caviar. If you'd rather dance all night, hit **Habana Village** in Adams Morgan, where you'll arrive too late for salsa lessons, but in plenty of time to fake it.

Friday

9am The cafeteria on the sixth floor of the **Library of Congress**'s Madison Building serves hearty fare, with a view of Capitol Hill, to boot. Just be sure to bring a photo ID, which you'll need to enter the building. After breakfasting, tour the magnificent Jefferson Building across the street, and don't miss the Reading Room Overlook.

10:30am If you're able to obtain timed tickets, tour the **Capitol** and, if you've secured gallery passes from your senator or representative, attend a session of Congress to observe the legislative process firsthand. If you're unable to go inside the Capitol, you can at least admire its exterior and the well-kept grounds, which hold architectural surprises, like the **Summer House**, and several grand statues. Finish up at the **U.S. Botanic Garden**, at the bottom of Capitol Hill. If the sun is shining and the weather warm, consider instead a bike ride through D.C.'s urban paradise, **Rock Creek Park**, and around the Mall to salute the memorials as you pedal by.

1pm Lunch From the Garden, it's a short walk across the Mall to join lobbyists and lawyers in their swank steak haven, **Charlie Palmer Steak**. A bit further is **The Monocle**, where you'll dine among senators, congresspeople, and their staff, and maybe even a Supreme Court justice or two.

3pm Cross the street to the **National Gallery of Art**, and luxuriate in the sight of Western masterpieces from the last five centuries. End with a tour of the **Sculpture Garden**, across the street from the gallery's west wing.

5pm Fridays in summer, the National Gallery stages **jazz concerts** 5-8pm in its Sculpture Garden. So treat yourselves to wine or beer and some tapas from the Pavilion Café, and stake out a choice spot. Or start your walk back to the Willard, stopping en route at any number of prime watering holes, like **The Caucus Room***, whose dining room is excellent and bar scene even more so.

7:30pm Dinner You're in for a romantic treat and sumptuous American cuisine at the **1789 Restaurant** in Georgetown. The simply elegant **Obelisk** in Dupont Circle is another excellent choice, if you prefer an intimate room and a foodie ambience. Reserve a table at **Marcel's** if the thought of Belgian-influenced French cuisine and a formal but lively setting appeal.

But if you'd rather have a rip-roaring time, postpone dinner and take in a 7:30pm performance of the **Capitol Steps**, a musical satire in which former Congressional staffers ruthlessly skewer political figures.

10pm Arrange for a **Tour de Force** limo to come pick you up at dinner's end for a romantic **moonlit tour** of the city. If you opted for Capitol Steps entertainment, you can finish up the night with a postshow steak frites, right across the street, at **Les Halles**, whose buzzing sidewalk seating and cigar lounge draw an upper-crust D.C. clientele. And if you dined at Marcel's, you might want to follow dinner with a **Kennedy Center** performance, and take advantage of Marcel's pretheater deal: free limo service to the Kennedy Center, returning again by limo after the show to Marcel's for dessert.

Midnight After your tour or your late dinner, it's time for a little bourbon tasting at Georgetown's **Old Glory BBQ**.

For this day's itinerary, obtain advance timed tickets to tour

CLASSIC · ITINERARY

the Washington Monument and the Holocaust Museum.

9am Wear your most comfortable walking shoes as you're going to cover a lot of ground this morning. Join the mix of Georgetown University grads, tourists, and soccer moms on the loose for Saturday brunch at the favorite **Old Ebbitt Grill***, around the corner from the Willard. The food's not superb, but the lively, quintessential D.C. atmosphere and location make up for it.

10am Stand in line for admission to the Washington Monument, from whose pinnacle panoramic views stretch for miles. Return to earth and set your sights on the **Lincoln Memorial**. Study Abe's face and his words inscribed on the walls before turning to admire the sweeping view of Mall, Washington Monument, and Capitol dome in the distance. Cross Independence Avenue to circle around the **FDR Memorial**, then follow the Tidal Basin path to reach the **Jefferson Memorial**.

12:30pm Lunch Find your way to the **Café MoZU** in the Mandarin Oriental Hotel and savor the fact that this repast is light-years beyond any other dining option this side of the Smithsonians.

2pm Tour the **Holocaust Museum**, keeping in mind that the permanent exhibit ends with the hour-long film *Testimony*, in which Holocaust survivors relate their personal histories.

6:30pm Back at the hotel, dress your sexy best, then start out the night with a cocktail at **Kinkead's*** bar.

8pm Dinner Make your way to the city's best restaurant, the creatively French **Citronelle** in Georgetown. If you'd rather dine on French bistro classics in a cozy setting, try **La Chaumiere**. Of course, Kinkead's is a blast and serves outstanding fresh fish and seafood dishes, so you can always stay put on that barstool and dine there.

11pm Follow up a feast at Citronelle with some classic Saturday night jazz at **Blues Alley**, just up the street. Not up for jazz? Head across town to catch the second show of whoever's playing at the **9:30 Club**.

1am Can't get enough music? Take in live jazz on the same street that made Duke Ellington famous. **U-topia** serves fine single malts and the music continues until 2:30am.

> **The Morning After**
> Dress in your unsexy best and repent of all your sins at St. John's, the "Church of the Presidents," on Lafayette Square, before joining several from the congregation for a champagne brunch at the **Hay-Adams Hotel** across the street.

Classic D.C.: The Key Neighborhoods

Capitol Hill is exactly that, the hill where lies the Capitol, but also the Supreme Court and the Library of Congress, essential sites in Washington. Beyond these neighborhood titans, scattered along Pennsylvania Avenue and side streets, are small restaurants, bars, markets, and townhouses, forming a community, where Hill staffers and generations of Washingtonians have long lived.

Downtown, at the junction of Pennsylvania Avenue and 15th Street NW, and on K St. and other streets near the White House, holds many executive branch bureaus, and so is a hot spot for corporate offices, Washington's historic hotels, and some of the city's finer restaurants and bars. K Street, which runs parallel to Pennsylvania Avenue, is known for its many law firms.

Foggy Bottom is home to International Monetary Fund and World Bank buildings, as well as George Washington University and the Kennedy Center for the Performing Arts. Located between Georgetown and the White House, south of Dupont Circle, this is a rather low-key neighborhood of charming townhouses and a number of good restaurants.

National Mall is the two-mile expanse from the foot of the Capitol to the Lincoln Memorial, flanked by Smithsonian museums and dotted with national memorials and the Washington Monument. Whether or not you visit the sites, you should at least amble the Mall to view them. No hotels or restaurants are situated on the Mall, but Washington's most luxurious hotel, the Mandarin Oriental, lies by itself off the Mall's southwest corner.

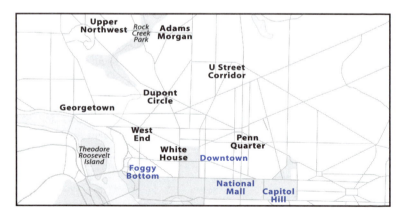

Classic D.C.:
The Shopping Blocks

Chevy Chase

Although the affluent neighborhood on the D.C.-Maryland border boasts few independent boutiques, the Collection at Chevy Chase has brought fashion's heavy hitters to the District, including Ralph Lauren, Barney's Co-Op, Max Mara, Tiffany & Co., Louis Vuitton, Cartier, Christian Dior, Jimmy Choo, and Bulgari. Wisconsin Ave. NW (Western Ave.), 301-654-2690

Dupont

In addition to designer standbys like Thomas Pink, Burberry, and Godiva, the area south of Dupont Circle on Connecticut Avenue boasts classy boutiques that have served D.C.'s power players for decades.

Betsy Fisher You'll find designer women's clothing that is at once classic and contemporary. (p.137) 1224 Connecticut Ave. NW (Jefferson Pl.), 202-785-1975

Brooks Brothers This shop is known throughout the world for elegantly tailored suits. 1201 Connecticut Ave. NW (Rhode Island Ave.), 202-659-4650

Rizik's Come for excellent suits and outerwear; also known for its evening wear and bridal collection. (p.140) 1100 Connecticut Ave. NW (L St.), 202-223-4050

Tiny Jewel Box You'll find vintage and antique jewelry, one-of-a-kind pieces, and contemporary items. 1147 Connecticut Ave. NW (M St. NW), 202-393-2747

Georgetown

Some 200 shops sell designer duds, antiques, and more, along M Street between 28th and 34th Streets, and Wisconsin Avenue between K Street and Reservoir Road.

Appalachian Spring This shop sells the work of American craftspeople, from blown-glass vases to jewelry. 1425 Wisconsin Ave. NW (O St.), 202-337-5780

Fornash Custom-design a clutch, handbag, or ribbon belt out of preppy plaids, prints, and polka dots. The Shops at Georgetown Park Mall, 3222 M St. NW (Wisconsin Ave.), 202-338-0774

Galerie L'Enfant This sprawling antique store specializes in 19th- and 20th-century pieces. 1442 Wisconsin Ave. NW (P St.), 202-625-2873

Georgetown Tobacco This shop carries cigars, pipes, humidors, and more. 3144 M St. NW (31st St.), 202-338-5100

Gore Dean Nineteenth-century antiques complement the store's own line of furniture. 3338 M St. NW (33rd St.) 202-625-9199

K Baby Cuddly cotton onesies, whimsical nursery décor, and designer diaper bags fill this upscale baby store. 3112 M St. NW (31st St.), 202-333-3939

Sherman Pickey The preppy set comes for embroidered corduroys and cable-knit cashmere. (p.140) 1647 Wisconsin Ave. NW (Reservoir Rd.), 202-333-4212

Classic D.C.: The Hotels

Hay-Adams Hotel • White House • Timeless (145 rms)
If it had nothing else, the Hay-Adams would always have its peerless location, directly across from the White House, with front-of-the-house guest rooms proffering views of the same. But the Hay has lots else. This jewel of a hotel keeps homemade cookies in a jar at the reception desk and wraps lovely toile fabrics over puffy beds and headboards in the exquisitely decorated bedrooms. Smartly attired staff are helpful and discreet. Best of all, maybe, the Hay-Adams doesn't try to be what it isn't. It's historic, not new; charmingly elegant, not swank. If you must have a spa or on-site fitness center, look elsewhere. But if you like the idea of sleeping in the same hotel where Amelia Earhart once stayed or where Brad and Angelina recently dined, or of drawing the drapes at night to the sight of the lit-up President's House across the way, then consider the Hay. Note: ask for a sixth-to-eighth-floor room on the H Street side for that view. $$$$+ One Lafayette Sq. NW (H St.). 202-638-6600 / 800-853-6807, hayadams.com

The Jefferson • White House • Timeless (100 rms)
Recent turnovers of management companies and owners have done nothing to disturb the special character and charming elegance of the Jefferson. Rooms are all different sizes and individually decorated, so it's worth inquiring about what's available; all have luxurious bedding, antiques, CD players, and original artwork, but some also feature a canopy or four-poster bed, fireplace, and views, like the eighth-floor suite whose windows reveal the Washington Monument. Since it opened in 1923, the Jefferson has stood in as a home away from home for famous guests, including a *New York Times* reporter who stayed here for seven months, former Soviet president Mikhail Gorbachev, and President George W. Bush and family during his first inaugural celebration. Always a pleasure is the cozy red-walled lounge off the lobby, a fine place for a single malt scotch or two. By the way, those documents displayed on the wall? Many of them are original and bear TJ's own signature. $$$$ 1200 16th St. NW (M St.), 202-347-2200 / 866-270-8118, thejeffersonwashingtondc.com.

The Renaissance Mayflower Hotel • White House • Grand (657 rms)
When Harry Truman needed a place to live while the White House was being renovated, where did he go? The Mayflower. Ditto FDR during his preinaugural period. But the hotel dwells less on its history (for a more historic feel, look to the Willard) than on its experience. Built in 1925, the Mayflower has evolved into a well-oiled machine of a hotel, whose recent dramatic renovation helped turn it into a 21st-century luxury property. Guest rooms are beautiful, with golden walls, thick carpeting, and marble bathrooms, and provide the latest amenities, like high-speed internet access and individual climate controls. For a room with extra amenities and downtown views, ask for an eighth-floor (club level) room, facing Connecticut Avenue. Meanwhile, down in the lobby, Washington's elite are pow-wowing over breakfast in the Café Promenade or joining up for a drink later in the day at the Town and Country pub—a favorite watering hole, thanks to barkeep Sambonn Lek, and the hotel's central location near the White House and

the K Street corridor. $$$$ 1127 Connecticut Ave. NW (L St.), 202-347-3000 / 800-228-7697, renaissancehotels.com/WASSH

The Ritz-Carlton, Washington, D.C. • West End • Modern (299 rms)
The staff at the Ritz wear earpieces and talk into wired wristbands, which only adds another layer of VIP ambience to the hotel. This Ritz is so discreet it doesn't even have a lobby. Instead, you have to be guided to the off-center, paneled reception area, where spiced cider is at the ready to refresh you as you check in. Spacious guest rooms are extraordinarily fine, furnished with hand-carved wooden headboards and armoires, tapestry-like fabrics at the windows and on the bed, and cornices hugging the ceiling. Bathrooms are enormous, with a wall-wide mirror, toilet behind a louvered door, and tub separate from the glass-enclosed shower. The best rooms overlook a Japanese garden with bubbling pools and waterfalls. Downstairs, afternoon tea awaits in the lush lounge, or if you prefer, drinks in the paneled gentleman's clubby pub; live music plays nightly, a pianist early on, a jazz quartet for later in the evening (until midnight Friday and Saturday). The hotel's vast sports center is the city's best and has everything: basketball courts, indoor heated pool, and a full-service spa. $$$$+ 1150 22nd St. NW (M St.), 202-835-0500 / 800-241-3333, ritzcarlton.com

Sofitel Lafayette Square • White House • Modern (237 rms)
The Sofitel is a breath of French air in the capital, employing a French staff, serving French haute cuisine in its restaurant, Café 15, and often catering to French guests, although its clientele is more generally international business people, and lawyers especially. Very popular is Le Bar, the large lounge across the lobby from the restaurant; at any time of day, a chic crowd is lounging in its deep armchairs. The big picture windows that frame Le Bar also enclose guest rooms situated on the H Street and 15th Street sides of the hotel. These are the deluxe rooms, more light-filled and a little more spacious than the superior rooms, which overlook other buildings. Windows in second- and third-floor deluxe rooms are nearly floor to ceiling. Décor throughout is contemporary and upscale, featuring black marble bathrooms, long desks, fresh flowers, and duvet-covered beds. And it's just minutes from the White House. $$$$ 806 15th St. NW (H St.), 202-730-8800 / 800-763-4835, sofitel.com

Willard InterContinental Washington, D.C. • Downtown • Grand (334 rms)
The Willard is not trendy. But historic, glamorous, dazzling, luxurious, and urbanely obliging? Yes, it's all that. Which is why the hotel's clientele includes everyone from Matt Damon and Robert DeNiro to the king and queen of Norway. Located near the White House, the Willard has welcomed luminaries since its early 1800s beginnings. Abraham Lincoln and his family were guests before Lincoln's inauguration. A century later, Dr. Martin Luther King, Jr., finished his "I Have a Dream" speech here. Read all about the Willard's past in an exhibit beyond the lobby, or hear all about it in the Round Robin bar, where bartenders regale you with stories. Dine in the Willard Room and you'll see the movers and shakers of Washington and the world. Deluxe rooms overlook Pennsylvania Avenue and the Washington Monument. Standard rooms facing 14th Street are larger than the smaller but quieter standards facing the courtyard. And though the Willard is not trendy, it does keep up to date: it added a luxurious spa in 2005. $$$$+ 1401 Pennsylvania Ave. NW (14th St.), 202-628-9100 / 800-827-1747, washington.interconti.com

Classic D.C.: The Restaurants

The Bombay Club • White House • Indian
Best Indian Restaurants This is the eldest child of Ashak Bajaj, who also owns the Oval Room across the street and Rasika in the Penn Quarter, among others. A five-minute stroll from the White House, the Bombay sees a lot of that action, but then it sees a lot of action, period. *New York Times* reporters and stars like Goldie Hawn and Kurt Russell turn up, pleased to find an easy pace, an elegant room, a fair-weather patio, a cozy bar, and an extensive menu. Specialties include tandoori dishes and vegetarian entrées, as well as locally loved items, like chicken tikka masala and mustard shrimp. *Sun 11:30am-2:30pm and 5:30-9pm, Mon-Thu 11:30am-2:30pm and 6:30-10:30pm, Fri 11:30am-2:30pm and 6-11pm, Sat 6-11pm.* $$ 815 Connecticut Ave. NW (I St.), 202-659-3727, bombayclubdc.com

BreadLine • White House • Bakery/Deli
Those waiting in this bread line are hungry, all right: hungry for Mark Furstenburg's divine bread stuffed with sublime fillings, like baguette with grilled eggplant, zucchini, roasted red peppers, and olive tapenade; or layers of top-quality prosciutto de Parma, mascarpone, gorgonzola, and fig jam thrust between slices of walnut bread. The BreadLine is such a staple of the close-by White House crowd, it might as well be called the Mess Annex. Open for breakfast, the joint really starts jumping for lunch at about 11:30am, with people crammed into the limited seating areas, including outdoors, when the weather allows. *Mon-Fri 7:30am-3:30pm.* $- 1751 Pennsylvania Ave. NW (17th St.), 202-822-8900, thebreadlinedc.blogspot.com

Café MoZU • Southwest • Asian-American
The southwest corner of the National Mall is Siberia, as far as dining goes. So it's worth trotting just two blocks south to the Mandarin Oriental Hotel to find culinary salvation. The hotel's hottest restaurant, CityZen, serves dinner only. But that's OK, because Café MoZU, open basically all day, offers the perfect respite from sightseeing. In a window-fronted room overlooking the Tidal Basin and the Jefferson Memorial, waiters graciously present Asian-influenced American food, such as green tea–encrusted tuna salad and Asian crab cake accompanied by avocado wasabi cream. Diners are a mix of ID-tagged government workers and well-coiffed hotel guests. *Sun 7am-2pm and 6-10:30pm, Mon-Sat 6:30am-10:30pm.* $$ Mandarin Oriental, 1330 Maryland Ave. SW (12th St.), 202-787-6868, cafemozu.com

The Capital Grille • Penn Quarter • Steak House
Best Power Lunch Spots This restaurant is synonymous with "inside Washington," at least to those insiders who frequent it (very important people, they consider themselves). You might see an ex-Congressman sitting at the bar having had one too many at lunch, or Hollywood celebs like Michael Douglas and Kiefer Sutherland being feted at dinner. It's a Washington scene and the Grille prides itself on that, as well as on its rib eye and dry-aged steaks, hamburgers, and

800-label wine list, and its location, within eyesight of the Capitol and walking distance of the Mall. *Sun 5-10pm, Mon-Thu 11:30am-3pm and 5-10pm, Fri-Sat 11:30am-3pm and 5-11pm.* $$$ 601 Pennsylvania Ave. NW (Sixth St.), 202-737-6200, thecapitalgrille.com

The Caucus Room* • Penn Quarter • American

Best Power Lunch Spots Dine here for lunch or dinner Tuesday through Thursday, when Congress is in session, and you'll be sitting among buzz-making lobbyists, lawyers, media types, and politicians. When Congress is out, it's a dead zone, with most of the dinner patrons headed for one of the nearby theaters. Either way, service is grand in this traditional, leather-laden establishment, and the food, though pricey, is well executed: oyster stew, sesame-coated seared rockfish, filet mignon, and the famous coconut cake for dessert. Ask to be seated in the main dining room, or in the huge bar, to be where the action is. *Mon-Fri 11:30am-2:30pm and 5:30-10:30pm, Sat 5:30-10:30pm.* $$$ 401 Ninth St. NW (D St.), 202-393-1300, thecaucusroom.com

Charlie Palmer Steak* • Capitol Hill • Steak House

Best Politico Sightings This house of outsized egos, beef, and prices lies cozily close to the Capitol, as you'll have no trouble noticing, especially if you're able to snare table 23 or another next to the floor-to-ceiling picture window. (Winter reveals a better view; in summer, only the dome is visible.) Some find the restaurant's plush décor and the unabashed powermongering on display so, so ... excessive. But as American spectacle, it's quite a treat. Sink your teeth into a perfectly done slice of rib-eye, sip a cunning vintage chosen from the 10,000-bottle inventory, and enjoy the show. *Sun 5-10pm, Mon-Fri 11:30am-2:30pm and 5:30-10pm, Sat 5-10:30pm.* $$$ 101 Constitution Ave. NW (First St.), 202-547-8100, charliepalmer.com/steak_dc

Citronelle • Georgetown • Haute French (G)

Best Hot Chefs Bon vivants must dine at Citronelle. Chef Michel Richard so delights in reinventing French cooking that his happy energy pervades the tiered dining room, filled nightly with an international crowd, suburbanites, Hollywood and political celebrities, and Gen-Xers coming into their own. Those who can manage it book the chef's table (minimum of six diners, $275 each), inside the display kitchen, where they are entertained as much by Richard's ebullience as by his cuisine. But main dining room patrons are likewise transported, by tournedos of halibut with foie gras nuggets and green peppercorn sauce, tuna Napoleon niçoise, and the like. Jackets required for men. *Sun 6:30-10:30am and 6-9pm, Mon-Sat 6:30-10:30am and 6-9:30pm.* $$$$ Latham Hotel, 3000 M St. NW (30th St.), 202-625-2150, citronelledc.com

Equinox • White House • New American (G)

When the restaurant owner is also its chef, diners can expect a certain consistency, and at Equinox, diners get it, in the form of Todd Gray's intelligent takes on the likes of truffled white bean soup with crispy pancetta or marinated bison tenderloin. This is cuisine prepared with the freshest, often organically grown, ingredients of the season. A favorite among foodies, Equinox doesn't exude a foodie pretentiousness, more an exuberance, suitable to a successful restaurant frequented by K Street lobbyists and Pennsylvania Avenue "administrators." The front glassed-in atrium allows you to guess who's coming to lunch or dinner year-round; the elegant dining room is the quieter, more romantic spot. *Sun 5-9pm, Mon-Thu 11:30am-2pm and 5:30-10pm, Fri 11:30am-2pm and 5:30-10:30pm, Sat 5:30-10:30pm.* $$$ B≡ 818 Connecticut Ave. NW (I St.), 202-331-8118, equinoxrestaurant.com

Galileo • West End • Italian
Best Always-Hot Tables Galileo jumps daily for lunch and dinner, with diners crowding into the window-front bar, waiting for their table to be ready. Sometimes the wait is a little longer than you'd want, but that only heightens the anticipation. This is the domain of owner Roberto Donna, originally from the Piedmont area of Italy, which is the cuisine's emphasis, from the bagna cauda antipasti to the black olive salmon with pepper. The dining room looks a little worn these days and the Italian waiters barely speak English, but taste the extraordinary food and look around to see a whole table of TV news anchors, and believe it: you're having a classic Washington experience. *Sun 5-10pm, Mon-Thu 11:30am-2:15pm and 5:30-10pm, Fri 11:30am-2:15pm and 5:30-10:30pm, Sat 5:30-10:30pm.* $$$ B≡ 1110 21st St. NW (L St.), 202-293-7191, galileodc.com

Gerard's Place • White House • French (G)
Best Romantic Dining This cozy, simply decorated dining room seats no more than 55 and is family run. Considered one of D.C.'s best restaurants, it's all about the food: very French creations, like sautéed salmon with chestnuts and roasted garlic sauce, or the signature poached Maine lobster with ginger, lime, and sauternes sauce. Thursday and Saturday evenings are busiest and booked way in advance by lawyers and out-of-towners on weeknights and wealthy suburbanites on weekends. Couples like the table in the back alcove, though the entire room, with fresh flowers, white linens, and fabric-covered walls, speaks romance. *Mon-Thu 11:30am-2pm and 5:30-9pm, Fri 11:30am-2pm and 5:30-9:30pm, Sat 5:30-9:30pm.* $$$ ▭ 915 15th St. NW (McPherson Sq.), 202-737-4445

Kinkead's* • Foggy Bottom • Seafood
Downstairs, a large bar holds center stage and a pianist tinkles jazz Tuesday through Saturday evenings. Regulars enjoy each other's company and the seafood, some of the freshest in town. Upstairs in the dining room, the best tables are those sidling the booths, in view of the display kitchen, within earshot of the live jazz. After 13 years, Kinkead's is known for fine service and its fried clams and pepita-crusted salmon over a ragout of crab, shrimp, corn, and chilies. You might come here in the mood for love, but you'll have a better time if you're in the mood for fun. *Daily 11:30am-11pm.* $$$ B≡ 2000 Pennsylvania Ave. NW (20th St.), 202-296-7700, kinkead.com

La Chaumiere • Georgetown • French Bistro
Other D.C. French restaurants have come and gone in La Chaumiere's 30-year lifetime, but none has ever offered exactly what this convivial French country bistro continues to do so well: provide a comfortable atmosphere, charming service, and French staples, like steak au poivre, fish stew, and soufflés. With its rush-bottom chairs, central fireplace, and nightly specials (Thursday's cassoulet is fabulous), La Chaumiere might seem a bit old-fashioned. Judging by the full house of French diners, office crowd, and Georgetowners, one might conclude: Old-fashioned is in. *Mon-Fri 11:30am-2:30pm and 5:30-10:30pm, Sat 5:30-10:30pm.* $$ ≡ 2813 M St. NW (28th St.), 202-338-1784

CLASSIC · RESTAURANTS

Laboratorio del Galileo • West End • Haute Italian (G)
Best Chef's Tables Restaurant critics agree on this: Roberto Donna's Laboratorio is the best, or certainly among the very best places to eat in town. Laboratorio is a chef's table restaurant within Donna's larger restaurant, Galileo. Open most Thursday through Saturday evenings and booked way in advance, the open kitchen set in a private, 32-seat dining room is a theater, really, where Donna performs, with several assistants, joking, commanding, chatting with his diners, and most important, cooking: one course after another until it adds up to 10 or 12! This is rich, rich food, in small portions, yes, but still, foie gras, followed by chestnut soup with pancetta, followed by cheesy pastas, and on and on, until you feel like a stuffed truffle. *Thu-Sat one seating at 7:30pm. $$$$* 1110 21st NW (L St.), 202-293-7191, galileodc.com

Lafayette Room • White House • American
Best Brunches No one dines at the Lafayette Room for the buzz; the draw here is white tablecloth and crystal chandelier elegance, classic fine dining, intimacy, and front-row views of Lafayette Park and the White House. Weeknights, patrons are likely to be hotel guests—anyone from Brad and Angelina to visiting foreign dignitaries. Come noon Sunday, the room is awash with pearl-adorned Washingtonians, arriving fresh from church with an unholy appetite for mimosas and orange-infused French toast. *Sun 7-11am, Mon-Fri 6:30-11am, 11:30am-2pm, and 5:30-10pm, Sat 7-11am and 11:30am-2pm. $$$* Hay-Adams Hotel, One Lafayette Sq. (H St.), 202-638-2570, hayadams.com/dining

Les Halles • Penn Quarter • French Brasserie
The Gallic spirit lives strong at Les Halles, which sponsors an annual Bastille Day celebration so popular that the city actually closes a bit of Pennsylvania Avenue for it, amazing in this red-tape town. Year-round, Les Halles is always celebrating something, whether choucroute (a sausage and sauerkraut dish) in February or the arrival of the year's Beaujolais nouveau every November. Daily diners include theatergoers, hangar steak lovers, and good-time Charlies postponing the inevitable return to work or home. Les Halles, with its sidewalk cafe, Parisian brasserie ambience, and menu of steaks, croque monsieurs, and other French fare, makes it hard for some to find the door. *Daily 11:30am-midnight. $$* 1201 Pennsylvania Ave. NW (12th St.), 202-347-6848, leshalles.net

Marcel's • Foggy Bottom • Belgian-French (G)
Best Fine Dining Marcel's is serious about its Flemish-influenced French cuisine, served in a beautiful dining room to a slightly older, affluent clientele, who enjoys entrées like boudin blanc with celery root puree, or veal osso buco. Several twists make this a lively spot for all sorts: the sight of chef/owner Robert Wiedemaier at play in the front-door-facing kitchen; the wine bar, where you can lounge, dine, and listen to jazz nightly; and interesting choices, like the pretheater menu, which feeds you dinner, then limos you to the Kennedy Center and back for your postshow dessert course. *Sun 5:30-9:30pm, Mon-Thu 5:30-10pm, Fri-Sat 5:30-11pm. $$$* 2401 Pennsylvania Ave. NW (24th St.), 202-296-1166, marcelsdc.com

The Monocle • Capitol Hill • American
Only-in-D.C. Restaurants No other restaurant comes close to the Monocle's convenient location: literally in the Senate's parking lot. Naturally, its location predis-

poses the restaurant to a Congressional clientele, with a Supreme Court justice or two thrown in from time to time. The best time to be here to stare at your senators and representatives is at dinner when Congress is in session. Many members come here for dinner or for one of the fundraisers going on nonstop upstairs. Lunchtime sees more of a lobbyist and congressional staff crowd, with staffers recongregating in the lively bar after work. In business since 1960, the Monocle is an absolute fixture on the Washington scene, not so much for the food, which does an adequate job on burgers, pork chops, and salads, but for the fascinating sight of Washington's prime players at ease. *Mon-Fri 11:30am-midnight.* $$ 107 D St. NE (First St.), 202-546-4488, themonocle.com

Montmartre • Capitol Hill • French Brasserie

The chic French owner greets and seats you, but maybe has you stop at the bar first for a drink, if the table's not ready and you look in need. Montmartre is a neighborhood restaurant, whose diners are likely to be 40-somethings who know their way around a menu that offers brandade de morue (salted cod and potato mousse) and poitrines de pintade rotis (roasted guinea hen). The glass-fronted dining room is small, its open kitchen warming the entire space. *Sun-Thu 11:30am-2:30pm and 6-10pm, Fri-Sat 11:30am-2:30pm and 6-10:30pm.* $$ 327 Seventh St. SE (Pennsylvania Ave.), 202-544-1244, montmartre.us

National Gallery of Art Cafes • National Mall • Cafe

Like its breathtaking art collection, the National Gallery's restaurants offer something for everyone. The East Wing's concourse-level Cascade Café features pizza, hot entrées, sushi, sandwiches, salads, and soups; an espresso and gelato bar sells freshly made gelato and sorbetto, but also super sandwiches. Diners sit in the skylit cafeteria facing a huge window-wall down whose exterior cascades of water fall. This is the noisiest and largest, but probably the cheapest option. The West Building's Garden Café often links its menu to a particular exhibit, serving Provençal fare during the Cézanne show, for example. Best of all for views is the Sculpture Garden's Pavilion Café, where you can order chicken dijonnaise panini or turkey-and-brie wraps and drinks, and sit on the terrace or inside the glass-walled structure regarding the sculpture, the National Archives Building, and the passing scene. *Daily, check website for restaurant hours.* $ Constitution Ave. NW (7th St.), 202-737-4215, nga.gov/ginfo/cafes.shtm

Obelisk • Dupont Circle • Italian (G)

Best Fine Dining Owner Peter Pastan knows exactly what he wants to give diners: an intimate dining room, intelligent service, a short prix-fixe menu of two or three exquisitely prepared choices for each of five courses, and the time to savor them. Obviously the combination works, for Obelisk has been filling tables every Tuesday through Saturday night for 18 years. The menu changes daily, but count on tasting the freshest ingredients in dishes such as pheasant-filled agnolotti or bass with hedgehog mushrooms and guanciale (a kind of bacon). People often dress up to come here, though it's not required and, in fact, a better time might be had if you dress casually, eat seriously, talk passionately. *Tue-Sat 6-10pm.* $$$ 2029 P St. NW (20th St.), 202-872-1180

The Occidental • Downtown • American

Best Power Lunch Spots If this century-old restaurant does not generate a constant buzz, that's because it doesn't need to. Located within the Willard Hotel com-

CLASSIC · RESTAURANTS

plex near the White House, this is a restaurant for mostly male regulars from nearby offices at lunchtime and for deal-makers and theatergoers at dinner. The signature chopped salad and crab cake remain on a menu that increasingly tends toward fish. Décor, like the waiters' uniforms, is black and white: the restaurant is famous for its 2,000 autographed old photos of Washington legends. The practice of displaying them started in the 1920s, though some of the photos are even older. Faces like Teddy Roosevelt's and Winston Churchill's you'll recognize, but most you won't. *Sun 5-9:30pm, Mon-Thu 11:30am-3pm and 5-10pm, Fri-Sat 11:30am-3pm and 5-10:30pm.* $$ B≡ 1475 Pennsylvania Ave. NW (15th St.), 202-783-1475, occidentaldc.com

Oceanaire Seafood Room • Penn Quarter • Seafood

Oceanaire cultivates a party atmosphere, making it hard for younger Dilberts to return to their cubicles by lunch hour's end. Some don't, aided and abetted by the restaurant's open-all-day policy. Nightly happy hour in the oyster bar pulls in the after-work crowd, and everyone stays until closing. The dining room, designed like a cruise ship, serves big portions of shellfish, specials like red snapper with black-olive vinaigrette, crab cakes, and baked Alaska. Hefty cocktails are from another era, with names like Harvey Wallbanger and Singapore Sling. *Sun 5-9pm, Mon-Thu 11:30am-10pm, Fri 11:30am-11pm, Sat 5-11pm.* $$$ B≡ 1201 F St. NW (12th St.), 202-347-2277, theoceanaire.com

Old Ebbitt Grill* • Downtown • American

Opened in 1856 around the corner and operating since 1980 at this location, the Old Ebbitt has staying power. One reason is, the place almost never closes, sending night owls home at 2am weekdays, 3am Fridays and Saturdays, then reopening five hours later for daily breakfast. It's a reliable destination at all hours, as you'll see for yourself if you seek a propping-up. Oysters, crab cakes, and other dishes made with crab, like the Chesapeake Eggs Benedict served at the ever-popular weekend brunch, are the standouts. *Mon-Fri 7:30am-1am, Sat-Sun 8:30am-1am; bar Sun-Thu until 2am, Fri-Sat until 3am.* $$ B≡ 675 15th St. NW (G St.), 202-347-4801, ebbitt.com

Old Glory BBQ* • Georgetown • American

Come to this rowdy watering hole for ribs and a few bourbons. *See Classic Nightlife, p.134, for details.* $ B≡ 3139 M St. NW (Wisconsin Ave.), 202-337-3406, oldglorybbq.com

The Oval Room • White House • New American

"Condi used to hang out here," a customer muses to the bartender, as he looks toward the main dining room filling up for lunch. Secretary of State Condoleeza Rice is too busy to stop in now, but other administration officials do, along with the lawyers and corporate execs from nearby K Street offices, the White House, and its executive office buildings. Lunch is busier than dinner, the modern American menu the same at both meals, though served in larger portions with higher prices at dinner, excellent barbecued oysters and grilled pork tenderloin with crispy polenta among the items offered. Those in the know ask for tables eight, nine, and ten in the corner, good for private conversation and keeping watch over the crowd. *Mon-Fri 11:30am-2:30pm and 6-10:30pm, Sat 6-10:30pm.* $$ B≡ 800 Connecticut Ave. NW (H St.), 202-463-8700, ovalroom.com

The Palm • Dupont Circle • Steak House
Longtime waiters are either gruff or just waiting for a chance to banter with you. They know the prime-aged New York strip steak is the best and don't back away. But they also stand by the lump crab cakes, which prove to be a trio of moist, fresh-tasting perfections. The chopped house salad is a winner, though only if you like a little taste of anchovy. Any night's a good night for spotting a member of Congress or media personality. If the steak house is slow the day you're dining, study the caricature-covered walls to see who's been here in the past 34 years, and who might be coming through the door any second. *Sun 5:30-9:30pm, Mon-Fri 11:45am-10:30pm, Sat 5:30-10:30pm.* $$$ B= 1225 19th St. NW (M St.), 202-293-9091, thepalm.com

The Prime Rib • West End • Steak House
This is the place to see men in suits (jacket and tie are required) doing manly things, like eating large portions of beef and potatoes and drinking undiluted cocktails served by tuxedoed waiters, in a gentleman's club–like black- and gold-toned dining room. Well, that's true, but so is this: Women come here, too; the prime rib, is of course superb, but so is the crab imperial; and live music at both lunch and dinner (jazz standards, natch) leavens the mood. Definitely old-style but ever popular—it seems all that Washington politicos and businesspeople the world round want is a little respect and a juicy slice of red meat, as time goes by. *Mon-Thu 11:30am-3pm and 5-11pm, Fri 11:30am-3pm and 5-11:30pm, Sat 5-11:30pm.* $$$$ B= 2020 K St. NW (20th St.), 202-466-8811, theprimerib.com

1789 Restaurant • Georgetown • American (G)
Best Romantic Dining Favorite chef Ris Lacoste has left, but no worries, her replacement Nathan Beauchamp is already getting rave reviews with his Modern American cuisine featuring champagne-marinated salmon and venison rutabaga served with chestnuts and red currants. The 1789 is famously romantic, which must have guided Nicole Kidman's decision to celebrate Keith Urban's 38th birthday here. Housed in a two-story, six-room Federal townhouse, the 1789 is unapologetically refined and traditional, one of the last places in town to require that men wear a jacket. *Sun 5:30-10pm, Mon-Thu 6-10pm, Fri 6-11pm, Sat 5:30-11pm.* $$$ B= 1226 36th St. NW (Prospect St.), 202-965-1789, 1789restaurant.com

Sushi-Ko • Georgetown • Sushi
Considered by sushi aficionados to be the best sushi bar in the city, Sushi-ko is also its oldest, at 30 years. Top chefs Michel Richard of Citronelle, Johnny Monis of Komi, and Jose Andres of Jaleo stop in when they can to sample chef Koji Terano's signature dishes, such as seared white tuna tataki and ceviche trio of salmon, or whatever Terano has that moment created, maybe grilled baby octopus with mango. The restaurant offers a list of burgundies that is surprisingly suited to the cuisine. *Sun 5:30-10pm, Mon 6-10:30pm, Tue-Thu noon-2:30pm and 6-10:30pm, Fri noon-2:30pm and 6-11pm, Sat 5:30-11pm.* $$ = 2309 Wisconsin Ave. NW (Calvert St.), 202-333-4187, sushiko.us

Tabard Inn* • Dupont Circle • New American
This cheerful dining room at the back of a hip (some say hippie) hotel is a local favorite, a training ground for lesser-known chefs who move on eventually to bigger-name places, much to the regret of regulars. At lunchtime, diners arrive from nearby Dupont Circle embassies and offices. At dinner, the black-and-white-

checker–floored room, with its original art and windows overlooking the terrace, fills with tables of girlfriends, after-work noshers, couples, and business types. The place is noisy and crowded, the food is reliably wonderful (pray that Pedro Matamoros is still chef: caramelized diver scallops, house-smoked salmon and pastrami, pork and foie gras terrine, dreamy desserts), and the ambience is looser than usual for wound-up Washingtonians. *Sun 8-10am, 10:30am-2pm, and 6-9pm, Mon-Wed 7-10am, 11am-2:30pm, and 6-9pm, Thu-Fri 7-10am, 11am-2:30pm, and 6-9:30pm, Sat 8-10am, 11am-2pm, and 6-9:30pm.* $$ Tabard Inn, 1739 N St. NW (17th St.), 202-331-8528, tabardinn.com

Taberna del Alabardero • White House • Spanish (G)
Old World personified is the Taberna. Think chandeliers and balconies, gold-leaf and brocade furnishings, and gracious formality. The traditional Spanish cuisine is authentic; just ask the World Bankers and visiting Spanish dignitaries oft seen dining here. Known for its bacalao (salt cod), paellas, venison, and Spanish wine list, the restaurant also serves tapas at lunch and dinner, and in between, too, 3-5:30pm weekdays, a good thing to note if you're touring near the White House and find yourself hungering for a little deep-fried squid or shrimp and crab croquette. *Mon-Fri 11:30am-10:30pm (tapas only 3-5:30pm), Sat 5:30-10:30pm.* $$$ 1776 I St. NW (18th St.), 202-429-2200, alabardero.com

U-topia* • U Street • American
Come for live jazz and high-quality food in an idyllic setting. *See Classic Nightlife, p.136, for details.* $ 1418 U St. NW (14th St.), 202-483-7669, utopiaindc.com

Vidalia • Dupont Circle • Southern
Subterranean Vidalia may be, but the dining room is luminous and lively, especially on a Saturday night. With its clever use of spacing and glass partitioning, the restaurant allows diners to enjoy private conversations, but feel part of a larger party. You can see the sommelier and a server consulting in the glass-enclosed wine room, the 20-something couple dining at the bar at the front of the restaurant, the party of 20 in the middle of the room celebrating a birthday, and everybody slurping up the food. This is Modern Southern fare, which means a mélange of oysters with country ham and artichoke on brioche toast, trout with sweet onion andouille crust, and Georgia pecan pie. *Mon-Thu 11:30am-2:30pm and 5:30-10pm, Fri 11:30am-2:30pm and 5:30-10:30pm, Sat 5:30-10:30pm.* $$$ 1990 M St. NW (20th St.), 202-659-1990, bistrobis.com

The Willard Room • Downtown • French
Only-in-D.C. Restaurants When you walk into the Willard Room and see the high ceiling, ornate furnishings, massive columns, and overall elegance, and you sit down at an immaculate table with waiters standing by for you to catch their eye—well, you feel like somebody powerful. As for your fellow diners, even if you don't recognize them, they look important, simply by virtue of being there. That's the Willard effect. The food matches the décor and service: elegant preparations of French classics, like lobster bisque, Dover sole, and chateaubriand. *Mon-Thu 7:30-10am, 11:30am-2pm, and 6-10pm, Fri 7:30-10am, 11:30am-2pm, and 5:30-10pm, Sat 5:30-10pm.* $$$$ 1401 Pennsylvania Ave. NW (14th St.), 202-637-7440, washington.interconti.com

Classic D.C.: The Nightlife

The Bar at the Ritz-Carlton, Washington, D.C. • West End • Hotel Bar
The motto of the Ritz Carlton staff is: "We are ladies and gentlemen serving ladies and gentlemen." You'll find that credo in action in the 22nd Street hotel, where bartenders will ably guide a classy, older clientele through a list of specialty cocktails, dessert martinis, gourmet coffee, and scotch. In addition to nightly jazz (8:30-midnight Fri and Sat), weekends see culinary entertainment in the form of lobby tastings. Recent offerings include the "Chocolate Decadence" buffet, and the "Where in the World Is Mmmm ... on M St.," a series that explores the culture and culinary trends of different countries. *Sun-Thu 11am-1am, Fri-Sat 11am-1:30am.* 1150 22nd St. NW (M St.), 202-835-0500, ritzcarlton.com

Blues Alley • Georgetown • Cabaret
Best Live Music Though the name may be confusing, you're likely to echo the sentiments of Dizzy Gillespie when you enter this converted 18th-century carriage house: "Now *this* is a jazz club." Blues Alley is the country's oldest continuing supper club, serving up New Orleans cuisine and some of the country's top jazz outfits from Chick Corea to Pat Martino. The club oozes ambience, and the cozy feel is ideal for couples. Be sure to check the schedule in advance as weekend dates for well-known acts tend to sell out quickly. Though dinner isn't mandatory, be aware that there is a $10 per-person food and drink minimum. *Daily 6pm-12:30am.* 1073 Wisconsin Ave. NW (M St.), 202-337-4141, bluesalley.com

The Capitol Steps • Downtown • Cabaret
Before there was *The Daily Show*, there was the Capitol Steps. Congressional staffers formed the comedy group in 1981 to ask hard-hitting questions about our government, like "Who put the mock in democracy?" Playing on the news of the day, the cast of the show skewers politicians from both sides of the aisle with new takes on old standards like "Don't Go Fakin' You're Smart," and "House of the Right-Wing Son." Because performances only occur on Friday and Saturday, shows can sell out. Be sure to reserve ahead of time. *Fri-Sat 7:30-9:30pm.* 1300 Pennsylvania Ave. NW (13th St.), 202-312-1555, capsteps.com

The Caucus Room* • Penn Quarter • Cigar Bar
This is the ultimate bipartisan drinking and dining establishment for Washington's elite. *See Classic Restaurants, p.125, for details.* 401 Ninth St. NW (D St.), 202-393-1300, thecaucusroom.com

Charlie Palmer Steak* • Capitol Hill • Restaurant Bar
Best Politico Sightings Forget your Birkins and Blahniks—the status accessory at this bar is the Blackberry, the wireless handheld device that aids D.C.'s infamous addiction to mixing business and pleasure. In the shadow of the Capitol Building, senators and their staffers strategize at a bar that overlooks the dining room, ensuring maximum see-and-be-seen opportunities. However, this isn't your typical Hill establishment: Dark wood and low lighting are replaced with airy cream walls, wine bottles suspended in glass and stainless steel, and

sleek modern furniture. Eavesdrop on the latest power plays while munching on a bar menu of lobster corn dogs. *Sun 5-10pm, Mon-Fri 11:30am-2:30pm and 5:30-10pm, Sat 5-10:30pm.* 101 Constitution Ave. NW (First St.), 202-547-8100, charliepalmer.com/steak_dc

Finn macCool's • Capitol Hill • Bar

Finn macCool was Ireland's King Arthur, and the bar bearing his name is appropriately a step above your average public house. The ceilings are higher, the space lit by medieval chandeliers and a roaring fire, and the walls adorned with Celtic tapestries. But Finn macCool's keeps with the pub tradition of making all feel welcome. Old couples and young friends alike settle into buttery leather chairs in the upstairs lounge for a pint of Smithwick's or an after-dinner Irish coffee. On Saturdays, the first-floor bar gets raucous with live Irish rock bands. *Sun-Thu 11am-1:30am, Fri-Sat 11am-2:30am.* 713 Eighth St. SE (G St.), 202-547-7100, finnmaccoolsdc.com

Habana Village • Adams Morgan • Bar

Best Dance Clubs Set aside a full night to work through all three floors of the district's top Latin bar. Grab mojitos and light Cuban fare in the charming first-floor dining room as the first band warms up. Then draw inspiration from the mural of salsa queen Celia Cruz as you ascend to the second floor. Here women are never at a loss for partners, and the darkness cloaks the missteps of less suave dancers. By 2am, you may need a break. Head to the third floor for yet a third live band—this one a bit mellower. *Wed-Sat 6:30pm-3am. Wed-Sat lessons offered 7:30-9:30pm* ($10 for one hour, $15 for two hours). C Men 1834 Columbia Rd. NW (Mintwood St.), 202-462-6310, habanavillage.com

IMAX Jazz at the National Museum of Natural History • National Mall • Jazz

The museums along the National Mall tend to empty when the sun goes down. But if you want a chance to experience the Smithsonian sans crowds, head to the National Museum of Natural History. Arrive by 5pm on Fridays to get a glimpse of the Hope diamond before the 5:30pm closing time, then buy tickets for the after-hours double feature: 3D IMAX flicks and live jazz. Unlike that of U Street's jazz clubs, the atmosphere here allows for a mix of music and chatting. The wine list is lacking in fancy vintages, so opt for the specialty cocktails and decadent dessert selections—from fruit tarts to fresh gelato. *Wed-Sat 6:30pm-3am.* C Constitution Ave. NW (10th St.), 202-633-7400, mnh.si.edu/jazz/

JR's Bar & Grill • Dupont Circle • Gay Bar

New to town and want an entrée to the city's gay scene? Stop for a drink at JR's Bar & Grill, a *Cheers*-style mainstay on the 17th Street strip. Stained-glass windows cast a glow on the dark wood bar, where friendly bartenders will fill your glass and fill you in on what's hot any given night of the week. It's most pleasant to come to JR's for a laid-back drink early in the evening. Specials draw crowds later on, but you can take a break on the second floor for a game of pool or to check out the crowd below. Expect to find a late-20s to early-40s crowd. *Fri-Sat 2pm-3am, Sun-Thu 4pm-2am.* 1519 17th St. NW (Church St.), 202-328-0090, jrswdc.com

The Kennedy Center Roof Terrace Restaurant & Bar • Foggy Bottom • Bar
Best Drinks with a View There are few D.C. experiences as thrilling as walking through the towering Hall of Nations at the Kennedy Center. The legendary performing arts complex is culture on a grand scale, and the soaring ceilings and nouveau Art Deco feel of the center's Roof Terrace Restaurant & Bar are a worthy match. The bar fills up around 10pm with theatergoers enjoying a postshow cocktail amid panoramic views of Georgetown and the Potomac River. There are plans in the works for an outdoor summer wine bar. *Sun 11am-2pm, Sun-Wed 5-8pm, Thu-Sat 5-8:30pm, and after performances.* 2700 F St., NW (25th St.), 202-416-8555, kennedy-center.org/visitor/restaurant_terrace.cfm

Kinkead's* • Foggy Bottom • Restaurant Bar
A large bar holds center stage and a pianist tinkles jazz Tuesday through Saturday evenings. *See Classic Restaurants, p.126, for details.* 2000 Pennsylvania Ave. NW (20th St.), 202-296-7700, kinkead.com

Le Bar • Downtown • Bar
It's no secret that the country's founders—from Jefferson to Franklin—were avid Francophiles. Though cross-pond relations may be more fraught these days, no amount of "freedom fries" could do away with D.C.'s love affair with France. Enter Hotel Sofitel's Le Bar. The handiwork of French designer Pierre-Yves Rochon, the Euro-chic bar features plush armchairs, a dark mahogany bar, and bold modern paintings. Early evening hours play host to an attractive after-work crowd, while expats and European visitors swill fashionably late. *Daily 10am-midnight.* Hotel Sofitel, 806 15th St. NW (H St.), 202-737-8800, sofitel.com

Off the Record • Downtown • Bar
Best Politico Sightings Perhaps it's the proximity to the White House. Or maybe it's the building's illustrious past as an intellectual salon of 19th-century luminaries from Mark Twain to Teddy Roosevelt. Whatever the reason, the historical charm of Off the Record is palpable. Its subterranean location keeps it off the tourist track and encourages garrulousness among the notoriously tight-lipped White House staffers that populate its plush red banquettes. The cocktails mixed by John Boswell, four-time winner of the best D.C. bartender award, also help. Puff a cigar and eavesdrop on the power players around you: It's history in the making. *Sun-Thu 11:30am-midnight, Fri-Sat 11:30am-12:30am.* The Hay-Adams, One Lafayette Sq. NW (H St.), 202-638-6600, hayadams.com/dining/off_record.htm

Old Ebbitt Grill* • Downtown • Restaurant Bar
Old Ebbitt Grill is Washington's oldest saloon, with a prime downtown location that makes it a crossroads for politicians, journalists, theatergoers, and tourists alike. On weekends, the three main bars are packed until after midnight. *See Classic Restaurants, p.129, for details.* 675 15th St. NW (G St.), 202-347-4801, ebbitt.com

Old Glory BBQ* • Georgetown • Bar
Thirsty? Drink all 81 varieties of bourbon on offer at this classic Georgetown bar, and it'll immortalize you on a plaque on the wall. Those with less lofty alcoholic ambitions can still enjoy this rowdy watering hole. Avoid the crush at the bar by piling into a booth amid exposed brick and dark wood. Order some ribs, try a few bourbons, or opt for one of the seasonal beers it has on tap. For a bar in a

college area, the crowd skews older at night. *Sun 11am-2am, Mon-Thu 11:30am-2am, Fri-Sat 11:30am-3am.* 3139 M St. NW (Wisconsin Ave.), 202-337-3406, oldglorybbq.com

Round Robin • Downtown • Hotel Bar
Best Hotel Bars No tour guide in D.C. will be able to give you the history lesson that bartender Jim Hewes relates while muddling your mint julep. The drink tastes just like it did in the 1850s when famous orator Henry Clay handwrote the recipe. Immortalized by Walt Whitman and celebrated by countless politicians, the Round Robin's polished mahogany bar fills with well-heeled patrons from 4pm until after 10pm on the weekends. Recent additions include the "All the President's Cocktails" menu, which is rife with political humor (the Gerald Ford is a longneck Budweiser). *Sun noon-midnight, Mon-Sat noon-1am.* Willard InterContinental Hotel, 1401 Pennsylvania Ave. NW (14th St.), 202-628-9100

Russia House • Dupont Circle • Bar
Best International Scenes Longtime D.C. residents often fail to stop into Russia House, assuming the building is yet another of the embassies whose grand facades populate the neighborhood. Indeed, the curved staircase and red silk walls reinforce the notion. However, the only diplomatic relations encouraged in this lounge are those between the guests, the vodka, and the caviar. The bar serves up 50 different vodkas. Don't make the faux pas of drinking it with a mixer. When in Russia House, make like the Eastern-Euro expats around you and do shots. *Mon-Thu 5pm-midnight, Fri 5pm-2am, Sat 6pm-2am.* 1800 Connecticut Ave. NW (Florida Ave.), 202-234-9433, russiahouselounge.com

Sky Terrace at the Hotel Washington • White House • Hotel Bar
Best Drinks with a View Being next-door neighbors with the White House has afforded the Hotel Washington many a benefit since its 1917 opening. At one point, nearly 50 congressmen lived there (apparently following the maxim "Keep your friends close and your enemies closer"). Though it's no longer home to politicos, the hotel's location affords some of the most spectacular views of the city from its sky terrace. The casual restaurant and bar makes a perfect first stop as panoramic views of the White House and monuments help visitors get the lay of the land. However, because it's not heated, the terrace is only open in season. *Apr-Oct daily 11:30am-12:30am.* Hotel Washington, 2800 Pennsylvania Ave. NW (28th St.), 202-342-0444

Tabard Inn Lounge* • Dupont Circle • Hotel Bar
It's named for the inn in Chaucer's *Canterbury Tales,* and the nooks and crannies, roaring fireplace, and book-lined walls of this Victorian hotel's lounge cry out for storytelling and secret-sharing. Chat with other travelers and locals cozied up on the communal couches. Play chess while watching live jazz on Sunday nights. In the summer, grab a seat at the sunny private cafe for afternoon drinks. The intimate nature of the space makes it hard to accommodate large groups, so it's better to come in twos and threes. *Daily 4pm-midnight.* 1739 N St. NW (17th St.), 202-785-1277, tabardinn.com

Top of the Hill • Capitol Hill • Bar
Navigate through the down-and-dirty first-floor Pourhouse and past the dress-code–enforcing bouncer to get to this upstairs cocktail lounge. The strict no-sneakers-and-baseball-caps rule is one of the measures in place to ensure that

this bar rises above the young and rowdy vibe of other Hill establishments. Although it attracts a relatively sophisticated crowd, don't expect the polish of the downtown bars. The leather couches have been well broken in, and the bar has a shabby-chic feel. But these factors all combine to give an ideal entrée into D.C.'s political world. Expect high noise levels in the after-work hours, except during presidential debates or the State of the Union when nearly all D.C. bars fall attentively silent. *Mon-Fri 5:30pm-close, Sat 7pm-close.* 319 Pennsylvania Ave. SE (Third St.), 202-546-7782, politiki-dc.com/top.php

Town and Country Lounge • Dupont Circle • Bar

The plush red couches and leather armchairs may be inviting, but to truly experience Town and Country, grab at seat at the bar. Thirty-year veteran Sam Lek has perfected the recipe for bartending almost as well as he has perfected the mix of the 101 martinis on the menu: "The secret to a good bartender is a sense of humor, a warm smile, and a calming presence. Besides, everything looks a little better after one of my martinis." The affable Lek will levitate your money or make change out of thin air while chatting about local history and just about anything else you'd like to know about the area. Prime swilling hours? Friday for happy hour and after 10pm on Saturdays. *Daily 11am-1am.* Mayflower Hotel, 1127 Connecticut Ave. NW (Desales St.), 202-347-3000

U-topia* • U Street • Cabaret

In a perfect world, local jazz musicians would play cover-free shows to a softly lit room of rapt listeners. In a perfect world, they would sip from an extensive list of wines and aged single malts. In a perfect world, the restaurant wouldn't trade ambience for high-quality cuisine, and the whole operation would be presided over by an artist whose work adorns soaring brick walls. All overwrought metaphors aside, U-topia is the perfect spot for both postdinner drinks and long, intimate meals. Live music runs until 1:30-ish during the week and 2:30-ish on weekends. *Sun-Thu 11am-2am, Fri 11am-3am, Sat 5pm-3am.* 1418 U St. NW (14th St.), 202-483-7669, utopiaindc.com

Classic D.C.: The Attractions

Betsy Fisher • Dupont Circle • Store
You have to be buzzed into this exclusive Dupont Circle boutique, but once inside you'll find a staff eager to help you determine which sophisticated pieces are needed to spice up your wardrobe. From transitional work-to-bar pieces by Three Dot to flirty dresses by Nanette Lepore and denim by Oprah favorite Pure Color, the staff has a good eye for selecting pieces that will fit your lifestyle. *Sun noon-4pm, Mon-Wed 10am-7pm, Thu-Fri 10am-9pm, Sat 10am-6pm.* 1224 Connecticut Ave. NW (Jefferson Pl.), 202-785-1975, betsyfisher.com

Corcoran Gallery of Art • White House • Art Museum
Best Art Museums This very proper and big Beaux Arts building across from the White House was founded in 1869 and is famous for its elegant, skylit spaces and permanent collection of Cole, Remington, and other classic 19th-century American artworks. But then you walk in one day and find a video installation that interplays waterfall footage with scenes from American history or an exhibit of contemporary pieces that explore the idea of psyche and alter ego. So it's not all what you'd expect. Also at the Corcoran: European paintings, medieval tapestries, a popular gospel brunch every Sunday, and regular concerts. $- *Wed, Fri-Sun 10am-5pm, Thu 10am-9pm.* 500 17th St. NW (New York Ave.), 202-639-1700, corcoran.org

Embassy Row • Dupont Circle • Neighborhood
D.C. is home to some 172 embassies, most of them distributed along Mass Ave. and throughout the Dupont Circle neighborhood. Tour Mass Ave. and you'll encounter cool statuary, like Gandhi across from the Indian Embassy and Churchill outside the British; embassy personnel in their native garb; and standout architecture, including the Beaux Arts 1901 mansion that houses the Indonesian Embassy (at 2020) and the postmodern Finnish Embassy (at 3301). Start near the National Cathedral and follow the avenue down to Dupont Circle; do it the other way, and it's all uphill, gradual though it is. The embassies themselves are not open to the general public. embassy.org

Franklin Delano Roosevelt Memorial • Southwest • Site
On a picturesque plot in the thick of cherry-tree country along the Tidal Basin is this memorial to the only U.S. president to serve four terms, FDR, in office from 1933 to 1945. Each of the outdoor galleries depicts a different term using sculpture, waterfalls, and inscriptions ("I never forget that I live in a house owned by all the American people and that I have been given their trust"—from a Fireside chat delivered in 1938). It's appropriate that this memorial to FDR lies near the memorial to Jefferson, whom FDR greatly admired. West Basin Dr. SW (Independence Ave.), 202-426-6841, nps.gov/fdrm

Grounds of the U.S. Capitol • Capitol Hill • Park
These 58.8 acres immediately surrounding the Capitol, within its 274-acre complex, offer not only a great vantage point from which to appreciate the building's grand facade, but a pleasant spot to wander when touring lines are too

long. Designed by Frederick Law Olmsted, famous for sculpting New York's Central Park, the park is planted with more than 100 varieties of trees and bushes and thousands of seasonal flowers. Hill staffers are acquainted with a few of the more private features of the grounds. Stumble upon a small, hexagonal brick structure in the park's northwest pocket and you'll discover the 1880 Summer House, a shaded haven with benches, an ornamental fountain, and, quite possibly, a romantic rendezvous in progress. Bounded south by Independence Ave. SW, north by Constitution Ave. NW, east by First St. NE/SE, and west by First St. NW/SW, 202-225-6827, aoc.gov

Hillwood Museum and Gardens • Upper Northwest • Museum/Garden

Marjorie Merriweather Post, the heiress to the C.W. Post cereal fortune and a businesswoman in her own right, collected art throughout her life and travels. In 1955, Post settled into this grand Georgian-style country house on 25 acres and lived here until her death in 1973, bequeathing that the estate be opened as a museum. The mansion is filled with decorative arts from 18th-century France and imperial Russia; her lush 12-acre gardens include a French parterre, roses, 2,000 orchids, a Japanese-style garden, a Russian dacha, and wooded paths throughout. Reservations are required, for admission and for dining in the cafe. $ *Tue-Sat 10am-5pm.* 4155 Linnean Ave. NW (Tilden St.), 202-686-5807, hillwoodmuseum.org

I Spa at the Willard • Downtown • Spa

Best Luxury Spas In August 2005, the Willard's 5,000-square-foot I Spa opened, and from discreet accounts, seems to be doing quite nicely by its often-famous, well-traveled guests. Services include 11 different massages (Swedish to Pregnancy); body treatments, like the 50-minute Jet Lag Bath, designed to rejuvenate tired skin and muscles; and facials, manicures, and pedicures. Metrosexuals will like the Gentleman's Facial; couples can choose the Romantic Retreat Package, in the VIP couple's suite. The facility includes a small fitness center, steam rooms, and saunas. Word's out, and locals are making their way here, too. *Mon-Sat 9am-7pm, Sun 9am-5pm.* $$$$ Willard InterContinental Washington Hotel, 1401 Pennsylvania Ave. NW (14th St.), 202-942-2700, washington.interconti.com

Jefferson Memorial • Southwest • Site

Best Monumental Sculptures Thomas Jefferson was our third president, author of the Declaration of Independence, George Washington's secretary of state, and John Adams' vice president. But that's not all. The man had an interest in everything and was good at quite a lot of it, whether architecture (he designed the University of Virginia) or music (he played the violin). This 19-foot statue of Jefferson stands within the domed memorial, looking toward the White House. Inscriptions on the marble walls include, of course, the one that starts, "We hold these truths to be self-evident: that all men are created equal ..." Read on. Ohio Dr. SW (Tidal Basin), 202-426-6841, nps.gov/thje

Kennedy Center for the Performing Arts • Foggy Bottom • Site

You'll get your exercise when you visit this vast complex, but stroll, don't sprint, down the grand stretches of the Hall of Nations, the Grand Foyer, and the outdoor terraces. In fact, go ahead and join one of the free tours, which take place throughout the day. That way, you get to poke your head in to see the President's

CLASSIC • ATTRACTIONS

Box, and find out that the spectacular red and gold curtains hanging in the Opera House are a gift from Japan, measure 47 feet high, and weigh 3,000 pounds. The center is full of extraordinary art given by states in this country and nations around the world. At the very least, if you're here for neither performance nor tour, walk out to the River Terrace for a mesmerizing view of the Potomac, or up to the Roof Terrace to circumnavigate the entire exterior and enjoy a grand view of the city. *Daily 10am-9pm (and later, according to performance schedule).* 2700 F St. NW (New Hampshire Ave.), 202-467-4600, kennedy-center.org

Library of Congress • Capitol Hill • Site
Before and after Google, there was and always will be this repository of knowledge, the Library of Congress, the largest library in the world, with 130 million items and growing, including 29 million books, 2.7 million recordings, 12 million photographs, and 58 million manuscripts. Created in 1800 to serve as a resource for Congress, the Library remains open to the public for research and visiting. And though scholarship is primarily what the Library is all about, the Library's beautiful 19th-century architecture (don't miss the Reading Room Gallery Overlook), rotating exhibits of items from its collections, and lively event schedule are all good reasons to stop here. *Thomas Jefferson Building Mon-Sat 10am-5pm; James Madison Building Mon-Fri 8:30am-9:30pm, Sat 8:30am-6:30pm.* 101 Independence Ave. SE (First St.), 202-797-8000, loc.gov

Lincoln Memorial • National Mall • Site
Best Monumental Sculptures Tourists must look like little children scampering around his feet to the pensive, 19-foot-high Lincoln, who sits in this chamber facing the Capitol, his wise eyes cast down. People from around the world pay tribute to our 16th president, and read out loud the words etched on the walls of the templelike memorial: "Four score and seven years ago our fathers brought forth on this continent, a new nation, conceived in liberty and dedicated to the proposition that all men are created equal ..." In addition to the Gettysburg Address, the walls bear the words of other addresses, as well as large murals illustrating themes of unity and freedom. On August 28, 1963, Dr. Martin Luther King, Jr., delivered his "I Have a Dream" speech here; an inscription marks the exact spot. Western end of the Mall (23rd St.), 202-426-6842, nps.gov/linc

National Archives • National Mall • Site
Best Patriotic Adventures Here's your chance to see our country's founding documents, up close and in person, though behind glass (drum roll, please): the Declaration of Independence, the Constitution of the United States, and the Bill of Rights. Seriously, isn't this the kind of thing that brought you to Washington? The Archives displays these and other documents in the Rotunda (including an original of the 1297 Magna Carta, the only one in the US), where huge murals re-create historic scenes. It's worth spending a little time here to watch the documentaries and play around with interactive exhibits. Expect long lines for entry in spring, or call for tour reservations. *Labor Day–late-Mar 10am-5:30pm, Apr–Memorial Day weekend 10am-7pm, Memorial Day–Labor Day 10am-9pm.* Constitution Ave. NW (Seventh St.), 202-357-5000, archives.gov

National Gallery of Art and Sculpture Garden • National Mall • Art Museum
Best Art Museums It's possible that nothing in D.C. will make you feel more like you're in a world capital than a tour of the National Gallery. On display are paintings, sculptures, decorative arts, and works on paper dating from the Middle Ages to the present, mostly European, but also American. Its permanent collection holds 106,000 works; special exhibitions highlight major artists or significant periods, whether Cezanne, Winslow Homer, or Dadaism; and gallery programs range from Sunday evening concerts to ice skating in the popular Sculpture Garden. International visitors love the Gallery, and you will see a kind of sophisticated traveler and bohemian student here that you won't see elsewhere in the city. *Sun 11am-6pm, Mon-Sat 10am-5pm (summer hours Sun 11am-7pm, Mon-Thu, Sat 10am-7pm, Fri 10am-9:30pm).* On Constitution Ave. NW (Seventh St.), 202-737-4215, nga.gov

Renwick Gallery • White House • Art Museum
This historic 1858 building across from the White House is a favorite among lovers of American decorative arts, for works like the intriguing "Ghost Clock" (take a closer look) on display from its permanent collection. Some visitors bypass arts and crafts galleries altogether to make a beeline for the second-floor Grand Salon. Designed to resemble a Victorian-era picture gallery, the salon's 40-foot-high walls are covered in paintings. *Daily 10am-5:30pm.* 1661 Pennsylvania Ave. NW (17th St.), 202-633-2850, americanart.si.edu

Rizik's • Dupont Circle • Store
Opened as a couture dress-making shop more than 90 years ago, Rizik's has clothed diplomats, politicians, and society ladies for state dinners, fundraising events, and inaugural balls. Though the store now offers a full range of other wardrobe options like suits, blouses, and outerwear, it's the special occasion and bridal collections like Helen Morley, Flores & Flores, and Bellville Sassoon that stand out. The Dupont Circle store offers a range of services for its tony clientele, from fur storage and restyling to personal shopping. *Mon-Wed, Fri-Sat 9am-6pm, Thu 9am-8pm.* 1100 Connecticut Ave. NW (L St.), 202-223-4050, riziks.com

Rock Creek Park • Various • Park
Best Outdoor Activities This 2,000-acre park is the city's largest outdoor recreational area. A bike and pedestrian path winds all the way through, paralleling first the Potomac River near the Kennedy Center and Georgetown, and then the Rock Creek as it continues on, past the National Zoo, to its end, 12 miles along, in the Maryland suburbs. In between are great forests of beech and sycamore; deer, foxes, and assorted species of birds; hiking trails; and facilities for tennis, horseback riding, picnicking, exercise, and nature study, plus a planetarium and historic Civil War forts. From the Potomac River near the Kennedy Center, northwest through the city into Maryland, 202-895-6070, nps.gov/rocr

Sherman Pickey • Georgetown • Store
Not even a Martha's Vineyard yacht club could rival this store for the title of nation's preppiest venue. Nestled in the heart of prepster land, Sherman Pickey is stocked with more patterned ribbon belts than you can pop a collar at as well as lines like Petit Bateau and Lacoste. Sherman Pickey caters to four-legged friends with dog treats, pet collars, and leashes. *Sun noon-5pm, Tue-Sat 10am-6pm.* 1647 Wisconsin Ave. NW (Reservoir Rd.), 202-333-4212, shermanpickey.com

CLASSIC · ATTRACTIONS

A Tour de Force • Various • Tour
Best Romantic Trysts Prepare to be seduced by the sight of the sprawling, white, wedding-cake-tiered Capitol illuminated by night, followed by the sight of the lit-up Lincoln Memorial, cast against the dark sky. Other companies offer moonlight tours, but Jeanne Fogle's A Tour de Force is the best. Fogle designs a tour to suit your preferences, picks you up and delivers you wherever you like, provides background narration filled with anecdotes and history, and allows you to hop in and out for closer looks, as you like. Depending on timing, tours take two to four hours. Available for individuals and couples, not just groups, Fogle's tours benefit from her 22 years of experience. Reserve an SUV, rather than a limo, says Fogle, the better for viewing. A Tour de Force offers assorted other tours as well. $$$$ 703-525-2948, atourdeforce.com

Union Station • Capitol Hill • Site/Store
Insider D.C. Experiences Twenty-nine million people "visit" Union Station every year, making it easily the most popular destination in Washington. Travelers account for much of that traffic, for this is both an Amtrak and a Metro train station. But it's also a shopping mall lined with 120 stores and a historic attraction. Built in 1907, Union Station is an example of Beaux Arts architecture, its grand archways, vaulted ceilings, marble floors, and enormous halls making it a traditional location for inaugural balls. Stores range from chains like Ann Taylor to specialty stores like Destination D.C. *24/7, stores Sun noon-6pm, Mon-Sat 10am-9pm.* 50 Massachusetts Ave. NE (First St.), 202-289-1908, unionstationdc.com

U.S. Botanic Garden • Capitol Hill • Garden
Yes, it's historic and beautiful, but it's the "stinky plant" that's gotten this place the most publicity in recent times. When the rarely blooming titan arum gets ready to pop, Washingtonians charge down to the Botanic Garden to catch sight of the giant plant that stands about five feet tall, weighs 100 pounds, blooms for about 48 hours—and reeks of rotting meat. If the stinky plant isn't going on, thousands of other sweeter-smelling, spectacular-looking plants always are. Built in 1933, the greenhouse now features a 24-foot-high walkway that allows a grand view of both the jungle below, and the Capitol situated at the top of the hill. *Daily 10am-5pm.* 100 Maryland Ave. SW (Independence Ave.), 202-225-8333, usbg.gov

U.S. Capitol • Capitol Hill • Site
Best Patriotic Adventures The other branches of government certainly disagree, but here at headquarters, the legislative branch believes that this is where the greatest power lies. The House of Representatives occupies the southern side of the complex, the Senate the northern side. Your senators' and representatives' doors are always open, and though you're unlikely to meet them, you might watch them, and democracy, in action in the Senate and House chambers (obtain gallery passes in person or by mail from your member's office), when Congress is in session. Alternatively, or if time allows, tour the Capitol for a lesson in American history, starting in 1800, when Congress first occupied the Capitol; and to admire its architecture and art depicting famous scenes and figures from history. Note: Tours require tickets; expect lines in high season; call in advance for the latest admission procedures. *Mon-Sat 9am-4:30pm.* East Capitol St. (First St. NE/NW), 202-225-6827, aoc.gov

U.S. Holocaust Memorial Museum • Southwest • Museum
Who said this? "The government of the United States ... gives to bigotry no sanction, to persecution no assistance."? George Washington, in a 1790 letter to the Hebrew Congregation of Newport, Rhode Island—though he did, alas, own slaves. And this? "I don't believe that the big men, the capitalists and the politicians all alone, are guilty of the war. Oh no, the little man is just as guilty, otherwise the peoples of the world would have risen in revolt long ago." Anne Frank in a diary entry dated May 3, 1944. Using quotations like these, and photographs, artifacts, video monitors, and other devices that give context and take you chronologically and heartrendingly through the experience, this four-level museum bears witness to the Holocaust. *Daily 10am-5:30pm (until 7:50pm Tue and Thu, mid-Apr–mid-Jun).* 100 Raoul Wallenberg Pl. SW (Independence Ave.), 202-488-0400, ushmm.org

Washington Monument • National Mall • Site
Best Monumental Sculptures Just because you can see it from a distance at points all over the city doesn't mean you have *seen* the Washington Monument. Without a visit, you'd miss the 70-second zip in an elevator to the pinnacle and the panoramic view awaiting you: the city, the Potomac River, all the way to the Shenandoah Mountains 60 miles away. Measuring more than 555 feet high, the monument is one of the tallest freestanding masonry buildings in the world. Started in 1848, it took another 40 years to finish. Tickets required but free. *Daily 9am-5pm.* National Mall (15th St.), 202-426-6841, nps.gov/wash

Washington National Cathedral • Upper Northwest • Site/Garden
Best Views of D.C. Facts and figures about the cathedral astound: this is the sixth-largest cathedral in the world, the second-largest in the United States, and it sits on the highest point of the city; it took 83 years to complete, weighs 150,000 tons, and its exterior is almost the length of two football fields. Guided tours cover details about some of the 215 stained-glass windows and other art, architectural, and garden features, as well as the history of the cathedral. All of the cathedral's many programs, including tours, concerts, and carillon performances, revolve around the church's Episcopal service schedule. *Gardens: daily to dusk; cathedral: Sun 8am-6:30pm, Mon-Fri 10am-5:30pm (7:45pm June-Sept), Sat 10am-4:30pm.* Massachusetts Ave. NW (Wisconsin Ave.), 202-537-6200, cathedral.org

The White House • White House • Site
Visit Washington, D.C., and not see the White House? Only you'll have to be content with an exterior view; interior tours are limited to groups of ten who've coordinated with their congressional office six months in advance. So if you haven't arranged that, do this: Stroll along Pennsylvania Avenue's 84-foot-wide pedestrian plaza stretching between 15th and 17th Streets for a "front door" look at the executive mansion. Consider the facts: that this is the oldest federal building in the capital and the residence of every president but George Washington. Torched by the British in 1814, the President's Mansion was rebuilt by 1817, using the original sandstone walls and interior brickwork. 1600 Pennsylvania Ave. NW (17th St.), 202-456-7041, whitehouse.gov

PRIME TIME D.C.

Everything in life is timing (with a dash of serendipity thrown in). Would you want to arrive in Pamplona, Spain, the day *after* the Running of the Bulls? Not if you have a choice and enjoy the world's most exciting experiences. With our month-by-month calendar of events, there's no excuse to miss out on any of D.C.'s greatest moments—when its energy is at its peak. From the classic to the whimsical, the sophisticated to the outrageous, all the events that are worth your time are right here.

Prime Time Basics

Eating and Drinking

D.C. is the home of the power lunch, and it tends to stretch from 11:30am until 1:30pm. Dinner runs from 6:30pm to 9:30pm on weekdays and later on weekends. Brunch starts at 11am, though Capitol Hill rises and shines earlier for breakfast. Worker bees head to happy hour from 5:30pm to 7:30pm, lingering later on sunny spring and summer days. Bars get hopping by 10:30pm and stay busy until about 1am on weeknights, except on the Hill, where they empty out earlier. On the weekends, last call is 2:30am, with most places shutting the doors by 3am. After-hours clubs stay open until 5am. Late-night food options are easy to come by in nightlife hot spots like Dupont, Adams Morgan, and along U Street, but are practically nonexistent downtown and on Capitol Hill.

Weather and Tourism

The ebb and flow of visitors to Washington relates less to weather than to politics. When Congress is in session, the city bustles, hotels and restaurants are full, and traffic goes at a snail's pace. Peak season, politically speaking, runs in two stints, roughly mid-September right up to Thanksgiving and late January through June. Weekends, summer, holidays, and the weeks between Thanksgiving and late January are off-peak, since that's when senators, representatives, and all who do business with them head home. Those weeks in January especially can be shockingly slow.

Seasonal Changes

Month	Fahrenheit High	Low	Celsius High	Low	Hotel Rates
Jan	44	30	5	-1	L
Feb	46	29	8	-1	H
Mar	54	36	12	2	H
Apr	66	46	19	8	H
May	76	56	25	14	H
June	83	65	29	19	H
July	87	69	31	20	L
Aug	85	68	30	20	L
Sept	79	61	26	16	H
Oct	68	50	20	10	H
Nov	57	39	14	4	H
Dec	46	32	8	0	L

H-High Season L-Low

Mar-May: Weather does play a part in tourism, of course, especially when it comes to springtime and the blooming of the cherry trees along the

PRIME TIME BASICS

Tidal Basin. In fact, the 10-to-14-day blooming period, which occurs annually sometime between March 20 and April 17, is a season unto itself, attracting more visitors to the capital than at any other time of the year. Cherry blossoms aside, springtime in Washington can be magnificent, though it usually starts out rather cold. When the winds die down, and the sun comes out, and the temperatures warm, typically in mid-May, there is no better place to be.

June-Aug: Summers are hot and humid, and anyone who arrives without sunscreen and sunglasses will want to purchase these items immediately, since so many of Washington's memorials and other attractions offer little shade or protection from the sun.

Sept-Nov: Fall is easier to take, starting out warm in September and turning brisk by late October, matching the quickening pace of the city as it gets back to business.

Dec-Feb: Winters are moderately cold, with temperatures usually hovering just above freezing. The season generally holds at least one snowstorm, or worse, an ice storm; situations that both city government and local drivers remain notoriously, perhaps stubbornly, inept at handling.

National Holidays

New Year's Day	January 1
Martin Luther King Day	Third Monday in January
Valentine's Day	February 14
Presidents' Birthday	Third Monday in February
Memorial Day	Last Monday in May
Independence Day	July 4
Labor Day	First Monday in September
Columbus Day	Second Monday in October
Halloween	October 31
Veterans' Day	November 11
Thanksgiving Day	Fourth Thursday in November
Christmas Day	December 25
New Year's Eve	December 31

Listings in blue are major celebrations but not official holidays.

The Best Events Calendar

January
- **Presidential Inauguration**
- Restaurant Week
- Washington Antiques Show

February

March
- National Cherry Blossom Festival

April
- Filmfest D.C.
- Smithsonian Craft Show

May
- Virginia Gold Cup
- Washington National Cathedral Flower Mart

June
- Capital Pride Festival
- National Capital Barbecue Battle
- **Smithsonian Folklife Festival**

July
- Bastille Day Celebration
- Capital Fringe Festival
- **Fourth of July Celebration**
- Screen on the Green Film Festival

August
- Legg Mason Tennis Classic

September
- Adams Morgan Day
- **Kennedy Center Open House Arts Festival**
- Library of Congress National Book Festival

October
- Halloween

November
- Washington Craft Show

December
- National Christmas Tree Lighting and Pageant of Peace

Night+Day's Top Five Events are in blue.
High Season is from Feb-June and Sept-Nov represented by blue background.

The Best Events

January

Presidential Inauguration
Swearing-in ceremony: west front steps of the U.S. Capitol; motorcade down Pennsylvania Avenue to the White House; balls and celebrations throughout the city, presidential-inauguration.com

The Lowdown: This quadrennial political event is also the capital's biggest, most spectacular social affair, with at least 50,000 out-of-towners arriving to party with the incoming powers-that-be. Celebrations start on the eve of Inauguration Day and continue throughout January 20, with inaugural balls, both official and unofficial, capping the day. Regardless of who the newly elected president is, schmoozing is a prime activity, and Democrats, Republicans, Hollywood film stars, and rich and famous glamour couples hobnob into the wee hours for days upon end.

When and How Much: *On January 20 every four years, following a presidential election. The 56th inauguration takes place January 20, 2009.* Tickets are scarce for the swearing-in ceremony but might be available from your representatives' or senators' offices. The inaugural committee sells tickets to watch the president's motorcade pass by on Pennsylvania Avenue, but usually reserves more than half of the space along the parade route for spectators without tickets. Inaugural ball tickets cost about $150 each and attendance to some of the balls is by invitation only. Hottest ticket in town? The one that will get you in to the ball sponsored by the home state of the incoming president.

Restaurant Week
At participating restaurants citywide; for more information, Washington Convention and Tourism Corporation, 202-789-7000, washington.org/restaurantwk

The Lowdown: Observe Washingtonians at their most rapacious and stoke your own appetite while you're at it during this event that aims to fill the city's restaurants during the off seasons. So popular that the capital now stages two a year (the second usually takes place during the doldrums of August), Restaurant Week invites diners to enjoy a three-course meal for a bargain fixed price, at either or both lunch and dinner, for the entire designated week. As many as 140 restaurants participate, including some of Washington's finest.

When and How Much: *Twice a year, usually a full week starting on a Monday the second week in January and the first week in August.* In January 2006, the price was $20.06 for lunch and $30.06 for dinner, not including beverage, tax, or gratuity. Mention "Restaurant Week" when making a reservation.

Washington Antiques Show
Omni Shoreham Hotel, 2500 Calvert St. NW (Connecticut Ave.), 202-388-9560, washingtonantiques.org

The Lowdown: Wealthy Washington socialites and highbrow collectors browse the art, antiques, furnishings, and jewelry displayed by nearly 50 dealers at this annual antiques show, which, at 51, is one of the oldest in the country. Though the quality of the items is not what it was in the days when curators for the White House and State Department Diplomatic Rooms shopped here, this is serious stuff nonetheless, with hefty prices to prove it.

When and How Much: *Four days, usually a Thursday through Sunday, in early January.* The opening day luncheon and lecture usually sells out to a local see-and-be-seen crowd; dealer chats on Friday afternoon and appraisals on Saturday morning are also on offer. $15 one-day or $25 four-day pass.

March

National Cherry Blossom Festival
Citywide; event locations vary, 202-661-7584, nationalcherryblossomfestival.org

The Lowdown: This is one of D.C.'s premier events, attracting one million people to celebrate a rite of spring: the blooming of the 3,700 cherry trees planted around the Tidal Basin and on the Washington Monument grounds. Japan gave the U.S. a gift of the original trees in 1912, and the city's commemoration of that event has blossomed, like the trees, into something extraordinary. The whole city gets into the act, with restaurants concocting cherry blossom menu specials, museums mounting Japanese art exhibits, and the National Park Service hosting daily performances on a stage in the thick of the blossoms. The festival culminates with a parade down Constitution Avenue of lavish floats, marching bands, the works.

When and How Much: *The city schedules the two-week festival to coincide with the trees' two-week blooming, which usually occurs late March into early April (if Mother Nature cooperates).* Most events are free, but tickets for grandstand seats along the parade route are $15 (ticketmaster.com). The prime day to be here is the last day, since that's when the parade takes place.

April

Filmfest D.C., Washington's International Film Festival
Different venues around town, including traditional movie theaters and concert halls, 703-218-3456, filmfestdc.org

The Lowdown: Every year highlights the works of a different country or region of the world. The D.C. Commission on the Arts and Humanities coordinates the festival, nearly 20 years old and growing strong. Washingtonians were slow to turn away from their DVD players and neighborhood blockbusters, but now turn out in great numbers for screenings, which include more than 100 features, documentaries, and short films from around the globe.

When and How Much: *Twelve days in April (often Wednesday through the following Sunday).* $9 admission per film. Opening night is the best time to go, when a star actor or director with a film in the festival kicks off the event with an introduction and talk.

Smithsonian Craft Show
National Building Museum, 401 F St. NW (bet. Fourth and Fifth Sts.), 888-832-9554, smithsoniancraftshow.com

The Lowdown: Recognized as "the nation's most prestigious juried exhibition and sale of contemporary American crafts," the Smithsonian Craft Show features works deemed both artistic and functional in 12 categories, from basketry to wearable art. The jury chooses only 120 of approximately 1,200 applicants, and showgoers can expect to pay for these one-of-a-kind creations. One-of-a-kind is also a good description of the show's exhibit space.

When and How Much: *Four days in mid- to late April, with a preview gala the Wednesday before the show, which starts on Thursday.* Daily admission $15. Try to attend the preview gala for sights of Washington hotshots and glamorous socialites—and for the chance of snatching up some precious bauble before the show opens to the public.

May

Virginia Gold Cup
Great Meadow, The Plains, Virginia, 540-317-1215, vagoldcup.com

The Lowdown: Run since 1922, this steeplechase race takes place 40 miles from D.C., and draws 45,000 people in their best spring finery to drink champagne and party hard in the Virginia countryside.

When and How Much: *First Saturday in May;* car admission pass is $85. *(A second race, the International Gold Cup, takes place the third Saturday in October, same place, same price, but half the crowd.)*

Washington National Cathedral Flower Mart
Massachusetts and Wisconsin Aves. NW, 202-537-6200, nationalcathedral.org

The Lowdown: The highest spot in Washington, D.C., is right here, at the pinnacle of the central tower in the cathedral, which presides over the city from atop Mount St. Albans, 676 feet above sea level. Twice a year, the cathedral allows the public to climb the spiral staircase to the Gloria in Excelsis Bell Tower and exult in the view; the annual Flower Mart is the occasion for one of them. (The cathedral's annual open house in September is the other.) The Flower Mart, too, is a treat, each year honoring a different embassy, and offering gardening and home boutiques, food booths, and live music.

When and How Much: *Friday and Saturday of the first full weekend in May.* Sometimes a nominal fee for the tower climb; admission is free.

June

Capital Pride Festival
Parade at Dupont Circle, festival on Pennsylvania Ave. NW, 202-797-3510, capitalpride.org

> The Lowdown: D.C. hosts the country's fourth-largest gay pride event. Politicians show their support, cowboys ride mechanical bulls on floats, and drag queens strut their stuff along the parade route that winds through the Dupont Circle area. It's all a lot of fun, but partly serious, too, as the event is also a fundraiser for event sponsor the Whitman-Walker Clinic, which provides services to those infected with HIV.
>
> When and How Much: *Nine-day celebration beginning on the first Saturday in June and culminating the following Saturday in a nighttime parade, followed by a street festival on Sunday.* The street festival, attracting some 200,000 people, is not to be missed, with musical performances on several stages and a closing dance party, spun by a DJ. Free.

National Capital Barbecue Battle
Pennsylvania Ave. NW (bet. Ninth and 14th Sts.), 301-860-0630, barbecuebattle.com

> The Lowdown: Judging by the crowds who turn out for this event, everybody likes barbecue. Rain or shine, the battle takes place, with competitions, demonstrations, free food samples, and live music, mostly rock, and rhythm and blues, by local legends like the Nighthawks and Mary Ann Redmond. People pig out and the bands play on.
>
> When and How Much: *The last Saturday and Sunday in June.* Admission $10.

Smithsonian Folklife Festival
National Mall, 202-275-1150, si.edu/center/festival.html

> The Lowdown: Imagine how all the people of the world live and eat, and dress, and the kinds of songs they sing and the music they make. Well, that's the idea behind the Folklife Festival. Each year the Smithsonian shines a light on one or more world cultures, and its artistic and musical traditions, and invites performing artists and artisans, storytellers and workers from those communities to Washington to share their experiences. Past exhibits have included a re-created Asian Silk Road, a horse racetrack, a Japanese rice paddy, and a polka hall. It's always a crowded, hot, sweaty—and fascinating—time.
>
> When and How Much: *Takes place over the course of two weekends in late June and early July, 10 days in all, and always including July 4.* For the most fun and least heat, attend one of the evening concerts or dance parties. Free.

THE BEST EVENTS

July

Bastille Day Celebration
Les Halles Restaurant, 1201 Pennsylvania Ave. NW (12th St.), 202-347-6848, leshalles.net

The Lowdown: Francophiles, European visitors, and good old American office workers wind up midday at Les Halles to drink wine, eat frites, and watch the famous Bastille Day race. The city closes Pennsylvania Avenue between Seventh St. NW and Les Halles, at 12th St. NW, the mayor says a few words, and the race is on. Actually, there are three races, one for children, one for Les Halles customers, and one for waiters. The waiter's contest is the one you want to watch and it starts about 1:45pm. Waiters from restaurants all over town palm a tray with a split of champagne and a filled wine glass, and walk fast down the avenue, hoping to be the first to return to Les Halles with everything still upright and unspilled. Show up at noon and join the others crowding the sidewalks. Don't book a table, since the view's outside and Les Halles grills sandwiches, crepes, and frites on the street. The party continues into the night.

When and How Much: *July 14.* The celebration is free; food prices vary.

Capital Fringe Festival
At 20 venues on or near Seventh Street NW, 202-294-6909, capfringe.org

The Lowdown: The Capital Fringe Festival makes its debut July 2006, showcasing experimental performances, local and visiting, in theater, dance, music, and other disciplines. The festival takes its cues from the annual Edinburgh Fringe Festival that takes place in Scotland every summer. Organizers hope to present 1,000 events in all and to explore more provocative and politically riskier spectacles than those on offer in the capital's traditional theater settings.

When and How Much: *This 11-day event in late July beginning on a Thursday and ending on a Sunday features five events each day at each venue.* Tickets average $10 per event.

Fourth of July Celebration
Constitution Ave. (bet. Seventh and 17th Sts. NW), the National Mall, 202-619-7400

The Lowdown: The day begins in front of the National Archives with a reading of the Declaration of Independence and the playing of period music. At noon, the National Independence Day Parade progresses down Constitution Avenue, with school marching bands and military units interspersed with elaborate floats and entertainers. Then it's off to the National Mall with thousands of fellow patriots to watch fireworks burst in the night sky above the Washington Monument, set off in time to the National Symphony Orchestra's renditions of "The 1812 Overture" and "Stars and Stripes Forever."

When and How Much: *July 4.* The Mall is crowded by afternoon with picnickers. Fireworks start after 9pm. Free.

PRIME TIME

Screen on the Green Film Festival
National Mall grounds (bet. Fourth and Seventh Sts.)

The Lowdown: College-age kids, families, and young worker bees end up here, with a blanket and picnic, to watch Robert Redford and Barbra Streisand in *The Way We Were* and Bogie in *The Big Sleep,* projected on a gigantic screen set up on the National Mall. The outdoor film festival always shows classics, and the scene is so popular that people come right after work to reserve their spot.

When and How Much: *Five consecutive Monday nights starting mid-July; films begin at sundown, around 8:30pm.* Free.

August

Legg Mason Tennis Classic
Fitzgerald Tennis Center, 16th St. NW (Kennedy St.), 202-721-9500, leggmasontennisclassic.com

The Lowdown: This U.S. Open Series event attracts as many as 72,000 people. Fans turn out to watch the likes of Andre Agassi and Andy Roddick compete for big bucks. The classic benefits a good cause, too: the Washington Tennis & Education Foundation, a nonprofit organization established to improve the lives of kids in lower-income communities by introducing them to tennis and other educational and community-based activities.

When and How Much: *The first week of August, starting on a Saturday and going through the following Sunday.* Individual tickets are $9-$44 for certain sessions; ticket packages are available through Ticketmaster (ticketmaster.com).

September

Adams Morgan Day
Columbia Rd. NW, 18th St. NW, and other streets in Adams Morgan, 202-232-1978, adamsmorgandayfestival.com

The Lowdown: For such a little neighborhood, Adams Morgan has a big fan club. So when residents and businesses throw a block party to celebrate themselves, they invite everyone on and off the block to come, and come they do, in the thousands. Dance and music performances, art exhibits, food samplings, and other activities represent the many nationalities of Adams Morganers.

When and How Much: *Second Sunday in September.* Free.

THE BEST EVENTS

Kennedy Center Open House Arts Festival
Kennedy Center, 2700 F St. NW (25th St.), 202-467-4600, kennedy-center.org

The Lowdown: The Kennedy Center, or the nation's theater, as it refers to itself, is open to the public every day for tours, free performances nightly on the Millennium Stage, and general wandering around (great views to be had of the city and the Potomac River). Once a year, to celebrate its birthday, the center invites the public to sample a little more, by holding this all-day fair of some 30 dance, music, and theater performances by local, national, and even international artists. It's superpopular, and offers something for everyone, though families do turn out in big numbers.

When and How Much: *A Saturday or Sunday in early to mid-September. Free.*

Library of Congress National Book Festival
National Mall (bet. Seventh and 14th Sts. NW), 202-707-8000, loc.gov/bookfest

The Lowdown: Book lovers of every genre and fans hoping to meet their favorite authors gather for this festival cosponsored by the Library of Congress and First Lady Laura Bush. In pavilions erected across the Mall, festivalgoers play with LOC computer kiosks to access the library's vast holdings of digitized music, movies, and recordings; listen to authors discuss and read from their works; and discover which authors hail from their home states.

When and How Much: *Last Saturday in September. Free.*

October

Halloween
Throughout Georgetown and Dupont Circle neighborhoods

The Lowdown: The fun begins on the Tuesday before Halloween with a High Heel Drag Race down 17th St. NW, between P and S Sts., in the Dupont Circle neighborhood. Thousands watch as 100 or so participants in full outré regalia wobbily compete. Bars and restaurants along the route prepare special drinks and dishes for the occasion. On Halloween, in Georgetown especially, but throughout the city, Washingtonians of all ages and persuasions dress outlandishly and carry on for all they're worth until the wee hours.

When and How Much: *Tuesday before Halloween and October 31. Free.*

November

Washington Craft Show
Washington Convention Center, 801 Mt. Vernon Pl., NW (Seventh St.), 202-249-3000, craftsamericashows.com

The Lowdown: Handmade paper sculptures, burnished wooden bowls, and whimsical glass jewelry and ornaments are some of the crafts on display in this event, which features 185 of the nation's leading craft artists. Like its sister event, the Smithsonian Craft Show, held in April, this is a juried competition, and only masters in their fields win a place here. The schedule includes art and interior design talks throughout each day and a gala awards dinner honoring the best on opening night.

When and How Much: *Three days, Friday through Sunday, during the third weekend in November. $14 admission.*

December

National Christmas Tree Lighting and Pageant of Peace
The Ellipse, south of the White House, 202-208-1631, pageantofpeace.org

The Lowdown: With one swift motion, the president or the school child he designates presses a button and illuminates the gorgeously decorated National Christmas Tree, and the capital's Christmas season is off to a joyous start. A military band officiates and entertainers like CeCe Winans perform. Every night thereafter throughout December, musical groups take the stage on the Ellipse.

When and How Much: *Opening ceremony begins at 5pm, early in December; tickets are required but free, and distributed first come, first serve that morning at the Ellipse Visitor Pavilion, southwest corner of 15th and E Sts. NW. Nightly musical performances are free and require no tickets.*

HIT the GROUND RUNNING

In this section, you'll find all the indispensable details to enhance your trip—from tips on what to wear and how to get around to planning resources that will help your vacation come off without a hitch. You'll also find suggestions for making business trips a pleasure, as well as some fun, surprising facts that will let you impress the locals.

City Essentials

Getting to D.C.: By Air

Ronald Reagan Washington National Airport (DCA)
703-417-8000, mwaa.com/national

DCA is located four miles south of Washington, on the Potomac River and accessible via the George Washington Memorial Parkway, in Arlington, Virginia.

Ronald Reagan Washington National Airport, or "National," as it's called, sits just across the Potomac River from the city of Washington, making it easily the most convenient of the area's three airports. The fact that National is the only D.C. airport with its own Metro stop recommends it further; board a train at National's Metro station and five stops and 15 minutes later you're in the heart of the city. National is a "short-haul" airport, which means it offers nonstop service to destinations no further than 1,250 miles from Washington, with the exception of six cities: Denver, Las Vegas, Los Angeles, Phoenix, Salt Lake City, and Seattle. The airport's 14 passenger airlines provide daily nonstop flights to a total of 69 U.S., 1 Caribbean, and 2 Canadian cities.

National has two terminals: the original, "Historic Terminal A," used by a handful of airlines; and the million-square-foot, three-level main terminal that the airport added in 1997, which handles the lion's share of flights. The main terminal is labeled C at its northern end and B at its southern end. Architect Cesar Pelli's design for this terminal incorporates 30 commissioned artworks into the architectural features, so that as you walk through the main terminal, you might notice a Frank Stella inlaid marble-and-glass mosaic medallion on the concourse floor, or a mural by Sam Gilliam on a Metro bridge wall. The expansion also created climate-controlled pedestrian

Nonstop Flying Times to Washington, D.C.

From	Airport Code	Time (hr.)
Atlanta	ATL	2
Boston	BOS	1½
Chicago	ORD	2
London	LHR	8
Los Angeles	LAX	5
Miami	MIA	3
Montreal	YUL	2
New York	JFK	1
San Francisco	SFO	5
Tokyo	NRT	12

Airlines Serving D.C. Airports

Airlines	Website	800 Number	BWI	DCA	Dulles
Aeroflot	aeroflot.org	800-995-5555			D
Air Canada	aircanada.ca	888-247-2262	E	B	C
Air France	airfrance.us	800-237-2747			B
AirTran Airways	airtran.com	800-247-8726	D	A	B
Alitalia	alitaliausa.com	800-223-5730			H
Alaska Airlines	alaskaair.com	800-426-0333		B	D
America West	americawest.com	800-235-9292	D		D
American Airlines	aa.com	800-433-7300	C	B	D
American Eagle	aa.com	800-433-7300			D
ATA	ata.com	800-453-9282		A	
ANA (All Nippon Airways)	fly-ana.com	800-235-9262			B
Austrian Airlines	austrianair.com	800-843-0002			D
British Airways	britishairways.com	800-247-9297	E		D
Continental Airlines	continental.com	800-525-0280	D	B	B
Delta Air Lines	delta.com	800-221-1212	C	B	B
Ethiopian	flyethiopian.com	800-445-2733			D
Frontier	flyfrontier.com	800-432-1359	D	B	
JetBlue	jetblue.com	800-538-2583			B
Korean Air	koreanair.com	800-438-5000			B
LAB Bolivia	labairlines.com	800-337-0918			H
Lufthansa	lufthansa.com	800-645-3880			B, C
MAXjet	maxjet.com	888-435-9629			B
Midwest	midwestairlines.com	800-452-2022	D	A	
Northwest Airlines	nwa.com	800-225-2525	D	A	B
SAS	scandinavian.net	800-221-2350			B
Saudi Arabian	saudiairlines.com	800-472-8342			H
South African	flysaa.com	800-722-9675			B
Southwest	southwest.com	800-435-9792	A, B		B
Spirit	spiritair.com	800-772-7117		A	
TACA	grupotaca.com	800-400-8780			H
Ted	flyted.com	800-225-5833			C
United Airlines	united.com	800-241-6522	D	B	C, D, G
US Airways	usairways.com	800-428-4322	D	B, C	Z
Virgin Atlantic	virgin-atlantic.com	800-862-8621			B

bridges connecting the terminal to the Metro station and to parking garages, and some fabulous shops, bars, and restaurants—100 at last count.

Nearly all of your dining, drinking, and shopping options are located on the second level of the main terminal, and the best of these lie within National Hall, that length of concourse you traverse before passing through security to reach your gate. Legal Seafoods and its fab lobster rolls; Five Guys, the local favorite joint for burgers; and California Pizza Kitchen are among your choice eats. Shopping best bets include chains, like Crabtree & Evelyn and Brooks Brothers, but also only-in-D.C. Smithsonian and National Geographic museum boutiques and a branch of the local independent bookstore, Olsson's. More stores and cafes, as well as a couple of pubs, await you on the other side of security, but these are mostly of the grab-and-go variety.

Business travelers can look to the airport's business service center at the C end of the main terminal for foreign currency exchange, photocopying, faxing, and other services. Nearly 60 phone stations with data ports are located throughout the main terminal.

Into Town by Taxi: Rates from the airport are based on miles traveled and range from $10 to $20, depending on your destination.

Into Town by Airport Shuttle Service: SuperShuttle (202-296-6662 or 800-258-3826, supershuttle.com) vans are available outside the baggage claim area on the lower level. These are shared ride vans, whose fares run about $12 for the first person and $8 for each additional person in your party.

Into Town by Public Transit: Metro's Blue and Yellow lines stop at National Airport, where pedestrian walkways lead straight from the station to the middle level of the main terminal B/C. If your airline is located in Terminal A, you'll need to walk out to the curb and catch a free airport shuttle to the Metro station; you can also walk from Terminal A into the main terminal and follow the signs to the pedestrian walkways and the Metro station. Base fare is $1.35, and increases depending on how far and when you're traveling.

Into Town by Car: National Airport is about 15 minutes by car from downtown Washington, depending on traffic; between 7am and 9am and between 3pm and 7pm, rush hour can double or triple the time, particularly if you're en route to the airport during that afternoon period. See box for rental car options.

Rental Cars: All of the following major rental car companies have locations at all three airports. At Washington Dulles International Airport, courtesy shuttle vans pick you up at designated spots outside the baggage claim area to take you to their lots for vehicle pickup. Avis, Budget, Dollar, Hertz, and National are onsite at National Airport, and you simply follow the pedestrian walkway or take the shuttle to garage A, where the rental cars are kept. If you've rented a car from National Airport's offsite agencies, Alamo, Enterprise, and Thrifty, you must walk outside the terminal near the baggage claim area to catch your agency's shuttle to the lot. In Baltimore, a free shuttle picks you outside baggage claim and transports you to the off-site facility ten minutes away.

Agency	Website	800 Number
Alamo	alamo.com	800-462-5266
Avis	avis.com	800-331-1212
Budget	budget.com	800-527-0700
Dollar	dollar.com	800-800-4000
Enterprise	enterprise.com	800-261-7331
Hertz	hertz.com	800-654-3131
National	nationalcar.com	800-227-7368
Thrifty	thrifty.com	800-367-2277

Limos
- Red Top Sedan, redtopsedan.com   800-296-3300
- RMA Worldwide Chauffeured Transportation,   800-878-7743
  rmalimo.com

Washington Dulles International Airport (IAD)
703-572-2700, mwaa.com/dulles

IAD is located about 26 miles west of Washington, D.C., at the junction of Route 28 and Route 267, the Dulles Access and Toll Road, in Chantilly, Virginia.

Washington Dulles International Airport, "Dulles" for short, is the area's largest airport, and getting bigger all the time, as its ten-year, $3.4 billion construction program progresses toward completion, scheduled for 2009. The airport is fully operational, though it doesn't always appear that way as you proceed past tarp-covered areas of the terminal and walk great distances to reach your gate. It will be grand when it's finished, but for now, disregard the mess and noise and keep on moving.

Currently, 19 international and 12 domestic airlines fly to Dulles, offering nonstop daily service to 77 U.S. and 37 foreign cities. The airport has a main terminal, which houses the ticketing, baggage claim, security, and ground transportation functions, as well as just one concourse, Z, holding US Airways gates. All other airlines use the five concourses, A, B, C, D, and G, located in separate midfield terminals. Travelers to Dulles sometimes don't realize that they have arrived at remote terminals and need to board one of Dulles's bulky mobile lounges, or, if you arrive in Terminal B, follow the new passenger walkway to reach the main terminal. This is one of those situations where it's a good idea to just follow the crowd, which should take you directly to the lounges. These shuttles operate nonstop and take just a few minutes to travel the half-mile or so across the air field to the main terminal. (By 2009, the airport plans to replace most of the lounges with an underground automated train system that will zip passengers between the main terminal and midfield concourses.)

Dulles's nearly 100 dining and shopping options are getting better all the time, too, and the best are located in the midfield terminals, close to departure gates. Recent restaurant additions include a Daily Grind for coffee lovers (main terminal), an outpost of the well-reviewed local establishment Harry's Tap Room for discriminating diners (two locations: main terminal and Concourse B), a branch of Potbelly Sandwich Works (Concourse B), and three excellent venues for sipping your favorite beverage: the Vino Volo wine lounge (Concourse C), which serves wine by the glass or in flights, along with appetizer-portioned dishes; the Tequileria (Concourse B), a restaurant focused on tequila, which serves Mexican food; and the Gordon Biersch brewery (Concourse D), for fresh-brewed–beer lovers.

Dulles offers the same variety of stores as those at National, including Borders Bookstore (three locations: Concourses B, C, and D), Brooks Brothers (Concourse B), and the Smithsonian Museum Store (Concourse B). But Dulles has two additional venues worth noting: Rent-A-Cellular Business Service, for cellular phone rentals, and the Massage Bar, where sore-muscled travelers can receive foot, back, and neck rubs in 15- and 30-minute sessions; both concessions are in Concourse B.

Located throughout Dulles are ATMs and foreign currency exchange stations, and phones with data ports. Business service centers are positioned at either end of the ticketing (upper) level of the main terminal, and provide the usual: photocopying, faxing, and insurance. Also good to know: Dulles has seven public computer terminals with internet access, in wall-mounted telephone enclosures in concourses B, C, and D.

Dulles Airport is about 45 minutes by car from downtown Washington, depending on traffic; between 6am and 9am and between 3pm and

7pm, rush hour can at least double the time, particularly if you're en route to the airport during that afternoon period.

Into Town by Taxi: Rates from the airport are metered and range from $50 to $60, depending on your destination.

Into Town by Airport Shuttle Service: SuperShuttle (202-296-6662 or 800-258-3826, supershuttle.com) vans are available outside the baggage claim area on the lower level. These are shared ride vans, whose fares run about $22 for the first person and $10 for each additional person in your party.

Into Town by Public Transit: Not recommended. Travel to Washington via public transit requires that you either take a bus to the Metro station in Falls Church and ride the Metro's Orange line from there, or take a Metrobus all the way from Dulles into the city. This is the least expensive but also the slowest way to go.

Baltimore/Washington International Thurgood Marshall Airport (BWI)
Off I-195, which stems off I-95, near Linthicum, Maryland, 800-435-9294, bwiairport.com

Located about 32 miles from downtown Washington, D.C., BWI, newly renamed to honor the Baltimore native who rose to become the first black Supreme Court justice, is the least convenient of D.C. area airports, but notable for several reasons. BWI usually offers the best fares to the region, thanks to Southwest Airlines, whose 165 daily flights make up about 50% of BWI's business. In fact, it's quite possible that you will pay more for a taxi (about $63) than you might for your flight here. BWI's international airlines include IcelandAir, which does not fly to either National or Dulles. And BWI, like Dulles, is in the midst of a tremendous expansion that already has added pedestrian skywalks between terminal and garages. SuperShuttle also operates at BWI, and its fares hover around $30 for one person, $10 for each additional person in your party. All the major car rental agencies have offices on airport property, accessible by shuttle from the main terminal.

Getting to D.C.: By Land

By Car: Washington, D.C., lies on the I-95 north-south corridor, on a line with Baltimore, Philadelphia, and New York to the north, and Richmond and Charleston to the south. Also from the north, I-70 runs from Pennsylvania into Maryland, becoming I-270 at Frederick, Maryland, and continuing to the outskirts of D.C. From points west, Route 50 travels from West Virginia, and I-66 from the pretty Virginia countryside around Front Royal, Virginia, toward Washington. From the southwest, I-81 is the major highway, running through the middle of North Carolina and Virginia to meet up with D.C. If you're traveling to D.C. from an eastern direction, you'll be coming from the Eastern Shore or the Mid-Atlantic beaches, following Route 50 to get here. All of these roads converge on the Capital Beltway, I-495/I-95, which encircles the city of Washington, allowing drivers who want to bypass the city to do so, while posting exits for others who need to drive to points "inside the beltway."

Driving Times to D.C.

From	Distance (mi.)	Approx. Time (hr.)
Atlanta	638	10½
Boston	443	8
Chicago	702	11½
Miami	1,058	16½
New York	230	4
Philadelphia	144	2½

By Train: Amtrak (800-872-7245, amtrak.com) offers rail service nationwide, but its Boston to Washington route is its most traveled, with nearly hourly service offered daily between the two cities, and stops at major stations along the way, including Philadelphia and New York. Most popular for travelers along this northeast route are Amtrak's Metroliner and Acela Express trains, which provide high-speed service. The Metroliner travels between D.C. and New York, with stops in Philadelphia and a few other cities; the Acela travels between Boston and D.C., with stops in New York and Philadelphia. Amtrak operates twice-daily service between Washington and cities in the south, like Charleston, South Carolina, and Orlando, Florida. Amtrak trains arrive at Union Station, whose front doors present travelers with a superb view of the Capitol, a few streets away. From Union Station, you're a short walk, taxi ride, or subway ride from D.C.'s downtown and major attractions.

CITY ESSENTIALS

D.C.: Lay of the Land

D.C.'s compact 67-square-mile territory centers on the U.S. Capitol, from which the city extends into quadrants: northwest, northeast, southwest, and southeast. The layout today remains true to the 1792 vision of Pierre Charles L'Enfant, who modeled his plan on the design of various European cities. L'Enfant set the Capitol on a hill, the President's House on a lower plain overlooking the Potomac River, and connected the two by a grand avenue, Pennsylvania Avenue. Other wide boulevards named for states, New Hampshire, Rhode Island, Massachusetts, and so on, radiate diagonally and meet at traffic circles and squares. Numbered streets run in numerical order north and south, and lettered streets run in alphabetical order east and west, turning into two-syllable names and then three-syllable names the further away from the city center you travel.

The grid formula makes it easy to figure out a location, especially when it comes to the lettered and name streets. For example, the White House, at 1600 Pennsylvania Ave. NW, is between 16th and 17th streets in the northwest quadrant. Every street name includes one of the four directional suffixes: NW, NE, SW, or SE, and this is a crucial detail to note, since, for instance, 1600 Pennsylvania Avenue SE is a far cry and an entirely different kind of neighborhood from 1600 Pennsylvania Avenue NW.

Most of Washington's major tourist attractions lie in the northwest and southwest sections, notably the Smithsonian museums, the war and presidential memorials, and the Washington Monument, all of which stand on or near the National Mall. The Potomac River serves as a natural western border between the capital and Virginia.

Getting Around D.C.

By Car: It's official: According to a national study published in 2005, D.C.'s traffic is the third worst in the nation, following Los Angeles and San Francisco. Twice every weekday, commuters from Virginia and Maryland suburbs travel the Beltway, I-495, encircling the city, and traverse the 15 bridges over the Potomac and Anacostia rivers, to join District commuters on the series of main arteries, 16th Street, and Connecticut, Massachusetts, Wisconsin, New York, and other avenues, that lead finally to their work destinations. The term "rush hour" is an oxymoron, since it applies to the time between 5:30am and 9:30am and again between 3pm and 7pm, and lasts a full third of the day.

Most visitors to the capital do arrive by car, so should plan on encountering congestion on D.C.'s busy streets, even in off hours. Roadway maintenance and new construction in this ever-growing town are a way of life as well, with street closures and detours slowing traffic or sending it in unanticipated directions. Those experiences alone are usually sufficient to convince visitors to leave the car parked in the hotel garage, no matter how steep the daily fees, and to get around town on foot, by taxi, or public transit. But there are other inducements: Washington's traffic circles, lovely as they are, often provoke hysterics in the uninitiated driver. It is illegal to talk on a cell phone while driving, and police officers issue tickets to offenders. Finally, walking is truly the most pleasurable way, and Metro the quickest, to get where you're going in this beautiful city.

Metric Conversion

From	To	Multiply by
Inches	Centimeters	2.54
Yards	Meters	0.91
Miles	Kilometers	1.60
Gallons	Liters	3.79
Ounces	Grams	28.35
Pounds	Kilograms	0.45

To reach regions beyond D.C. and nearby Old Town Alexandria will likely require a car; if you haven't driven here you can rent a car from one of the many agencies, including a slew in Union Station's garage near Capitol Hill.

Parking: Like that of most cities, D.C.'s parking situation is disagreeable, to say the least, with not enough spaces available, astronomical rates charged by garages and lots, and overzealous meter men and maids ticketing your car as soon as the meter's red flag pops up. The worst areas are the most popular locations at their busiest times, of course: near the Mall on weekdays, and near the Verizon Center anytime, but especially when an event is on. (It can cost $20 to park in a lot for a

Parking Garages

Here are some of the biggest and most convenient parking facilities.
- Capitol Hill area: Union Station Garage (50 Massachusetts Ave. NE)
- Georgetown: Colonial Parking Garage at Georgetown Park Mall
   (3222 M St. NW, entrance on Wisconsin Ave.)
- Adams Morgan: Colonial Parking Garage
   (2328 Champlain St. NW, enter from 18th St.)
- Downtown, near National Mall: Interpark (655 15th St.)
- Downtown, near White House: Colonial Parking (1901 L St.)
- Downtown/Penn Quarter: Quikpark (1001 G St.)

couple of hours; a quarter at a meter buys you only 15 minutes.) Side streets in residential sections of Dupont Circle, Georgetown, Capitol Hill, and other neighborhoods usually allow for two-hour parking without a resident's permit, and again, parking police show no mercy. The key is to pay attention to the posted street signs, which note relevant parking restrictions.

By Public Transit: Metrorail (Metro) is the Washington Metropolitan Area Transit Authority's (202-637-7000, wmata.com) subway system. It is an indispensable way of traveling in and around the city and surrounding suburbs, and everyone, from students to administration stars, uses it. Metro has five color-coded lines, Red, Blue, Orange, Green, and Yellow, which criss-cross the city, intersecting at different junctions to allow transfers to other lines. The trains travel to 86 stations in all, including stops at Ronald Reagan Washington Airport, Union Station, the National Mall, various downtown locations, Dupont Circle, Capitol Hill, and other points at or near major tourist destinations. The system operates Mon-Thu 5:30am-midnight, Fri 5:30am-3am, Sat 7am-3am, and Sun 7am-midnight.

Metro is easy to use: you purchase fare cards in vending machines placed inside the entrance to each station, using coins or bills in denominations up to $20; machines marked "Passes/Farecards" accept both cash and credit cards. Base fare is $1.35, and the fee goes up from there to as much as $3.90, depending on how far you're traveling, and whether it's peak (weekdays 5:30-9:30am and 3-7pm) or off-peak time. To reach the station platform, you insert your fare card into the entry gate and snatch the card as it pops up, at the same time the gate opens to let you through. Hold on to your fare card, since you'll need it to insert in the exit gate to leave the station (again, you must retrieve your ticket when it pops up). Metro stations post maps and fare information signs to help you figure out where you're going and how much it will cost. Sometimes, though, it's faster and easier to ask someone nearby for assistance; Washingtonians are used to helping each other and out-of-towners navigate the Metro system, though morning rush hour is probably not the best time to approach them.

By Taxi: You'll find taxis lined up at Union Station and in front of major downtown hotels. In most parts of town, it's pretty easy to hail a taxi. If you telephone for a taxi, or have a restaurant or club telephone for one, you'll pay an extra $2 for the service, but the fee is well worth it if it's late and cabs are scarce. District taxis operate on the zone system, rather than using meters, and the base fare for one zone is $6.50. Additional charges may apply, for instance, for rush hour pickup, extra passengers, and so on.

- Capitol Cab 202-545-8900
- Diamond Cab 202-387-4011
- Yellow Cab 202-546-7900
- Yes Auto Cab 202-526-1152

By Bus: Although WMATA provides extensive bus transportation in addition to subway service, its bus system is currently overloaded, underfunded, and inefficient, so not recommended for out-of-town visitors. Two supplemental shuttle buses are of note, however: the Georgetown Metro Connection (georgetowndc.com/shuttle.php) and the D.C. Circulator (202-962-1423, dccirculator.com). The blue Georgetown Metro Connection buses fill the gap left by Metro, whose trains do not stop in Georgetown. The shuttles travel between three Metro stations, Rosslyn, Foggy Bottom, and Dupont Circle, and Georgetown, making stops throughout Georgetown and at each station every ten minutes 7am to midnight Mon-Thu, 7am-2am Friday, 8am-2am Saturday, and 8am-midnight Sunday. The one-way fare is $1.

The red and gray D.C. Circulator buses travel three routes: the gold route, which runs east and west between Georgetown and Union Station; the purple route, which loops continuously around the National Mall; and the red route, which runs north and south between the Southwest waterfront and the convention center. The red and gold routes operate daily 7am-9pm and the purple route runs 9:30am-6pm daily; all buses charge $1 for a one-way fare and stop at major sites along their routes.

Other Practical Information

Money Matters (Currency, Taxes, Tipping, and Service Charges): It's dollars ($) and cents (100 to the dollar). For currency conversion rates, go to xe.com/ucc. The United States does not apply a national sales (value-added) tax. However, the District applies a sales tax of 5.75% to purchased items, hotels add a 14.5% tax to their room rates, and restaurants and bars add a 10% charge to your food and beverage bills.

Numbers to Know (Hotlines)

Emergency, police, fire department, ambulance, and paramedics	911
Poison Control	800-222-1222
24-Hour Rape Crisis Line	202-333-7273
24-Hour Mental Health Crisis Hotline	202-561-7000

Along the highways, you'll find call boxes for emergency use.

Travelers Aid International	202-546-1127

24-Hour emergency rooms:

- George Washington University Hospital 202-715-4000
  900 23rd St. NW at Washington Circle

- Georgetown University Medical Center 202-687-0100
  4000 Reservoir Rd. NW

24-Hour CVS pharmacies:

- West End CVS 202-296-9877
  2240 M St. NW

- Dupont Circle CVS 202-785-1466
  6 Dupont Circle NW

Expect to tip taxi drivers and restaurant servers 15 to 20% and hotel housekeepers $3 or more per day.

Safety: D.C. can likely claim more policing organizations than any other city in the country: There's the local Metropolitan Police Department, National Park Service's U.S. Park Police and protection rangers, U.S. Capitol Police, U.S. Secret Service, and Metro's Transit Authority police, to name a few. Police and security officers are all over the place, guarding their individual jurisdictions, from the Lincoln Memorial to the subway, sometimes with security cameras and dogs. Crime still happens, though. In that respect, D.C.'s a city like any other. But the areas you're likely to travel are fairly safe, especially during the day. At night, keep your wits about you and walk on well-lit streets, preferably with others. Night and day, try not to draw attention to yourself as an out-of-towner (lose the conference ID badge, don't stand in the middle of a crowded sidewalk consulting your map).

Security: Safety is one thing, security another, and it may be security matters—the inconvenience of them, that is—that most concern you in the nation's capital. Since September 11, the city's federal or local agencies have installed protective barriers at places like the Washington Monument, restricted tours at the White House, and implemented clearance procedures in many government office buildings, national museums, and public spaces. The Capitol, Library of Congress, Smithsonian museums, and others require you to walk past metal detectors and allow staff to search your handbags, backpacks, and briefcases for prohibited items. In peak seasons, these searches translate into long lines for admission. So travel lightly for sightseeing and be prepared for a wait.

Gay and Lesbian Travel: Washington's gay and lesbian community has a long history and famous members, from poet Walt Whitman, who lived here during the Civil War, to Massachusetts Congressman Barney Frank. (Some in the community would have you believe that the city's planner, Pierre Charles L'Enfant, one-time FBI director J. Edgar Hoover, and perhaps even a president or two were gay.) Important gay rights milestone events have taken place here—D.C. was the site of America's first gay civil rights march, in 1965 in front of the White House, for example. At least three dozen national organizations dedicated to gay, lesbian, and transgender rights have their headquarters in D.C., including the country's oldest continuously active gay organization, the Washington Gay and Lesbian Activists Alliance, founded in 1971, which, coincidentally, is the same year the country's oldest continuously operating lesbian bar opened: Phase One, right here, on Eighth St. SE.

Dupont Circle is ground zero for the gay and lesbian community, home to bars like Cobalt and J.R.'s Bar and Grill, and bookstores like Lambda Rising. When the weather warms, kindred spirits sunbathe or toss Frisbees on "P Street Beach," a strip of Rock Creek Park where P and 23rd Streets come together. Dupont Circle is also the location for the annual Gay Pride Parade and other celebrations. For more information, pick up a copy of the weekly *Washington Blade,* distributed free at bookstores and other stores throughout the District, or visit the Washington Convention and Tourism Corporation's website, washington.org, and click on "Pride in D.C."

Traveling with Disabilities: Washington, D.C., is one of the most accessible cities in the world, but still offers challenges, especially when it comes to its many historic structures. Contact the Washington Convention & Tourism Corporation for more information, 202-789-7000. Also check out disabilityguide.org, or order a copy of its Washington, D.C., access guide, available by calling 301-528-8664.

CITY ESSENTIALS

Print Media: If you're flying into either Ronald Reagan Washington National Airport or Washington Dulles International Airport, pick up a copy of *Washington Flyer*, a free magazine published by the airport authority and a surprisingly interesting and up-to-the-minute observer of the Washington scene. The magazine is only available at the airport, so that's your only chance; you'll see stacks of them around the airports.

Radio Stations (a selection)

FM Stations

88.5	WAMU	NPR
89.3	WPFW	News, Jazzy Blues
90.1	WCSP	C-SPAN
90.9	WETA	NPR, BBC
96.3	WHUR	Modern R&B
97.1	WASH	Soft Rock
98.7	WMZQ	Country
101.1	WWDC	Alternative Rock
103.5	WTOP	Washington, News
104.1	WGMS	Classical
107.3	WRQX	Adult Contemporary

AM Stations

1670	National Park Service coverage of the National Mall

The *Washington Post*, washingtonpost.com, is the city's main newspaper, an invaluable source daily, but especially on Friday, when its *Weekend* section appears, full of nightlife and cultural activities listings. *Washington's City Paper* is a better and more comprehensive source for alternative entertainment, taking an irreverent tone and wider look at club happenings in particular.

A new flock of glossy lifestyle magazines recently debuted with great fanfare, with names like *D.C.*, *D.C. Style*, and *Capitol File*. Good enough for thumbing through, the magazines simply can't compete with the mother of them all, *Washingtonian*, the monthly locals love to critique, but read anyway for its restaurant reviews, inside scoops, and personality profiles.

Shopping Hours: Most stores are open weekdays from 10am to 5pm or 6pm, with some extending their hours on Thursdays until 9pm. Saturday hours are generally 10am to 9pm or 10pm, and on Sunday most stores are closed. Exceptions include Union Station stores, which are open Monday through Saturday 10am to 9pm and Sunday noon to 6pm; and Georgetown stores, which tend to stay open Monday through Saturday 10am to 9pm or 10pm and noon to 6pm or later on Sunday.

Attire: Washingtonians get a lot of flak for being fashion-oblivious. Some folks deserve it, like the ones who interpret the casual dress code at restaurants to mean "no style at all." Professional men and women tend to adhere to a conservative look: dark business suits and ties for men, dark suits and red outfits, for some reason, for women. The idea

HIT THE GROUND

Size Conversion

Dress Sizes

US	6	8	10	12	14	16
UK	8	10	12	14	16	18
France	36	38	40	42	44	46
Italy	38	40	42	44	46	48
Europe	34	36	38	40	42	44

Women's Shoes

US	6	6½	7	7½	8	8½
UK	4½	5	5½	6	6½	7
Europe	38	38	39	39	40	41

Men's Suits

US	36	38	40	42	44	46
UK	36	38	40	42	44	46
Europe	46	48	50	52	54	56

Men's Shirts

US	14½	15	15½	16	16½	17
UK	14½	15	15½	16	16½	17
Europe	38	39	40	41	42	43

Men's Shoes

US	8	8½	9½	10½	11½	12
UK	7	7½	8½	9½	10½	11
Europe	41	42	43	44	45	46

is that one wants to be taken seriously. Very seriously. Don't be fooled, though. Fashionistas do exist in the capital and they're the ones getting all the attention, disapproving (or envious?) though it may be.

For those who don't live here, anything goes, really. Both men and women might wear something black and sexy at night or low-rise jeans during the day, or vice versa. Dress for the season, remembering sunglasses and sunscreen in summer, heavy jackets, gloves, and scarves in winter, and comfortable shoes all year round. Pack an umbrella, especially in autumn, the rainiest season.

When Drinking Is Legal: The legal drinking age is 21, and District police take this seriously. Always carry your ID. Washington, D.C., restaurants, bars, and nightclubs are licensed to serve liquor until 2am Sunday through Thursday and until 3am Friday and Saturday.

Smoking: The D.C. City Council voted in January 2006 to expand its smoking ban in restaurants and public buildings to include bars, so by 2007 all establishments in the District will be smoke-free. Smoking outdoors is permitted, unless otherwise noted.

CITY ESSENTIALS

Drugs: Learn from the unfortunate experience of D.C.'s former mayor, Marion Barry, who in 1990 was caught smoking crack—while he was still in office—and did major jail time, and who in January 2006, sad to say, tested positive once again for cocaine, despite his rehabilitation and current position as a D.C. city councilman: The District makes no exceptions for drug users. Illegal drugs are illegal, period.

Time Zone: Washington, D.C., falls within the Eastern time zone (EST). A note on daylight savings time: clocks are set ahead one hour at 2am on the first Sunday in April and back one hour at 2am on the last Sunday in October.

Additional Resources for Visitors

Washington, D.C., Convention and Tourism Corporation Call ahead to order free brochures, maps, and tour information. Check online for visitor information, including descriptions of Washington's more than 100 hotels. The WCTC operates a hotel reservation service (800-422-8644) and frequently sponsors packages. The WCTC is more a call-in, online, and mail resource than a walk-in visitors center. 901 Seventh St. NW, 4th floor, 202-789-7000, washington.org

D.C.'s walk-in visitors centers include: the **White House Visitor Center** *daily 7:30am-4pm.* 1450 Pennsylvania Ave. NW, the **Smithsonian Information Center** *daily 8:30am-5:30pm.* 1000 Jefferson Dr. SW, and **National Park Service kiosks**, located at different sites on the National Mall.

Foreign Visitors

Foreign Embassies in the U.S.: Every country with whom the U.S. government maintains diplomatic relations has an embassy in Washington, D.C. Embassy.org/embassies lists all addresses and phone numbers.
Passport requirements: travel.state.gov
Cell phones: North America operates on the 1,900MHz frequency. For cell phone rentals and purchases, go to telestial.com/instructions.htm. Note: It is illegal in Washington, D.C., to use a cell phone while driving.
Toll-free numbers in the U.S.: 800, 866, 877, and 888.
Telephone directory assistance in the U.S.: 411
Electrical: U.S. standard is AC, 110 volts/60 cycles, with a plug of two flat pins set parallel to one another.

The Latest-Info Websites

Go to washington.org, dc.gov, washingtonpost.com, dcist.com, ontaponline.com, fly2dc.com.
And, of course, **pulseguides.com**.

Party Conversation—A Few Surprising Facts

- The man whose fortune established the Smithsonian Institution, James Smithson (1765–1829), was a wealthy British scientist who never actually visited the United States—alive, that is. His bones arrived in 1904 and are buried in a crypt in the Smithsonian Castle.

- Think scandal is new to the nation's capital? Think again. From Thomas Jefferson's dalliance with his slave, Sally Hemings; to Warren Harding's corrupt administration in which cabinet members accepted bribes to help private developers obtain federal oil reserve lands; to the audacious shenanigans of numerous members of Congress (like John Jenrette, Democratic congressman from South Carolina, arrested in 1979 on corruption charges but better known for having sex on the Capitol steps with his wife, Rita); to Richard Nixon (Watergate) and Bill Clinton (Monica Lewinsky), it seems that the powerful are especially prone to temptation.

- D.C. has earned the moniker "Hollywood on the Potomac" for the hundreds of movies shot here, including *Mr. Smith Goes to Washington*, *Strangers on a Train*, *All the President's Men*, and *The Exorcist*, as well as, more recently, *Syriana*, *Wedding Crashers*, *National Treasure*, and *Minority Report*.

- D.C.'s most famous native son in the arts is jazz great Duke Ellington, who lived and performed along U Street, "Black Broadway," as it was called in the 1920s, '30s, and '40s.

- Some presidents have commented on their time in the White House. Choice quotes include these: "I am not fit for this office and should never have been here" (Warren Harding). "No president has ever enjoyed himself as much as I" (Theodore Roosevelt). "The four most miserable years of my life" (John Quincy Adams). "If you want a friend in Washington, get a dog" (Harry Truman).

- According to *Men's Fitness Magazine,* Washington, D.C., ranks 23 out of 25 in the magazine's listing of the top fittest cities.

- D.C.'s unique status as a city without a state means that residents pay federal taxes, but are not represented in Congress. Washingtonians have one delegate to the House of Representatives, who can introduce legislation and vote in committees—but not vote on the House floor.

The Cheat Sheet
(The Very Least You Ought to Know About D.C.)

Contained herein is a little encyclopedia of D.C. information that should send you in interesting directions, or anyway, keep you from getting lost.

Neighborhoods

Adams Morgan, to many Washingtonians, is synonymous with "nighttime playground of bars, clubs, and ethnic restaurants." It's also a residential community, where people from El Salvador, Guatemala, Honduras, Nigeria, Pakistan, and assorted other countries live in the old townhouses and apartment buildings that lie beyond the main streets of Columbia Road and 18th Street.

Capitol Hill, without the Capitol and its office buildings, the Library of Congress and the Supreme Court, would be a quaint little Dickens-esque district of narrow streets, 19th-century dwellings, and one-of-a-kind shops. The place bustles when Congress is in session and subsides when Congress is out.

Downtown refers to three different areas: K Street (also known as "Lawyers' Row") and other streets close to the White House; the section marked by 15th Street NW and Pennsylvania Avenue NW that lies closest to the National Mall; and Penn Quarter (see below), which is the area surrounding the Verizon Center, Massachusetts to Pennsylvania Avenues. New and old hotels, great restaurants, theaters, bars, and clubs proliferate, especially the closer to the Verizon Center you go.

Dupont Circle has a cosmopolitan air about it, due to the presence of foreign embassies, as well as the interesting mix of young, old, and unconventional Washingtonians who come here. Connecticut Avenue anchors the area, which is home to grand early 20th-century mansions, lots of art galleries and restaurants, bookstores and small shops, and a large gay and lesbian community.

Foggy Bottom/West End lies at the western edge of downtown, approaching Georgetown. George Washington University and the GWU Hospital buildings sprawl across these city blocks, which also include several hotels and restaurants and the Kennedy Center for the Performing Arts.

Georgetown has several faces: the developing waterfront for singles hangouts and boating sports, the Wisconsin Avenue/M Street shopping and dining mecca, and the private, historic, centuries-old streets, some of them cobblestone, that extend behind the "public face" of the town. Many of Washington's rich and famous live here; all of Washington, rowdy, chic, and preppy, shops here.

National Mall/Southwest is the location of the memorials and the Washington Monument, most of the Smithsonian museums, and the National Gallery of Art. Southwest of the Mall is mostly a residential area for low-income Washingtonians, but also boasts the most luxurious hotel in D.C., the Mandarin Oriental; developers hope to expand in that direction, adding further embellishments to the few that exist: Arena Stage, some nightclubs, tour boats, and the waterfront fish market.

Penn Quarter is the hottest part of town, adding something new—a hotel, restaurant, club, shop, movie theater, bar, even a bowling alley—every time you turn around. The Verizon Center (until recently called the MCI Center) is at the epicenter, figuratively and literally, of all this activity: its opening in 1997 as a sports and concert venue gave people a reason to stay and play downtown after work, and sparked vibrant development.

U Street Corridor is the hippest part of town, for anyone who likes funky shops, alternative music clubs, ethnic cafes, jazz joints, and staying up late. This deep-rooted African-American community was once the stomping grounds for Duke Ellington, Jelly Roll Morton, and other jazz greats; today, clubs like Twins continue the jazz tradition, while the decades-old Ben's Chili Bowl remains a favorite juke joint.

Upper Northwest is the collective name for residential neighborhoods in the upper reaches of the northwest quadrant, beyond downtown: Woodley Park, Tenleytown, Cleveland Park, and Friendship Heights are some of their names. This is where the affluent, mostly families, live, and where some attractions lie, including two huge hotels, the National Zoo, several excellent restaurants, the Washington National Cathedral, and the highest-end stores, like Neiman-Marcus, Tiffany's, and Barney's.

9 Theaters

Arena Stage Located in a less-traveled part of town, Arena Stage puts on eight productions annually, usually innovative takes on plays by American masters like Tennessee Williams and world premieres of up-and-coming artists. 1101 Sixth St. SW, 202-488-3300, arenastage.org

Folger Theatre Ensconced in the bosom of the Folger Shakespeare Library on Capitol Hill, this small theater is an indoors Elizabethan replica, whose productions are rather more accessible and every bit as entertaining (the comedies are especially hilarious and fun) as its famous sister's on Seventh St. 201 E. Capitol St. SE, 202-544-7077, folger.edu

Ford's Theatre Abraham Lincoln was fatally shot here, April 14, 1865, as he sat and watched a production of *Our American Cousin*. Dark for more than 100 years, the theater reopened in 1968. Today, the place is a tourist site run by the National Park Service, whose nighttime performances are often patriotic musicals or holiday shows. 511 10th St. NW, 202-426-6925, fordstheatre.org

Kennedy Center for the Performing Arts In fact, this magnificent center holds six theaters, two stage opera, concerts for all genres, dance performances, dramas, musicals, and children's programs. Wonderful views of the Potomac River and the city, as well as spectacular gifts from countries around the world that adorn the center (the enormous Hadelands crystal chandeliers in the concert hall are from Norway) make the center worth a stop, whether or not you're here for a show. 2700 F St. NW, 202-467-4600, kennedy-center.org

Lansburgh Theatre for the Shakespeare Theatre Company This world-renowned theater in the heart of the Penn Quarter draws a full house of serious Bard lovers, locals and visitors, for every production. The season always includes one or two non-Shakespeare productions, such as Molière's *Don Juan*. In 2007, the Shakespeare Theatre Company is opening a second stage, the Sidney Harman Hall, at 650 F St. NW, right around the corner from the Lansburgh; together the two theaters will produce seven plays a season. 450 Seventh St. NW, 202-547-1122, shakespearetheatre.org

National Theatre In existence since 1835, the National is the third-oldest theater in the country. These days the theater is a showcase for musicals, mostly, which Washingtonians can't get enough of. The theater is near the White House and the Willard Hotel. 1321 Pennsylvania Ave. NW, 202-783-3372, nationaltheatre.org

Studio Theatre This is D.C.'s main showcase for contemporary plays and performance art. Started in 1978, when it shared space with a dance studio, the Studio now occupies several buildings on trendy 14th Street, and continues to grow as it tries to accommodate its audience. 1501 14th St. NW, 202-332-3300, studiotheatre.org

Warner Theatre An eclectic mix of golden-oldie performers, comedians, ballets, and musicals rounds out the schedule at the Warner, once a place for vaudeville acts. Thanks to a renovation, the theater's interior looks much the same as it did in 1924, when it was built. 513 13th St. NW, 202-783-4000, warnertheatre.com

Woolly Mammoth Theatre Company This theater's tag line invites you to "Defy convention" by attending one of its plays, which range from world premieres of works by local playwrights to offbeat plays by famous artists. The *New York Times* has called the company "Washington's most daring." 641 D St. NW, 202-393-3939, woollymammoth.net

Great Parks and Gardens

C&O Canal Historical Park Behind the buildings fronting M Street in Georgetown is the picturesque C&O Canal and the towpath that parallels it, all the way to Cumberland, Maryland, 184.5 miles away. It's a popular place for couples and families to stroll (though not recommended after dark); the further away you get from Georgetown, the more serious the hiking and hikers. Bike and boat rentals and picnic spots are available along the way. Path access from Thomas Jefferson St., NW, just below M St., in Georgetown.

Constitution Gardens Originally these 50 acres lay beneath the Potomac River. Today serpentine paths wind through groves of trees and informal gardens on grounds that stretch between the Washington Monument and the Lincoln Memorial. A highlight is Signers Memorial: a footbridge crosses a lake to a little island and a semicircle of red marble blocks, each of which bears a signature replica of the 56 signers of the Declaration of Independence. West Potomac Park, northeast of the Lincoln Memorial.

Enid A. Haupt Garden This 4.5-acre garden offers shade and a place to sit for weary Smithsonian museumgoers. Weeping cherry trees, English boxwoods, and 19th-century cast-iron benches are some of its features. At 10th St. and Independence Ave. SW.

Potomac Park The grounds on which the memorials and the Washington Monument lie comprise a 720-acre park, or rather two parks: West Potomac Park, home to all of the memorials and the Washington Monument; and East Potomac Park, more of a green expanse, with its southern tip, known as Hains Point, offering a golf course, tennis courts, and a swimming pool. Cherry blossom trees proliferate in both parks, and so do hiking and biking paths and picnicking options. At the western edge of the National Mall, bordering the Potomac River.

Rock Creek Park Like New York City's Central Park, Rock Creek is an integral part of D.C.'s urban landscape. Washingtonians use the park daily to commute, whether by bike or on foot along the pedestrian path, or by car along the roadway, but also to enjoy the natural beauty of these wooded and flowering 2,000 acres. From the Potomac River near the Kennedy Center, northwest through the city into Maryland.

Theodore Roosevelt Island This tiny, one-half-mile long by one-fourth-mile wide, 91-acre wilderness preserve sits in the middle of the Potomac River, a pleasant paddle away from Georgetown. A trail leads back to the 17-foot-high bronze statue of Teddy, flanked by tablets inscribed with Roosevelt's quotes. Accessible by boat, by pedestrian bridge from Rosslyn, or by car, from the northbound lane of the George Washington Memorial Parkway.

U.S. Botanic Garden This immense conservatory looks out of place on the National Mall, but is a favorite spot for a different sort of Washington experience. Four thousand species of some 26,000 plants are on display. At the foot of Capitol Hill on the National Mall.

Washington National Cathedral Gardens The Bishop's Garden, Herb Garden, and other plots replicate Cloisters gardens from the Middle Ages; couples like to wander here, but then so do children who enjoy a good game of hide-and-seek. On Mount St. Alban, north of Georgetown.

CHEAT SHEET

Major Traffic Circles

In fact, Washington, D.C., has as many as 28 traffic circles, most crowned with a compelling statue of some historic personage. Designed to aid the flow of traffic as well as impede the path of enemies, the circles are central points of convergence for multiple streets. The following seven are the circles people most encounter or, dare we say, run into as they make their way around the city.

Columbus Circle A 15-foot-high statue of Christopher Columbus, stationed at the forefront of this circle, faces the U.S. Capitol. The statue is the preeminent feature of a large memorial fountain and plaza fronting Union Station. Drivers enter Columbus Circle only if headed to Union Station, or accidentally, having gotten into the wrong lane. In northeast D.C., at E St., Massachusetts, Louisiana, and Delaware Aves., and East First St.

Dupont Circle Like its neighborhood, Dupont Circle is a lively place, where people play chess and music, protest, or just chill on the benches or lawn. Its central memorial fountain honors Rear Admiral Francis Dupont (the Union's first naval hero in the Civil War). In northwest D.C., at Massachusetts, Connecticut, and New Hampshire Aves., and 19th St.

Logan Circle Logan Circle is also the name for this historic district, filled with four-story 19th-century townhouses. That bronze equestrian statue portrays Major General John A. Logan, a Civil War army commander. In northwest D.C., at Vermont and Rhode Island Aves., and 13th St.

Scott Circle War of 1812 hero Winfield Scott sits astride his horse, which sits in the middle of the green circle, which, in turn, sits overtop a tunnel allowing drivers a north-south alternative to circle navigation. East- and westbound traffic must do its best to get from one side of the circle to the other. In northwest D.C., at Rhode Island and Massachusetts Aves., and 16th St.

Sheridan Circle Said to be one of the finest examples of equestrian sculpture, the bronze statue centering this circle depicts Philip Sheridan, a Civil War Union cavalry commander, waving his hat to rally his troops, as he sits astride his horse, Rienzi, who appears in mid-gallop. On Embassy Row in northwest D.C., at Massachusetts Ave. and 23rd and R Sts.

Thomas Circle Most drivers never notice the fine statue of Civil War general George Henry Thomas gracing the center of this green. They are too busy trying to survive this whirlpool of a circle, which seems to suck in cars and spit them out in directions drivers can only hope are correct. An east- and westbound tunnel under the circle helps somewhat. A transportation project under way in 2006 may further improve the situation. In northwest D.C., at 14th and M Sts., Vermont and Massachusetts Aves.

Washington Circle The neighborhood of Foggy Bottom is home to this circle, whose chief adornment is a calm-faced Lt. General George Washington riding a frightened-looking horse, as the two are about to mount an attack during the Revolutionary War. In northwest D.C., at Pennsylvania and New Hampshire Aves., 23rd and K Sts.

6 Sports Teams

D.C. United The "Black and Red" may sound like an exotic cocktail to you, but in D.C. it refers to the city's soccer team, one of whose star players, Freddy Adu, made history when he joined the team at age 15 (he's now 17). The young team's increasing popularity means a new soccer stadium is in the works; for now, D.C. United plays at RFK Stadium. dcunited.com

Washington Capitals Regular season for D.C.'s ice hockey team runs January through April, but ice hockey lovers can catch games in September and October, too. The Caps play at the Verizon Center, where you'll always find a seat, since hockey has less of a following here than football and basketball. washingtoncaps.com

Washington Mystics If you're not familiar with the Mystics, that's too bad, since the women's basketball team often provides an exhilarating game experience. Check them out at the Verizon Center, during their May through August season. washingtonmystics.com

Washington Nationals Yes, as of 2005, Washington does have a baseball team. Again. This is the capital's second go-round with baseball; the first team, the Washington Senators, played its last game in 1971. The Nationals play to sell-out crowds at RFK Stadium until a new one is built. nationals.com

Washington Redskins Obsession with Washington's football team crosses race, nationality, religion, gender, income, and age divisions in this town of diehard fans. Store clerks, bus drivers, lobbyists, and school teachers wear red and gold throughout the season. The Redskins play at FedEx Field, in Landover, Maryland, just outside Washington. redskins.com

Washington Wizards With players like Antawn Jamison and Gilbert Arenas, D.C.'s men's basketball team pursues a high standing in the Eastern Conference. Tickets to Wizards' games at the Verizon Center tend to be pricey, but that's no problem for sports fanatics. washingtonwizards.com

5 Subway Lines

Blue Line Runs between Largo Town Center, east of the capital, in Maryland, and Franconia-Springfield, southwest of the capital in Virginia. Major stops include Smithsonian, Ronald Reagan Washington National Airport, and Metro Center.

Green Line Runs between Greenbelt, northeast of the capital, in Maryland, and Branch Avenue, in southeast D.C. Major stops include U Street/Cardozo, Mount Vernon Square/Convention Center, and Gallery Place.

Orange Line Runs between New Carrolton, northeast of the capital, in Maryland, and Vienna, west of the capital, in Virginia. Major stops include L'Enfant Plaza, Metro Center, and Foggy Bottom.

Red Line Runs between Shady Grove, northwest of the capital, in Maryland, and Glenmont, north of the capital, in Maryland. Major stops include Adams Morgan, Dupont Circle, Metro Center, and Union Station.

Yellow Line Runs between Mount Vernon Square/Convention Center, in the center of the city, and Huntington Station, south of the city, in Virginia. Major stops include Mount Vernon Square/Convention Center, Gallery Place, and L'Enfant Plaza.

Concert Venues

DAR Constitution Hall Its schedule is a little erratic, but worth checking out, since the historic, turn-of-the-20th-century hall is just the right size, at 3,746 seats, and offers fine acoustics that make for a truly excellent experience of a Bonnie Raitt, Strokes, Jagged Edge, or U.S. Air Force Band performance. 1776 D St. NW, 202-628-4780, dar.org

Kennedy Center for the Performing Arts This is the place for high-toned jazz, classical, blues, choral, and chamber concerts, performed in the center's ornate Concert Hall or in another of its theaters. The center's Millennium Stage in the Grand Foyer is the setting for free nightly concerts at 6pm, each presenting a different genre of music, including country and rock, by different kinds of artists. 2700 F St. NW, 202-467-4600, kennedy-center.org

9:30 Nightclub A full roster of performers keeps the mostly indie-rock 9:30 Club open nearly every night. Popular bands sell out in advance, but lesser-known acts may allow walk-up admission. Four bars, two levels, and minimal seating make this a club, not a hall. Yellowcard, Flogging Molly, and the Pogues are some of the names on tap. 815 V St. NW, 202-393-0930, 930.com

Verizon Center Headliner musicians and bands, from the Rolling Stones to Coldplay, take the stage in this 20,600-seat arena, which also serves as the city's main sports venue. 601 F St. NW, 202-628-3200, verizoncenter.com

3 Skyscrapers

Well, not quite. But Congress passed a building height restriction for the capital in 1910, ensuring the prominence of key buildings in the D.C. skyline.

U.S. Capitol "A pedestal waiting for a monument" is how Pierre Charles L'Enfant famously described Jenkins Hill, known today as Capitol Hill for the building that crowns it. The hill itself stands on a plateau 88 feet above sea level; from its base on the east front to the top of the Statue of Freedom, the Capitol measures 288 feet tall. East Capitol St. at First St. NW, 202-225-6827, aoc.gov

Washington Monument Standing 1.4 miles from the Capitol, the Washington Monument is the taller of the two buildings: situated on a hill 30 feet above sea level, the obelisk rises another 555 feet into the air, making it one of the world's tallest freestanding works of masonry. 15th St. NW, 202-426-6841, nps.gov/wash

Washington National Cathedral Higher still than the Capitol and the Washington Monument is the National Cathedral, which is located on Mount St. Albans, at 676 feet above sea level. At its highest point, the tip of the Gloria in Excelsis bell tower, the cathedral reaches a height of 301 feet, or 701 feet above the city. Massachusetts and Wisconsin Aves. NW, 202-537-6200, nationalcathedral.org

2 Rivers

Anacostia River This river starts in Maryland and crosses into the District, where it separates a poorer part of town from the rest of the capital. The eight-mile-long river flows southward until it meets the Potomac River at Hains Point.

Potomac River The Potomac travels 380 miles and measures 11 miles at its widest point. In Washington, the river forms the natural boundary between D.C. and Virginia, as it flows past the memorials, the Kennedy Center, and Georgetown.

1 Singular Sensation

The White House It's Washington's oldest federal building and both the city's and country's enduring symbol, no matter which president presides.

Coffee (quick stops for a java jolt)

Baked and Wired A combo coffeehouse and graphic design firm, this quirky Georgetown cafe specializes in like-Mom-makes-'em pies, cookies, and cakes. 1052 Thomas Jefferson St. NW (M St.), 202-333-2500

Busboys and Poets Artists and activists say they come for the spoken word and documentary screenings, but the real draw is the peanut butter, banana, and challah sandwiches. (p.102) 2021 14th St. NW (U St.), 202-387-7638

Dos Gringos A cheery rainbow palette mirrors the diverse neighborhood crowd at this friendly townhouse cafe, which serves up excellent vegetarian and vegan fare. 3116 Mt. Pleasant St. NW (Irving St.), 202-462-1159

Java House Come for the scenery—sunny sidewalk views of the bustling Dupont neighborhood—and stay for the coffee. The beans are roasted on the premises everyday and served in 60 different blends. 1645 Q St. NW (16th St.), 202-387-6622

Love Café Cupcakes, pound cakes, tarts, and éclairs: At this coffee shop, it's all about the decadent desserts. (p.96) 1501 U St. NW (15th St.), 202-265-9800

Murky The perfect place to fuel up before shopping at Eastern Market, Murky serves a smooth Northern-Italian style brew. 660 Pennsylvania Ave. SE (7th St.), 202-546-5228

Politics and Prose Off the beaten path in Northwest D.C., the District's most enduring independent bookstore and cafe draws high-powered intellectuals with its book readings, lectures, and community forums. 5015 Connecticut Ave. NW (Fessenden St.), 202-364-1919

Sparky's Espresso Café Cozy 14th Street hangout where the black-coffee crowd plays board games and recounts last night's shows. 1720 14th St. NW (R St.), 202-332-9334

Tryst D.C.'s second living room; perfect for everything from morning-after brunches to Wi-Fi work sessions to late-night coffee cocktails. (p.107) 2459 18th St. NW (Columbia Rd.), 202-232-5500

Just for Business and Conventions

The latest statistics show that approximately one-third of visitors to D.C. are here on business. Washington awaits them with open arms. In 2004, a new convention center opened, its 2.4 million square feet making it the city's largest building. The convention center is located in the heart of downtown, within walking distance of the Penn Quarter neighborhood and its many chic restaurants and attractions. Wherever your business takes you, the capital can well accommodate you.

Addresses to Know

Convention Centers

- Washington Convention Center
  801 Mount Vernon Pl. NW (Seventh St.), Downtown
  202-249-3000, dcconvention.com

City Information

- Washington, D.C., Convention and Tourism Corporation
  901 Seventh St. NW (I St.), 4th Floor
  202-789-7000, washington.org

- Official Washington, D.C., website, dc.gov.

Business and Convention Hotels

A number of the hotels that we recommend in our Washington, D.C., Black Book (see p.201) cater to business travelers and are near the convention center and downtown offices. Some additional choices include:

Capital Hilton Two blocks from the White House, this one's a favorite old shoe. 1001 16th St. NW (K St.), 202-393-1000 / 800-445-8667

Embassy Suites Washington Convention Center 1.5 miles from the convention center. 900 10th St. NW (K St.), 202-739-2001 / 800-362-2779

Four Points Sheraton Washington, D.C. Central downtown location convenient to convention center and K St. 1201 K St. NW (12th St.), 202-289-7600 / 800-368-7764

Grand Hyatt Washington Walking distance to convention center and downtown. 1000 H St. NW (10th St.), 202-582-1234 / 888-591-1234

Hampton Inn Convention Center Offers city views from top rooms. 901 Sixth St. NW (Massachusetts Ave.), 202-842-2500 / 800-426-7866

Renaissance Washington, D.C. Halfway between the White House and the Capitol, across from the convention center. 999 Ninth St. NW (K St.), 202-898-9000 / 800-408-3571

Business Entertaining

Escape from the conference room to do a little business over lunch or dinner at any of these polished establishments.

Acadiana Lively atmosphere, the real-deal New Orleans fare. (p.60) 901 New York Ave. NW (10th St.), 202-408-8848

The Caucus Room* Business, clientele, meat specialties: all big deals. (p.125) 401 Ninth St. NW (D St.), 202-393-1300

Corduroy Four Points Sheraton Hotel For quiet conversation and exceptional modern American cuisine. 1201 K St. NW (12th St.), 202-589-0699

Finn & Porter Sushi, seafood, and steaks in a soaring space. Embassy Suites Washington Convention Center, 900 10th St. NW (K St.), 202-719-1600

Fogo de Chão Carnivore's delight, Brazilian-style, in a glamorous setting. 1101 Pennsylvania Ave. NW (12th St.), 202-347-4668

Tosca Elegant dining room, exquisite, sophisticated Italian food. (p.67) 1112 F St. NW (12th St.), 202-367-1990

Also see: **Best Fine Dining** (p.23)
                  Best Only-in-D.C. Restaurants (p.34)
                  Best Power Lunch Spots (p.39)

Ducking Out for a Half-Day

Chances are, your business is taking place within view or a short walk of a fascinating Washington attraction, so head out the door and see what's up.

International Spy Museum Good for an entertaining hour or two away from the conference table. (p.78) 800 F St. NW (Eighth St.), 202-393-7798

National Mall Walk the Mall just to gaze at the sights, or if time allows, to visit the Capitol, the Washington Monument, and the numerous memorials. Fourth to 15th Sts., NW

Phillips Collection This gem is known for its Impressionist and modern art collections. (p.79) 1600 21st St. NW (Q St.), 202-387-2151

Also see: **Best Insider D.C. Experiences** (p.28)
                  Best Luxury Spas (p.32)

Gifts to Bring Home

Washington is full of shops that sell excellent mementos of the city.

International Spy Museum Gift Shop This shop is full of unusual souvenirs, from invisible ink to KGB flasks. (p.78) 800 F St. NW, 202-654-0950

Smithsonian Museum Giftshops Nearly every Smithsonian has creative, often unique-to-Washington gifts. National Mall

Union Station This shopping mall sells Americana, travel paraphernalia, political memorabilia, and more. (p.141) 50 Massachusetts Ave. NE, 202-371-9441

D.C. REGION

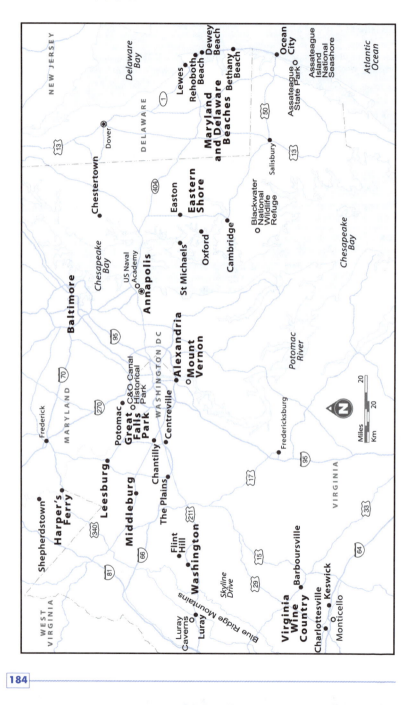

LEAVING D.C.

If you want a break from the D.C. scene, a number of excursions are yours for the choosing—from raucous weekend beach scenes to charming and relaxing wine country outings, from small-town diversions to historic landmarks. To experience where the locals go to unwind, choose from any of the destinations that follow.

Baltimore, Maryland

40 miles N

Hot Tip: Baltimore's traffic is nearly as bad as D.C.'s, so consider taking a commuter MARC train from Union Station, which has a stop at Camden Yards in downtown Baltimore, not far from the Inner Harbor and its attractions.

The Lowdown: Washingtonians are generally loath to admit that Baltimore has anything special. The Baltimore Orioles, they'd grant you that, and until recently, legions of Washingtonians regularly trekked to Camden Yards in baseball season to support the O's. Now that D.C. has its own baseball team, the Nationals, fewer fans make that trip. But District residents do visit Baltimore, and if you ask them about it, you discover that Baltimore has its own identity and a strong sense of itself. To be Baltimorean means something: it means a certain nasally "Bawlmer" accent and waitresses calling you "hun," it means constant small-world intersections, where you find out that your mother knows the friend of your co-worker's husband's sister, and that you are all quite possibly related; it means the real home of crab cakes, Babe Ruth, the "Star Spangled Banner," and a history uncomplicated by federal government. So what does take Washingtonians to Baltimore? Secure in the knowledge that their own museums and attractions are world-class, D.C. residents concede that Baltimore's Inner Harbor, Fells Point and Little Italy neighborhoods, National Aquarium, Walters Art Gallery, and Baltimore Museum of Art do have their appeal. (Note: Baltimore could also be done as a day trip.)

Best Attractions

American Visionary Art Museum Displays of folk art and unconventional creations by untrained artists. $ 800 Key Hwy., 410-244-1900, avam.org

Fort McHenry Where the "Star Spangled Banner," our flag of "broad stripes and bright stars," waved during the Battle of Baltimore in 1814, despite "the rockets' red glare, the bombs bursting in air." $- 2400 E. Fort Ave., 410-962-4290, nps.gov/fomc

Neighborhoods: Just east of the Inner Harbor is Little Italy, an enclave of Italian restaurants, churches, and Italian-speaking residents, where bocce ball is the home sport, and church festivals the major social event. Little Italy merges further east into the funky, hip, and historic Fells Point, a waterfront community of cobblestone streets and Baltimore's best bars. Fells Point Visitor Center, 808 S. Ann St., 410-675-6750, fellspoint.us, and Little Italy, littleitalymd.com

The Walters Art Gallery Its collection spanning 55 centuries, the Walters is best known for its antiquities and medieval collections, as well as for its French paintings. 600 N. Charles St., 410-547-9000, thewalters.org

LEAVING D.C. • OVERNIGHT TRIPS

Best Restaurants and Nightlife

Charleston This is the city's best restaurant; its menu features a seven-course tasting menu of slightly Southern-influenced American cuisine. $$$ 100 Lancaster St., 410-332-7373, charlestonrestaurant.com

Joy America Café A harbor-view restaurant in an eclectically artistic setting with an innovative menu. $$ American Visionary Art Museum, 800 Key Hwy., 410-244-6500

Pazo A renovated machine shop is Charm City's hottest restaurant, featuring balconies, an exhibition kitchen, many levels, and a chic crowd sprawled across low couches munching on assorted Spanish and Mediterranean tapas. $$ 1425 Aliceanna St., 410-534-7296, pazorestaurant.com

Sabatino's Southern and central Italian dishes arrive in huge portions at this 50-year-old Little Italy mainstay. $$ 901 Fawn St., Little Italy, 410-727-2667, sabatinos.com

Best Hotels

InterContinental Harbor Court Baltimore Old-fashioned elegance and gracious service combine with all the modern amenities you'd expect and a convenient harbor location. $$ 550 Light St., 410-234-0550 / 800-824-0076, harborcourt.com

Marriott Baltimore Waterfront Hotel This 32-story building sits right on the waterfront, within walking distance of both the trendy Fells Point neighborhood and the Inner Harbor's major attractions. $$ 700 Aliceanna St., 410-385-3000 / 800-228-9290, marriott.com

Renaissance Harborplace Hotel A traditional waterfront hotel with an indoor pool, restaurants, fitness facilities, and more. $$ 202 East Pratt St., 410-547-1200 / 800-535-1201, marriott.com

Contacts

Baltimore Area Convention and Visitors Association 100 Light St., 877-225-8466

Getting There: Weekdays only, you can catch a MARC commuter train from D.C.'s Union Station, which will take you to a Camden Yards station, and from there walk or taxi to specific destinations. If you drive, take the Washington Beltway, I-495, and exit to I-95 toward Baltimore. Travel I-95 into Baltimore, exiting at I-395, headed downtown. Follow the directions to the Inner Harbor, and bear right onto Pratt Street.

The Maryland and Delaware Beaches

120 miles E

Hot Tip: The summer is best, of course, for full fun in the sun, and this is where many Washingtonians head for leisure. But you'll have to time your drive carefully: Traffic-wise, Fridays, from 2pm on, and Saturday mornings are brutal, and Sunday afternoons just as bad for returning.

The Lowdown: The historic coastal towns of Maryland and Delaware are year-round enclaves of mostly modest dwellings and family farms, with lots of antique stores and, come summer, roadside stands selling fresh cantaloupes, tomatoes, and Silver Queen corn, a local variety known for its sweetness. The Maryland-Delaware shoreline is a whole other scene. Dotting the shore is a dessert tray of beaches, each with its own personality. At the northern end, in Delaware, Lewes is mostly for families. Oceanside Rehoboth and bayside Dewey Beach are where singles, partiers, and a gay contingent hang out, boogie boarding, sunbathing, and surfing during the day, drinking and clubbing at night. The beach is crowded, and so is Rehoboth's downtown, which is lined with spas, restaurants, and shops. Bethany Beach, also in Delaware, is a mainstay for families, who rent large houses and condominiums right on the beach, one of the prettiest and largest. Next to the south is Maryland's Ocean City, a rowdy, raucous beach town, where there are plenty of hotels, motels, and condos, as well as restaurants, bars, and touristy shops lining a boardwalk, but it's all a bit on the tacky side. Finally, at the southernmost tip is a nature-lover's haven, Assateague Island, Maryland, part seashore, part state park, part wildlife refuge.

Best Attractions

Assateague Island At this wildlife refuge, you can camp on the beach, go kayaking, hiking, fishing, birding, clamming, the whole naturalist's nine yards.

Beach activities Swimming, rafting, boogie boarding, and surfing are all possible. Keep an eye out for the schools of dolphins that travel up and down the coast, amazingly close to the beach.

Rehoboth This is the place to go if you want to have a good meal, to shop at a store that sells more than T-shirts, and to treat yourself to a spa. Singles-central (both gay and straight), Rehoboth has a vigorous night scene with live music venues and brewpubs. Shoppers also should know about the two miles of outlets on Route 1 north of town: no sales tax.

Best Restaurants

Blue Moon Celebrating 25 years, Blue Moon serves fine American cuisine in a rambling Victorian beach house. $$ 35 Baltimore Ave, Rehoboth Beach, 302-227-6515, bluemoonrehoboth.com

Café Solé A favorite lunch spot, Café Solé is known for its crab cakes. $$ 44 Baltimore Ave., Rehoboth Beach, 302-227-7107, rehoboth.com/cafesole

Espuma Modern Mediterranean dishes get rave reviews at this popular restaurant. $$ 28 Wilmington Ave., Rehoboth Beach, 302-227-4199, espumarestaurant.com

LEAVING D.C. • OVERNIGHT TRIPS

Best Hotels

The Bellmoor Inn and Spa This posh, 78-room hotel is unique for the beach area, with its elegant furnishings, pools, full-service spa, and terraces, gardens, and library. $$ 6 Christian St., Rehoboth Beach, 302-227-5800 / 800-425-2355, thebellmoor.com

House rentals right on the beach are optimum—if you can snag one. Best to call around New Year's for the coming summer. Return business keeps many of the rentals booked into eternity. See contact info for lodging help.

Melissa's Bed and Breakfast This year-round, six-guest-room, 1900s house is one block from the beach. $$ 36 Delaware Ave., Rehoboth Beach, 302-227-7504 / 800-396-8090, atmelissas.com

Contacts

Assateague Island National Seashore 410-641-3030, nps.gov/asis
Assateague State Park 410-641-1441, dnr.state.md.us/publiclands/eastern/assateague.html
Bethany Beach/Fenwick Island Chamber of Commerce 302-539-2100 / 800-962-7873, bethany-fenwick.org
Ocean City Convention and Visitors Bureau and Department of Tourism 800-626-2326, ococean.com
Rehoboth Beach/Dewey Beach Chamber of Commerce 302-227-2233 / 800-441-1329, beach-fun.com

---

Getting There: From the Washington Beltway, I-495, take Route 50 east past Annapolis and follow it over the Bay Bridge. Stay on Route 50 all the way to reach Ocean City. To head to Delaware's Rehoboth, Dewey, or Lewes beaches, veer left from Route 50 onto Route 404, staying on Route 404 past Bridgeville, where it merges with Route 18, then Route 9, to pick up Route 1 for Rehoboth, staying on Route 9 for Lewes. Follow the same directions for Bethany, but where 404 meets Route 113, head south on 113, then east on Route 26. To reach Assateague Island, take U.S. 50 east and south to Salisbury, then U.S. 13 south to Route 175 east to the island.

Maryland's Eastern Shore along the Chesapeake Bay

Hot Tip: Summer is probably not the best time to visit, simply because you'll get caught up in all the traffic headed to the beach further east. Otherwise, the Eastern Shore is a beautiful place to travel year-round.

The Lowdown: Maryland's Eastern Shore along the Chesapeake Bay is a place full of history and recreational activities. The towns of St. Michaels, Easton, Cambridge, Chestertown, and Oxford have been around since the 1700s, when colonists settled here, made their livelihood as watermen, fed their families with the crabs and fish from these waters, and developed their waterfronts into prosperous ports—activities that continue to this day. Not long ago, the word "quaint" would have accurately described these little burgs, but today the Eastern Shore hamlets, though certainly quieter and slower-paced than D.C., hum with the presence of the many Washingtonians who have either retired or made second homes here. And for area residents in search of a getaway, the Eastern Shore, with its picturesque, harbor-view main streets, lodging, and restaurants, and its many opportunities for sailing, antiquing, gallery-hopping, and kicking back, has always stood out as a cherished domain. Just like the beach, each of the bay towns projects its own ambience. St. Michaels is posh, Oxford rather genteelly endearing, Easton a tad touristy "downtown" but charming overall, Chestertown artsy and old-fashioned, and Cambridge a little rustic, with the presence of the 27,000-acre Blackwater National Wildlife Refuge.

Best Attractions

Antiquing Where centuries-old towns thrive, antique stores abound, and the Eastern Shore is no exception.

Blackwater National Wildlife Refuge The best time to visit this 27,000-acre preserve is in fall and winter, when mosquitoes and crowds are gone. American bald eagles, all manner of water fowl, otters, opossums, red foxes, and muskrats, and assorted other wildlife are here. 2145 Key Wallace Dr., Cambridge, 410-228-2677, fws.gov/blackwater

Boating the Eastern Shore is a sailor's paradise, but opportunities exist for inexperienced landlubbers, too: Take a narrated cruise on the Miles River in St. Michaels; ferry between the towns of St. Michaels and Oxford, only a ten-minute ride; or call ahead to the Blackwater National Wildlife Refuge to find out about canoe and kayak rentals, then join a guided paddling tour of the wildlife refuge.

Best Restaurants

Columbia A cozy setting for fabulous modern American cuisine. $$$ 28 S. Washington St., Easton, 410-770-5172, restaurantcolumbia.com

Inn at Easton Washingtonians drive out of the city to dine in this elegant dining room serving sophisticated fare with an Australian twist. $$$ 28 S. Harrison St., Easton, 410-822-4910 / 888-800-8091, theinnateaston.com

LEAVING D.C. • OVERNIGHT TRIPS

The Inn at Perry Cabin Gourmands love the fine continental cuisine served in this dining room overlooking the water. $$$ 308 Watkins Lane, St. Michaels, 410-745-2200 / 866-278-9601, perrycabin.com

Julia's A local favorite; elegant fare served in an appealing location right on the town square. $$$ 122 N. Commerce St., Centreville, 410-758-0471

Best Hotels

The Inn at Easton This 1790 inn in the heart of Easton has three rooms and four suites exquisitely decorated with a touch of Aboriginal Australian art. $$-$$$$+ 28 S. Harrison St., Easton, 410-822-4910 / 888-800-8091, theinnateaston.com

The Inn at Perry Cabin Ultradeluxe accommodations are attired in Laura Ashley fabrics in this 78-room Orient Express inn and hotel fronting the Miles River. $$$ 308 Watkins Lane, St. Michaels, 410-745-2200 / 866-278-9601, perrycabin.com

Robert Morris Inn Situated right on the banks of the Tred Avon River, this historic 1710 inn offers 34 rooms, some with water views and porches. The inn is open mid-April through November. $$ 314 N. Morris St., Oxford, 410-226-5111 / 888-823-4012, robertmorrisinn.com

Contacts

Chesapeake Bay Visitors Guide chesapeake-bay.com
Maryland Office of Tourism 866-639-3526, mdisfun.org

Getting There: From the Washington Beltway, I-495, take Route 50 east across the Chesapeake Bay Bridge and continue on Route 50 east: to Route 343 west to reach Cambridge; to Route 301 north, then Route 213 north across the Chester River Bridge to reach Chestertown; to Route 322, then east on Route 33 to reach St. Michaels; to Route 322 all the way to reach Easton; and to Route 322 to Route 333 south to reach Oxford.

125 miles SW

Virginia Wine Country

Hot Tip: The Virginia countryside is really beautiful in spring and fall, but people turn out in droves to tour wineries, especially on weekends in September and October. Try visiting weekdays or in off months, like April and November. But always call ahead, since many wineries are small and family-operated, and not always open on weekdays, with the smallest ones closed in winter.

The Lowdown: The number of wineries is tipping toward 100 in the state of Virginia, whose wines are increasingly gaining national and international acclaim. About half of the wineries are located east of the Blue Ridge Mountains in Central Virginia, with the city of Charlottesville as the hub. Though some of the wineries are quite new (12 opened in 2005 alone), winemaking has been going on here since Thomas Jefferson got it started at his Monticello estate in 1774. This is not only wine country but also early America country, and the landscape is riddled with historic buildings, farms, vineyards, and gorgeous scenery. Wineries are well marked on the roads, so one way to tour the area is simply to drive around and follow the signs showing a cluster of grapes. If you want to be sure of hitting some of the best, most scenic, and/or most historically interesting, follow one of the five Monticello Wine Trails (monticellowinetrail.org), each of which takes you to 3 or 4 of a total 21 wineries. For example, one mile from Jefferson's Monticello is Jefferson Vineyards, whose land was originally owned by Jefferson; today the winery, situated at the top of a winding hill, offers a breathtaking view of the Blue Ridge Mountains as well as tastings of chardonnay, viognier, and cabernet. North of Jefferson is Barboursville Vineyards; at 830 acres, it is one of the larger and older commercial wineries, and it features the ruins of a house designed by Jefferson in 1814 for James Barbour, governor of Virginia. The house burned down, hence the ruins, but Barbour's original 1804 Georgian manor house has been newly reincarnated as a luxury inn. The vineyard has 15 wines to sample.

Best Attractions

Central Virginia Wine Region Virginia Wineries Association About 50 wineries are scattered amid the rolling hills and along country roads between D.C. and Charlottesville, known as the "Wine Capital of Virginia." 800-828-4637, virginiawineries.org; Monticello Wine Trail, monticellowinetrail.org.

Charlottesville The city of Charlottesville is a college town with cosmopolitan leanings. The University of Virginia, whose buildings Jefferson also designed, and a main street lined with bookshops and fine restaurants are among its chief attractions.

Monticello This is the magnificent home that Thomas Jefferson designed and completed in 1809. The 2,000-acre mountaintop plantation includes the house filled with many of his inventions, and gardens, orchards, and vineyards. $ Thomas Jefferson Pkwy., Monticello, 434-984-9800, monticello.org

LEAVING D.C. • OVERNIGHT TRIPS

Best Restaurants

Clifton Inn The public is welcome to dine here, where the cuisine is as fine as the accommodations, with seating in a glassed-in verandah, formal dining room, chef's table in the kitchen, and at the bar. $$$ 1296 Clifton Inn Dr., Charlottesville, 434-971-1800 / 888-971-1800, cliftoninn.net

Michie Tavern Sure, it's hokey, but it's also old, dating from 1784, which explains the colonial attire, big hearth, pewter plates, and black-eyed peas on the menu. $$ 683 Thomas Jefferson Pkwy., Charlottesville, 434-977-1234, michietavern.com

Palladio Restaurant Enjoy locally sourced Italian cuisine in a pristine setting among scenic vineyards. $$$ Barboursville Vineyards, 17655 Winery Rd., Barboursville, 540-832-7848, palladiorestaurant.com

Best Hotels

Clifton Inn This historic 1799 home recently won entry in the exclusive Relais & Chateaux hotel association, overlooks the Rivanna River, and has a world-class restaurant and 14 stellar rooms in the manor and cottages. $$$$ 1296 Clifton Inn Dr., Charlottesville, 434-971-1800 / 888-971-1800, cliftoninn.net

The 1804 Inn at Barboursville An 18th-century cottage and an 1804 residence for Governor Barbour have been transformed into five luxurious suites, with balconies overlooking the countryside. $$$$ Barboursville Vineyards, 17655 Winery Rd., Barboursville, 434-760-2212, barboursvillewine.com

Keswick Hall at Monticello A grand, 45-room country house hotel sits on 600 beautiful acres in the foothills of the Blue Ridge Mountains; décor is Laura Ashley, with individually decorated rooms; amenities include afternoon tea, golf, dining, tennis, swimming pool. $$$$ 701 Club Dr., Keswick, 434-979-3440 / 800-274-5391, keswick.com

Contacts

Charlottesville/Albemarle Convention & Visitors Bureau 877-386-1102, charlottesvilletourism.org

Virginia Wineries Association 800-828-4637, virginiawines.org

---

Getting There: To reach Charlottesville: from the Washington Beltway, I-495, take I-66 west to U.S. 29, which you follow south all the way to Charlottesville. For more scenic routes, ask your inn or the tourism bureau for alternative directions.

65 miles SW

Washington, Virginia

Hot Tip: Spring and fall, especially the months of May and October, are most popular, and rates at the inns are significantly higher then. The town is lovely year-round, though. Consider coming for its annual Fourth of July celebration, which brings city slickers out from big Washington for a taste of small-town American life.

The Lowdown: Washington, Virginia, was on the map way before anyone in Washington, D.C., had ever heard of it. In fact, George Washington, in July 1749, at age 17, put this little town on the map, quite literally, when he laid out the five-by-two-block grid that remains the town today. The United States has 28 Washingtons, but this was the first one. Nearly 30 years ago, the little town of Washington suddenly came to the world's attention, thanks to two men, Patrick O'Connell and Reinhardt Lynch, who built their now-famous Inn at Little Washington on the site of what was once a gas station. The inn continues to receive thunderous applause for both its interior design and its restaurant and has won every conceivable award: James Beards, Relais & Chateaux, Mobil five stars and AAA five diamonds for both inn and restaurant. The "Pope of American cuisine," as chef O'Connell has been called, is himself charming, and he and Lynch graciously preside over a hideaway whose 15 bedrooms include "The Mayor's House," which has two fireplaces, a beamed ceiling, and a courtyard garden; and other rooms, some with canopy-covered sofas swathed in exotic fabrics or balconies overlooking the quiet town (population 162)—all with sumptuous, comfortable furnishings. The inn's guest list is global, though Washington journalists have a special fondness for it. In spite of all this notice, the little town of Washington has remained the quaint 18th-century village it's always been, which only adds to its overall appeal. Situated in Rappahannock County, surrounded by rolling hills and mountains, "Little" Washington is a good jumping-off point for exploring the area.

Best Attractions

Luray Caverns Guided hikes down into these underground caverns bring one face to face with awesome rock and crystal formations in cathedral-like rooms, including the one-and-only-in-the-world stalacpipe organ. Wear a jacket, since the temperature below is always about 54 degrees. $ 970 U.S. Hwy. 211 West, Luray, 540-743-6551, luraycaverns.com

Skyline Drive Blue Ridge Mountains Near Washington is Shenandoah National Park and its remarkable 105-mile scenic drive. Thornton Gap is the park entrance closest to the inn, and from there a 30-mile drive takes you north through the park. Luray, 540-999-3500, nps.gov/shen

Washington The town itself is a lovely place to wander, its buildings a mix of 18th century and the occasional colonial architecture. 540-675-3128, town.washington.va.us

Best Restaurants

Blue Rock Inn A bucolic setting in which to feast on traditional American fare. $$ 12567 Lee Hwy., Washington, 540-987-3190, bluerockinn.com

Four and Twenty Blackbirds In a more modest country setting, this restaurant nevertheless feeds you well on delicious, creative American fare. Live music on Saturdays. $$ 650 Zachary Taylor Hwy., Flint Hill, 540-675-1111, fourandtwenty.com

The Inn at Little Washington Patrick O'Connell's take on French classical cooking has been called "the gastronomic equivalent of sex." This is really where you want to eat; inn guests are guaranteed a table in the restaurant. $$$$+ Middle and Main Sts., 540-675-3800, theinnatlittlewashington.com

Best Hotels

Foster Harris House This 1900 country Victorian bed and breakfast is a fine, in-town second choice, with fireplaces, whirlpool, and a tranquil setting. $$ 189 Main St., 540-675-3757 / 800-874-1152, fosterharris.com

The Inn at Little Washington This is really where you should stay, or at least dine, or at least visit. Or at least enjoy a Bellini in the bar. $$$$+ Middle and Main Sts., 540-675-3800, theinnatlittlewashington.com

Middleton Inn Bed & Breakfast The highest-rated B&B in Virginia, the historic Middleton is set amid scenic pastures, with mountain views. $$ 176 Main St., 540-675-2020, middletoninn.com

Contacts

Rappahannock County Administration 290 Gay St., 540-675-5330, rappahannockcountyva.gov, rappahannock.com

Washington Town Hall 485 Gay St., 540-675-3128, town.washington.va.us

---

Getting There: From the Washington Beltway, I-495, take I-66 west to Gainesville, to U.S. 29 south to Warrenton, then route 211 west 25 miles to Washington, Virginia.

Annapolis, Maryland

Hot Tip: Annapolis is attractive year-round, but go in spring through fall if you want to get out on the water; spring also is when the restored gardens of the historic houses are in bloom.

The Lowdown: Annapolis is known as "America's sailing capital," because sailors from around the world pull into port here, especially in the fall, when the world's largest in-water sail and power boat show takes place; and also because Annapolis's 17-mile waterfront is home base for thousands of boats. Maryland's state capital since 1694, Annapolis was also the country's capital for nine months, following the signing of the Treaty of Paris in 1783, ending the Revolutionary War. All four Maryland signers of the Declaration of Independence lived in Annapolis, and their homes still stand. As much as these figures and facts might impress, a visit here comes down to a pleasant time strolling cobblestone streets, taking a boat tour, and browsing shops on the side streets leading to the wharf.

Best Attractions

U.S. Naval Academy Stroll the grounds of this 338-acre campus, founded in 1845; visit the maritime museum. 121 Blake Rd., 410-263-6933, usna.edu

Watermark Cruises Narrated boat tours offer grand views of Annapolis harbor, the Severn River, and the Naval Academy. $ 410-268-7600, watermarkcruises.com

William Paca House and Garden Paca was one of the signers of the Declaration of Independence. This Georgian house is where he lived, and the gardens have been restored to look as Paca designed them in the 1760s. $- 186 Prince George St., annapolis.org/paca-house-b.html

Best Restaurants

Harry Browne's A formal dining room serving American fare; also a sidewalk cafe and grill room. $$$ 66 State Cir., 410-263-4332, harrybrownes.com

O'Learys Seafood Restaurant You can see part of Annapolis harbor as you enjoy great service with your fresh fish and crab cakes. $$$ 310 Third St., 410-263-0884, olearys-seafood.com

Rockfish Rockfish serves upscale seafood in the form of excellent soft-shell crabs, raw oysters, and of course rockfish, in a spacious room with an exhibition kitchen and booths. $$$ 400 Sixth St., 410-267-1800, rockfishmd.com

Contacts

Annapolis and Anne Arundel County Conference and Visitors Bureau 26 West St., 888-302-2852, visit-annapolis.org
Annapolis Visitors Guide 410-263-7944, visitannapolismaryland.com
Historic Annapolis Foundation 18 Pinkney St., 410-267-7619, annapolis.org

Getting There: From the Washington Beltway, I-495, take Route 50 east to Exit 24, Rowe Blvd., and follow the signs to the visitors center.

LEAVING D.C. • DAY TRIPS

10 miles N

Great Falls Park, Maryland

Hot Tip: People flock here in huge numbers because it's easy to get to, it's truly spectacular, and it makes the city seem far away. It's most crowded at the first hint of a thaw in winter or on a crisp day in late summer.

The Lowdown: You'll need hiking boots, or at least sneakers, to visit the Great Falls, on the Maryland side of the Potomac River. What you're going for is the sight and sound of the normally placid Potomac River suddenly whipping, widening and crashing as it descends 76 feet in a series of rapids to fall upon the boulders below. From the Great Falls Tavern in the park, a short walk takes you to Olmstead Island walkway and overlook, where you stand about 100 feet above the river, with a front-row view of the falls. Lots of people prefer to enter the C&O Canal towpath just outside of the park, across from Old Angler's Inn. From this point, it's a one-mile hike to the overlook. In addition to the falls, people come to hike one of the well-marked trails of varying intensity, most of them easy to moderate. The woods and waters are teeming with beavers, songbirds, salamanders, and wildflowers. Some days, the trails can get as crowded as the Beltway, but on weekdays or in early morning, Great Falls, only ten miles from town, seems out of this world.

Best Attractions

Billy Goat Trail Everybody's favorite trail, it's laid out in three parts, the "A" section marked "strenuous," making a 3.7-mile loop via the towpath, and requiring scrambling over angled rocks, but rewarding climbers with beautiful views of Mather Gorge and the river. Sturdy shoes required. The two other sections are "moderate." C&O Canal Historical Park, Great Falls, Potomac

Great Falls Tavern Visitor Center The tavern was built in 1831 and offers rudimentary exhibits on the history of the C&O Canal. 11710 MacArthur Blvd., Potomac, 301-767-3714, nps.gov/choh

Best Restaurants

Old Angler's Inn In operation since 1860, Old Angler's is situated across the street from the parking lot and is a popular entrance to the C&O Canal towpath. The inn has a wonderful terrace outside with a blazing fireplace, serves fine American cuisine, and will not seat you if you look too scruffy. $$ 10801 MacArthur Blvd., Potomac, 301-299-9097, oldanglersinn.com

Contacts

Great Falls Tavern Visitor Center 11710 MacArthur Blvd., Potomac, 301-767-3714, nps.gov/choh

Getting There: From Georgetown, take M St. west, bearing left to pick up Canal Rd., which turns into the Clara Barton Pkwy. Follow it north to the end, turning left on MacArthur Blvd., passing the Old Angler's Inn, and following the boulevard to its end, in the Great Falls Visitor Center parking lot.

Harper's Ferry, West Virginia

Hot Tip: Come in late spring or early fall to have fun on the water.

The Lowdown: These 2,200 acres are a national park committed to commemorating several remarkable events, including those that happened the night of October 16, 1859, when abolitionist John Brown planned a rebellion he hoped would lead to the freeing of slaves in Virginia. It all went horribly wrong, and John Brown was hanged for treason, murder, and organizing a slave rebellion. In addition to its history, Harper's Ferry has an astounding location: at the juncture of the Shenandoah and Potomac rivers and the Blue Ridge Mountains, which form natural boundaries for the states of Maryland, Virginia, and West Virginia. Visitors can tour the restored 19th-century lower town, walking out to Jefferson's Rock, so named because this is where Thomas Jefferson proclaimed the view "one of the most stupendous scenes in Nature." Harper's Ferry offers two hiking trails, as well as driving tours through the park. But its main attractions are the thrilling tubing and rafting trips down the Shenandoah and Potomac rivers. Outfitters offer lots of options, from go-on-your-own flat-water tubing to outfitter-guided, high-speed rafting through white-water rapids.

Best Attractions

River Riders Lots of outfitters coordinate river trips, and this is one of them. Reservations are required to hold spaces and equipment, so call ahead. $$-$$$$ 800-326-7238, riverriders.com

Virginius Island Trail This easy 1.5-mile hike begins at the railroad trestle in Harpers Ferry's lower town and leads past lavender flowers and trees.

Best Restaurants

The Anvil Pub with bar food available up front and a formal dining room and menu in back. $ 1270 W. Washington St., Harper's Ferry, 304-535-2582

Betty's It's worth it to travel the eight or so miles to this cute little college town for sandwiches and hot lunch specials at this local landmark. $- 112 E. German St., Shepherdstown, 304-876-6080

Yellow Brick Bank Fancier décor and new American cuisine are on the menu at this popular restaurant. $$ 201 E. German St., Shepherdstown, 304-876-2208, yellowbrickbank.com

Contacts

Harper's Ferry Visitors Center 304-535-6298, nps.gov/hafe
Jefferson County Convention & Visitor Bureau 304-535-2627, hello-wv.com

Getting There: From the Washington Beltway, I-495, take I-270 north to I-70 west toward Hagerstown. Take Exit 52 to US 340 west and travel about 22 miles to the Harper's Ferry Visitor Center.

LEAVING D.C. • DAY TRIPS

35 miles W

Leesburg and Middleburg, Virginia

Hot Tip: Check the calendar for steeplechase races, usually held in May and again in the fall, to experience the best of this area.

The Lowdown: Despite Washington's rapidly encroaching exurbs, the two nearby towns of Leesburg and Middleburg hold on to their distinctive charms. Tiny Middleburg, circa 1787, consists of a main street flanked by boutiques, antique stores, art galleries, and pubs, and beyond that, horse farms and the rich estates of landed gentry. The slightly larger Leesburg is similar in its colonial architecture and Main Street attractions. This is Loudoun County, known for steeplechase races and other equestrian events; a covet-worthy setting at the foothills of the Blue Ridge Mountains, between two rivers; and numerous wineries and plantations. One Middleburg inn makes this easy day trip worth considering for an overnight one: the Goodstone Inn (36205 Snake Hill Rd., 540-687-4645 / 877-219-4663, goodstone.com) is a fabulous and luxurious retreat on 265 acres.

Best Attractions

National Air and Space Museum Steven F. Udvar-Hazy Center This annex of the Smithsonian's Mall Air and Space Museum houses more of the same: rockets and space equipment. 14390 Air & Space Museum Pkwy., Chantilly, 202-633-1000, nasm.si.edu

Oatlands Plantation Tour the 1803 mansion and gardens of this 261-acre plantation. $ 20850 Oatlands Plantation Ln., Leesburg, 703-777-3174, oatlands.org

Virginia Gold Cup Held on the first Saturday in May, this annual steeplechase horse race continues a tradition started in 1922. Pack the champagne, put on Ascot-like duds, and head for the Virginia hills. Great Meadows Race Course, The Plains, Virginia, 540-347-1215 / 800-697-2238, vagoldcup.com

Best Restaurants

Aster Finally, an in-town restaurant worthy of its moneyed setting; Aster serves gourmet modern American fare in a restored country house. $$$ 101 S. Madison St., Middleburg, 540-687-4080, asterrestaurant.com

Lightfoot A classically elegant setting in which to enjoy the traditional American cuisine. $$ 11 N. King St., Leesburg, 703-771-2233, lightfootrestaurant.com

Red Fox Inn The inn has been feeding weary travelers since 1758. $$$ Two E. Washington St., Middleburg, 540-687-6301 / 800-223-1728, redfox.com

Contacts

Loudoun Convention & Visitors Association 703-771-2617 / 800-752-6118, visitloudoun.org

Getting There: From I-495, take Route 66 west to Route 50 west to reach Middleburg. Take I-495 to the Dulles Toll Road (Route 267), until it becomes Dulles Greenway extension; follow signs for U.S. 15 to Leesburg.

Old Town Alexandria and Mount Vernon, Virginia

8-16 miles S

Hot Tip: These are year-round destinations, but particularly nice to visit, though more crowded, in spring and summer.

The Lowdown: Locals travel continuously back and forth between the District and this northern Virginia community, commuting to work, or to shop, dine, or tour. Old Town's shops and restaurants are similar to Georgetown's but this side of the Potomac is more tourist friendly. Old Town Alexandria outdoes Georgetown in another respect: This was George Washington's stomping ground and the town's colonial-era buildings include several where Washington dined, danced, discussed politics, and prayed. And speaking of George, a trip across the Potomac is a must if only to visit Mount Vernon, where Washington lived on and off for 45 years, starting in 1754. Mount Vernon's 500-acre estate lies eight miles south of Old Town.

Best Attractions

King Street, Alexandria From the waterfront at one end to the King Street Metro station at the other, King Street and its tributaries are lined with art galleries, clothing stores, historic attractions, clubs, and restaurants. Check out the 165 artists working in their studios at the Torpedo Factory (105 N. Union St., just off King St., 703-838-4565, torpedofactory.org), the European fashions at American in Paris (1225 King St., 703-519-8234), and the shoes at the Shoe Hive (115 S. Royal St., 703-548-7105, theshoehive.com).

Mount Vernon Estate and Gardens This is the plantation where GW lived and farmed, in between stints as commander in chief of the Continental Army during the Revolutionary War and as president of the United States. $ George Washington Memorial Pkwy., Mount Vernon, 703-780-2000, mountvernon.org

Best Restaurants

Geranio Lovely Italian fare served in the heart of Old Town. $$ 722 King St., 703-548-0088, geranio.net

100 King Street Usually packed and noisy with a young crowd enjoying tapas and martinis. $$ 100 King St., 703-299-0076, 100king.com

Restaurant Eve Eve serves modern American cuisine on a par with D.C.'s best restaurants. $$ 110 S. Pitt St., 703-706-0450, restauranteve.com

Contacts

Alexandria Convention and Visitors Association Ramsay House Visitors Center, 221 King St., 703-838-4200 / 800-388-9119, funside.com

Getting There: From Washington, find the Arlington Memorial or the 14th St. Bridge to reach the George Washington Memorial Parkway south, which becomes Washington Street in Old Town Alexandria; King Street crosses Washington Street. Mount Vernon lies eight miles further on George Washington Memorial Parkway.

D.C. BLACK BOOK

You're solo in the city—where's a singles-friendly place to eat? Is there a good lunch spot near the museum? Will the bar be too loud for easy conversation? Get the answers fast in the *Black Book*, a condensed version of every listing in our guide that puts all the essential information at your fingertips.

A quick glance down the page and you'll find the type of food, nightlife, or attractions you are looking for, the phone numbers, and which pages to turn to for more detailed information. How did you ever survive without it?

D.C. Black Book

Hotels

NAME TYPE (ROOMS)	ADDRESS (CROSS STREET) WEBSITE	AREA PRICE	PHONE 800 NUMBER	EXPERIENCE	PAGE
Four Seasons Hotel Grand (211)	2800 Pennsylvania Ave. NW (28th St.) fourseasons.com	GT $$$$+	202-342-0444 800-332-3442	Chic	57
Hay-Adams Hotel Timeless (145)	One Lafayette Sq. NW (H St.) hayadams.com	WH $$$$+	202-638-6600 800-853-6807	Classic	122
The Hotel George Trendy (139)	15 E St. NW (North Capitol St.) hotelgeorge.com	CH $$$	202-347-4200 800-576-8331	Chic	57
Hotel Helix Trendy (178)	1430 Rhode Island Ave. NW (14th St.) hotelhelix.com	DC $$	202-462-9001 800-706-1202	Hip	89
Hotel Madera Trendy (82)	1310 New Hampshire Ave. NW (N St.) hotelmadera.com	DC $$	202-296-7600 800-430-1202	Hip	89
Hotel Monaco Trendy (182)	700 F St. NW (Seventh St.) monaco-dc.com	PQ $$$	202-628-7177 800-649-1202	Hip	89
Hotel Palomar Modern (335)	2121 P St. NW (22nd St.) hotelpalomar-dc.com	DC $$$	202-448-1800 877-866-3070	Chic	57
Hotel Rouge Trendy (137)	1315 16th St. NW (Mass. Ave.) rougehotel.com	DC $$	202-232-8000 800-738-1202	Hip	90
The Jefferson Timeless (100)	1200 16th St. NW (M St.) thejeffersonwashingtondc.com	WH $$$$	202-347-2200 866-270-8118	Classic	122
Mandarin Oriental Modern (400)	1330 Maryland Ave. SW (12th St.) mandarinoriental.com/washington	SW $$$$+	202-554-8588 888-888-1778	Chic	58
Park Hyatt Washington, D.C. Modern (215)	1201 24th St. NW (M St.) parkhyattwashington.com	WE $$$$	202-789-1234 888-591-1234	Chic	58
The Renaissance Mayflower Grand (657)	1127 Connecticut Ave. NW (L St.) renaissancehotels.com/WASSH	WH $$$$	202-347-3000 800-228-7697	Classic	122
The Ritz-Carlton, Georgetown Trendy (86)	3100 South St. NW (31st St.) ritzcarlton.com	GT $$$$+	202-912-4100 800-241-3333	Chic	59
The Ritz-Carlton, Wash. D.C. Modern (299)	1150 22nd St. NW (M St.) ritzcarlton.com	WE $$$$+	202-835-0500 800-241-3333	Classic	123
Sofitel Lafayette Square Modern (237)	806 15th St. NW (H St.) sofitel.com	WH $$$$	202-730-8800 800-763-4835	Classic	123
Tabard Inn Timeless (40)	1739 N St. NW (17th St.) tabardinn.com	DC $$	202-785-1277	Hip	90
Topaz Hotel Trendy (99)	1733 N St. NW (17th St.) topazhotel.com	DC $$	202-393-3000 800-775-1202	Hip	90
Willard InterContinental Grand (334)	1401 Pennsylvania Ave. NW (14th St.) washington.interconti.com	DT $$$$+	202-628-9100 800-827-1747	Classic	123

Neighborhood (Area) Key

- **AM** = Adams Morgan
- **CH** = Capitol Hill
- **DC** = Dupont Circle
- **DT** = Downtown
- **FB** = Foggy Bottom
- **GT** = Georgetown
- **MP** = Mount Pleasant
- **NM** = National Mall
- **PQ** = Penn Quarter
- **SW** = Southwest
- **UN** = Upper Northwest
- **US** = U Street Corridor
- **VA** = Various
- **WE** = West End
- **WH** = White House

D.C. BLACK BOOK

Restaurants

NAME TYPE	ADDRESS (CROSS STREET) WEBSITE	AREA PRICE	PHONE SINGLES/NOISE	EXPERIENCE 99 BEST	PAGE PAGE
Acadiana Southern	901 New York Ave. NW (Ninth St.) acadianarestaurant.com	PQ $$	202-408-8848 B ≡	Chic American Originals	52, 60 17
Afterwords Cafe Bookstore/Cafe	1517 Connecticut Ave. NW (Dupont Cir.) kramers.com	DC $	202-387-1462 - ≡	Hip	92
Agua Ardiente* Latin American	1250 24th St. NW (M St.) agua-ardiente.com	FB $$	202-833-8500 B ≡	Chic	60
Al Crostino Italian	1324 U St. NW (14th St.) alcrostino.com	US $	202-797-0523 B ≡	Chic	60
Bangkok Bistro Thai	3251 Prospect St. NW (Potomac St.) 	GT $	202-337-2424 - ≡	Chic	60
Bardia's New Orleans Café Southern	2412 18th St. NW (Mintwood Pl.)	AM $-	202-234-0420 - ⎕	Hip	92
Belga Café Belgian	514 Eighth St. SE (E St.) belgacafe.com	CH $	202-544-0100 B ≡	Hip	86, 92
Ben's Chili Bowl Diner	1213 U St. NW (13th St.) benschilibowl.com	US $-	202-667-0909 B⎕ ≡	Hip Only-in-D.C.	84, 92 34
Bistro Bis French Bistro	15 E St. NW (N. Capitol St.) bistrobis.com	CH $$	202-661-2700 B ≡	Chic Always-Hot Tables	52, 60 16
Bistrot du Coin French Bistro	1738 Connecticut Ave. NW (Florida Ave.) bistrotducoin.com	DC $	202-234-6969 B ≡	Hip	84, 92
Blue Duck Tavern New American	1201 24th St. NW (M St.) blueducktavern.com	WE $$$	202-419-6755 - ≡	Chic	54, 61
The Bombay Club Indian	815 Connecticut Ave. NW (I St.) bombayclubdc.com	WH $$	202-659-3727 B ≡	Classic Indian Restaurants	116, 124 27
Bread and Chocolate Cafe	666 Pennsylvania Avenue SE (Seventh St.)	CH $-	202-547-2875 - ≡	Hip	86, 93
BreadLine Bakery/Deli	1751 Pennsylvania Ave. NW (17th St.) thebreadlinedc.blogspot.com	WH $-	202-822-8900 - ≡	Classic	124
Butterfield 9 New American	600 14th St. NW (F St.) butterfield9.com	PQ $$	202-289-8810 B ≡	Chic Romantic Dining	61 42
Cafe Asia* Asian	1720 I St. NW (17th St.) cafeasia.com	DT $	202-659-2696 B⎕ ≡	Hip	85, 93

Restaurant and Nightlife Symbols

Restaurants
Singles Friendly (eat and/or meet)
[] = Communal table
B = Food served at bar

(G) = Gourmet destination

Nightlife
Price Warning
C = Cover or ticket charge

Restaurant + Nightlife
Prime time noise levels
⎕ = Quiet
≡ = A buzz, but still conversational
≡ = Loud

Note regarding page numbers: *Italic* = itinerary listing; Roman = description in theme chapter listing.

Restaurants (cont.)

NAME TYPE	ADDRESS (CROSS STREET) WEBSITE	AREA PRICE	PHONE SINGLES/NOISE	EXPERIENCE 99 BEST	PAGE PAGE
Café Atlantico Nuevo Latino	405 Eighth St. NW (D St.) cafeatlantico.com	PQ $$	202-393-0812 B ≡	Chic Brunches	54, 61 19
Café Bonaparte European	1522 Wisconsin Ave. NW (P St.) cafebonaparte.com	GT $	202-333-8830 B =	Hip	93
Café Milano* Italian	3251 Prospect St. NW (Wisconsin Ave.) cafemilanodc.com	GT $$$	202-333-6183 B ≡	Chic Politico Sightings	52, 61 38
Café MoZU Asian-American	1330 Maryland Ave. SW (12th St.) cafemozu.com	SW $$	202-787-6868 - =	Classic	119, 124
Café Saint-Ex* American	1847 14th St. NW (T St.) saint-ex.com	US $	202-265-7839 B ≡	Hip	84, 93
The Capital Grille Steak House	601 Pennsylvania Ave. NW (Sixth St.) thecapitalgrille.com	PQ $$$	202-737-6200 B ≡	Classic Power Lunch Spots	124 39
Cashion's Eat Place* American	1819 Columbia Rd. NW (18th St.) cashionseatplace.com	AM $$	202-797-1819 B ≡	Chic Always-Hot Tables	53, 62 16
The Caucus Room* American	401 Ninth St. NW (D St.) thecaucusroom.com	PQ $$$	202-393-1300 B =	Classic Power Lunch Spots	125 39
Ceiba Latin American	701 14th St. NW (G St.) ceibarestaurant.com	PQ $$	202-393-3983 B ≡	Chic	54, 62
Charlie Palmer Steak* Steak House	101 Constitution Ave. NW (First St.) charliepalmer.com/steak_dc	CH $$$	202-547-8100 B -	Classic Politico Sightings	118, 125 38
Chinatown Express Chinese	746 Sixth St. NW (H St.)	PQ $-	202-638-0424 -	Hip	84, 93
Citronelle French (G)	3000 M St. NW (30th St.) citronelledc.com	GT $$$$	202-625-2150 B =	Classic Hot Chefs	125 25
CityZen New American (G)	1330 Maryland Ave. SW (12th St.) mandarinoriental.com/washington	SW $$$$	202-787-6006 B =	Chic Hot Chefs	52, 62 25
Creme Cafe Southern	1322 U St. NW (13th St.)	US $	202-234-1884 - ≡	Hip	94
DC Coast New American	1401 K St. NW (14th St.) dccoast.com	WH $$	202-216-5988 B ≡	Chic	62
The Diner Diner	2453 18th St. NW (Columbia Rd.) trystdc.com/diner	AM $	202-232-8800 B0 ≡	Hip	84, 94
Dino Italian	3435 Connecticut Ave. NW (Ordway St.) dino-dc.com	UN $$	202-686-2966 - -	Chic	63
Domku Bar & Café Eastern European	821 Upshur St. NW (Eighth St.)	UN $	202-722-7475 B0 =	Hip	94
Dragonfly* Sushi	1215 Connecticut Ave. NW (Rhode Island Ave.) dragonflysushibar.com	DC $$	202-331-1775 B ≡	Chic	63
Equinox New American (G)	818 Connecticut Ave. NW (I St.) equinoxrestaurant.com	WH $$$	202-331-8118 B =	Classic	125
Firefly American	1310 New Hampshire Ave. NW (20th St.) firefly-dc.com	DC $$	202-861-1310 B =	Hip	86, 94
Galileo Italian	1110 21st St. NW (L St.) galileodc.com	WE $$$	202-293-7191 B =	Classic Always-Hot Tables	117, 126 16

D.C. BLACK BOOK

NAME / TYPE	ADDRESS (CROSS STREET) / WEBSITE	AREA PRICE	PHONE SINGLES/NOISE	EXPERIENCE 99 BEST	PAGE PAGE
Gerard's Place / French (G)	915 15th St. NW (McPherson Sq.)	WH $$$	202-737-4445 -	Classic / Romantic Dining	117, 126 / 42
Hank's Oyster Bar / Oyster Bar	1624 Q St. NW (17th St.) / hanksdc.com	DC $	202-462-4265 / B =	Hip	94
Helix Lounge* / Bar Food	1430 Rhode Island Ave. NW (14th St.) hotelhelix.com/heldini	DC $-	202-462-9001 / B =	Hip	95
IndeBleu* / French-Indian	707 G St. NW (Seventh St.) / bleu.com/indebleu	PQ $$$	202-333-2538 / B =	Chic / Restaurant Lounges	53, 63 / 41
Indique / Indian	3512-14 Connecticut Ave. NW (Ordway St.) indique.com	UN $	202-244-6600 / B =	Chic / Indian Restaurants	53, 63 / 27
Jaleo / Tapas	480 Seventh St. NW (E St.) / jaleo.com	PQ $	202-628-7949 / B =	Hip	95
Johnny's Half Shell / Seafood	2002 P St. NW (20th St.) / johnnyshalfshell.net	CH $$	202-296-2021 / B =	Hip / American Originals	95 / 17
Kinkead's* / Seafood	2000 Pennsylvania Ave. NW (20th St.) kinkead.com	FB $$$	202-296-7700 / B =	Classic	126
Komi / New American	1509 17th St. NW (Church St.)	DC $$	202-332-9200 - =	Chic	64
L'Enfant Café / French	2000 18th St. NW (Florida Ave.) / lenfantcafe.com	AM $-	202-319-1800 / B =	Hip	95
La Chaumiere / French Bistro	2813 M St. NW (28th St.)	GT $$	202-338-1784 - =	Classic	126
Laboratorio del Galileo / Italian (G)	1110 21st St. NW (L St.) / galileodc.com	WE $$$$	202-293-7191 - =	Classic / Chef's Tables	117, 127 / 20
Lafayette Room / American	One Lafayette Sq. (H St.) / hayadams.com/dining	WH $$$	202-638-2570 - =	Classic / Brunches	127 / 19
Lauriol Plaza / Tex-Mex	1835 18th St. NW (Swann St.) / lauriolplaza.com	DC $	202-387-0035 / B =	Chic	64
Lebanese Taverna / Lebanese	2641 Connecticut Ave. NW (24th St.) / lebanesetaverna.com	UN $	202-265-8681 / B =	Chic	64
LeftBank* / International	2424 18th St. NW (Columbia Rd.) / leftbankdc.com	AM $	202-464-2100 / B◨ =	Chic	64
Leopold's Kafe & Konditorei / New American-Austrian	Cady's Alley, 3318 M St. NW (33rd St.) kafeleopolds.com	GT $	202-965-6005 / ◨ =	Chic	52, 64
Les Halles / French Brasserie	1201 Pennsylvania Ave. NW (12th St.) leshalles.net	PQ $$	202-347-6848 / B =	Classic	118, 127
Lima* / Latin American	1401 K St. NW (14th St.) / limarestaurant.com	DT $$$	202-789-2800 / B◨ =	Chic / Restaurant Lounges	65 / 41
Logan Tavern* / American	1423 P St. NW (15th St.) / logantavern.com	US $$	202-332-3710 / B =	Hip	84, 95
Love Café / Bakery/Cafe	1501 U St. NW (15th St.) / cakelove.com	US $-	202-265-9800 / ◨ =	Hip	96
Mama Ayesha's Restaurant / Middle Eastern	1967 Calvert St. NW (20th St.) / mamaayeshas.com	AM $	202-232-5431 - =	Hip / Vegetarian	86, 96 / 47

205

Restaurants (cont.)

NAME TYPE	ADDRESS (CROSS STREET) WEBSITE	AREA PRICE	PHONE SINGLES/NOISE	EXPERIENCE 99 BEST	PAGE PAGE
Marcel's Belgian/French (G)	2401 Pennsylvania Ave. NW (24th St.) marcelsdc.com	FB $$$	202-296-1166	Classic Fine Dining	*118*, 127 23
Market Lunch Diner	225 Seventh St. SE (C St.)	CH $-	202-547-8444	Hip	*85*, 96
Marrakesh Moroccan	617 New York Ave. NW (Sixth St.) marrakesh.us	PQ $$$	202-393-9393	Hip	96
Matchbox* Pizzeria	713 H St. NW (Seventh St.) matchboxdc.com	PQ $	202-289-4441	Hip	*84*, 97
Mendocino Grille and Wine Bar New American	2917 M St. NW (29th St.) mendocinodc.com	GT $$	202-333-2912	Chic	65
Merkado Asian-Latin	1443 P St. NW (14th St.) merkadodc.com	US $$	202-299-0018	Hip	97
Meskerem Ethiopian	2434 18th St. NW (Columbia Rd.) meskeremonline.com	AM $	202-462-4100	Hip	*84*, 97
Mie N Yu* Middle Eastern	3125 M St. NW (31st St) mienyu.com	GT $$	202-333-6122	Chic	65
Minibar at Café Atlantico American (G)	405 Eighth St. NW (D St.) cafeatlantico.com	PQ $$$$	202-393-0812	Hip Chef's Tables	*86*, 97 20
Mitsitam Native American	Independence Ave. SW (Fourth St.) nmai.si.edu	NM $-	202-633-1000	Hip Indian Restaurants	*83*, 97 27
The Monocle American	107 D St. NE (First St.) themonocle.com	CH $$	202-546-4488	Classic Only-in-D.C.	*118*, 127 34
Montmartre French Brasserie	327 Seventh St. SE (Penn. Ave.) montmartre.us	CH $$	202-544-1244	Classic	128
National Gallery of Art Cafes Cafe	Constitution Ave. NW (Seventh St.) nga.gov/ginfo/cafes.shtm	NM $	202-737-4215	Classic	128
Obelisk Italian (G)	2029 P St. NW (20th St.)	DC $$$	202-872-1180	Classic Fine Dining	*118*, 128 23
The Occidental American	1475 Pennsylvania Ave. NW (15th St.) occidentaldc.com	DT $$	202-783-1475	Classic Power Lunch Spots	*116*, 128 39
Oceanaire Seafood Room Seafood	1201 F St. NW (12th St.) theoceanaire.com	PQ $$$	202-347-2277	Classic	129
Old Ebbitt Grill* American	675 15th St. NW (G St.) ebbitt.com	DT $$	202-347-4801	Classic	*119*, 129
Old Glory BBQ* American	3139 M St. NW (Wisconsin Ave.) oldglorybbq.com	GT $	202-337-3406	Classic	*118*, 129
The Oval Room New American	800 Connecticut Ave. NW (H St.) ovalroom.com	WH $$	202-463-8700	Classic	129
Oya* French-Asian	777 Ninth St. NW (H St.) oyadc.com	PQ $$	202-393-1400	Chic Restaurant Lounges	*53*, 65 41
Palena Italian-New American (G)	3529 Connecticut Ave. NW (Porter St.) palenarestaurant.com	UN $$$	202-537-9250	Chic Hot Chefs	65 25
Palette American	1155 15th St. NW (M St.) palettedc.com	DT $$	202-587-2700	Hip	98

NAME	ADDRESS (CROSS STREET)	AREA	PHONE	EXPERIENCE	PAGE
TYPE	WEBSITE	PRICE	SINGLES/NOISE	99 BEST	PAGE
The Palm	1225 19th St. NW (M St.)	DC	202-293-9091	Classic	130
Steak House	thepalm.com	$$$	B ≡		
Perrys	1811 Columbia Rd. NW (Biltmore St.)	AM	202-234-6218	Hip	86, 98
Asian-American	perrysadamsmorgan.com	$$	B ≡	Brunches	19
Pesce	2016 P St. NW (20th St.)	DC	202-466-3474	Chic	66
Seafood	pescebistro.com	$$	- ≡		
Poste	555 Eighth St. NW (F St.)	PQ	202-783-6060	Hip	83, 98
New American	postebrasserie.com	$$	B ≡		
The Prime Rib	2020 K St. NW (20th St.)	WE	202-466-8811	Classic	130
Steak House	theprimerib.com	$$$$	B ≡		
Rasika	633 D St. NW (Seventh St.)	PQ	202-637-1222	Chic	54, 66
Indian	rasikarestaurant.com	$$	B◌ ≡	Trendy Tables	46
Rice	1608 14th St. NW (Q St.)	US	202-234-2400	Hip	84, 98
Thai	ricerestaurant.com	$	- ≡		
Rosa Mexicano*	575 Seventh St. NW (F St)	PQ	202-783-5522	Chic	66
Mexican	rosamexicano.info	$$	B◌ ≡		
1789 Restaurant	1226 36th St. NW (Prospect St.)	GT	202-965-1789	Classic	118, 130
American (G)	1789restaurant.com	$$$	B ≡	Romantic Dining	42
Sonoma Restaurant and Wine Bar*	223 Pennsylvania Ave. SE (Second St.)	CH	202-544-8088	Chic	66
New American	sonomadc.com	$	B◌ ≡	Trendy Tables	46
Sushi-Ko	2309 Wisconsin Ave. NW (Calvert St.)	GT	202-333-4187	Classic	130
Sushi	sushiko.us	$$	- ≡		
Tabaq Bistro*	1336 U St. NW (13th St.)	US	202-265-0965	Chic	67
Middle Eastern	tabaqbistro.com	$	B ≡		
Tabard Inn*	1739 N St. NW (17th St.)	DC	202-331-8528	Classic	130
New American	tabardinn.com	$$	B ≡		
Taberna del Alabardero	1776 I St. NW (18th St.)	WH	202-429-2200	Classic	131
Spanish (G)	alabardero.com	$$$	B ≡		
Teaism	400 Eighth St. NW (D St.)	PQ	202-638-6010	Hip	84, 99
Cafe	teaism.com	$-	◌ ≡		
Teatro Goldoni	1909 K St. NW (19th St.)	WH	202-955-9494	Chic	52, 67
Italian	teatrogoldoni.com	$$$	B ≡	Chef's Tables	20
TenPenh	1001 Pennsylvania Ave. NW (10th St.)	PQ	202-393-4500	Chic	67
Asian Fusion	tenpenh.com	$$	B ≡		
Tonic*	3155 Mt. Pleasant St. NW (Kilbourne Pl.)	MP	202-986-7661	Hip	86, 99
American	tonicrestaurant.com	$-	B◌ ≡		
Tosca	1112 F St. NW (12th St.)	PQ	202-367-1990	Chic	53, 67
Italian (G)	toscadc.com	$$$	B ≡	Fine Dining	23
Tryst*	2459 18th St. NW (Columbia Rd.)	AM	202-232-5500	Hip	99
Cafe	trystdc.com	$-	B◌ ≡		
U-topia	1418 U St. NW (14th St.)	US	202-483-7669	Classic	131
American	utopiaindc.com	$	- ≡		
Vegetate*	1414 Ninth St. NW (O St.)	US	202-232-4585	Hip	85, 99
Vegetarian	vegetatedc.com	$	B ≡	Vegetarian	47

Restaurants (cont.)

NAME TYPE	ADDRESS (CROSS STREET) WEBSITE	AREA PRICE	PHONE SINGLES/NOISE	EXPERIENCE 99 BEST	PAGE PAGE
Vidalia Southern	1990 M St. NW (20th St.) bistrobis.com	DC $$$	202-659-1990 B =	Classic	131
Viridian American	1515 14th St. NW (P St.) viridianrestaurant.com	US $	202-234-1400 B =	Hip Vegetarian	85, 99 47
The Willard Room French	1401 Pennsylvania Ave. NW (14th St.) washington.interconti.com	DT $$$$	202-637-7440 - =	Classic Only-in-D.C.	116, 131 34
Zaytinya* Mediterranean	701 Ninth St. NW (G St.) zaytinya.com	PQ $$	202-638-0800 BO =	Chic Trendy Tables	54, 68 46
Zengo* Asian-Latin	781 Seventh St. NW (H St.) modernmexican.com/zengodc	PQ $$	202-393-2929 BO =	Chic	51, 68
Zola* American	800 F St. NW (Eighth St.) zoladc.com	PQ $$	202-654-0999 B =	Chic American Originals	51, 68 17

Nightlife

NAME TYPE	ADDRESS (CROSS STREET) WEBSITE	AREA COVER	PHONE FOOD/NOISE	EXPERIENCE 99 BEST	PAGE PAGE
Agua Ardiente* Bar	1250 24th St. NW (M St.) agua-ardiente.com	FB C	202-833-8500 - =	Chic International Scenes	69 29
Avenue Bar	649 New York Ave. NW (Sixth St.) avedc.com	PQ C	202-347-8100 =	Hip	100
The Bar at the Ritz-Carlton Hotel Bar	1150 22nd St. NW (M St.) ritzcarlton.com	WE -	202-835-0500 - =	Classic	132
Bar Nun Bar	1326 U St. NW (14th St.) dcbarnun.com	US C	202-667-6680 - =	Hip	100
Bar Pilar Bar	1833 14th St. NW (T St.) barpilar.com	US -	202-265-1751 - =	Hip	100
Bardeo Bar	3311 Connecticut Ave. NW (Macomb & Porter Sts.) bardeo.com	UN C	202-244-6550 - =	Chic	69
Bedrock Billiards Pool Hall	1841 Columbia Rd. NW (Mintwood Pl.) bedrockbilliards.com	AM -	202-667-7665 - =	Hip	84, 100
The Big Hunt Dive Bar	1345 Connecticut Ave. NW (Dupont Cir.)	DC -	202-785-2333 =	Hip	101
The Black Cat Bar	1811 14th St. NW (S St.) blackcatdc.com	US C	202-667-7960 - =	Hip Live Music	86, 101 30
Blue Gin Lounge	1206 Wisconsin Ave. NW (M St.) bluegindc.com	GT C	202-965-5555 - =	Chic Singles Scenes	54, 69 45
Blues Alley Cabaret	1073 Wisconsin Ave. NW (M St.) bluesalley.com	GT C	202-337-4141 - =	Classic Live Music	119, 132 30
Bohemian Caverns Jazz Club	2003 11th St. NW (U St.) bohemiancaverns.com	US C	202-299-0801 - =	Hip	101
Bossa Bar	2463 18th St. NW (Columbia Rd.) bossa-dc.com	AM C	202-667-0088 - =	Hip	86, 101

D.C. BLACK BOOK

NAME TYPE	ADDRESS (CROSS STREET) WEBSITE	AREA COVER	PHONE FOOD/NOISE	EXPERIENCE 99 BEST	PAGE PAGE
The Brickskeller Saloon Bar	1523 22nd St. NW (P St.) thebrickskeller.com	DC -	202-293-1885 - ≡	Hip Local Favorites	*84*, 101 31
Busboys and Poets Bookstore/Lounge	2021 14th St. NW (V St.) busboysandpoets.com	US -	202-387-7638 🍴 ≡	Hip	*84*, 102
Cafe Asia* Restaurant Bar	1720 I St. NW (17th St.) cafeasia.com	DT -	202-659-2696 - ≡	Hip	102
Café Citron Caribbean	1343 Connecticut Ave. NW (Dupont Cir.) cafecitrondc.com	DC C	202-530-8844 - ≡	Hip	102
Café Milano* Restaurant Bar	3251 Prospect St. NW (Wisconsin Ave.) cafemilanodc.com	GT -	202-333-6183 - ≡	Chic	69
Café Saint-Ex* Bar	1847 14th St. NW (T St.) saint-ex.com	US -	202-265-7839 - ≡	Hip Local Favorites	*84*, 102 31
Capital City Records Dive Bar	1020 U St. NW (10th St.) capitalcityrecords.com	US -	202-518-2444 - ≡	Hip	*85*, 102
Capitol Lounge Dive Bar	231 Pennsylvania Ave. SE (Independence Ave.)	CH -	202-547-2098 - ≡	Hip	103
The Capitol Steps Cabaret	1300 Pennsylvania Ave. NW (13th St.) capsteps.com	DT C	202-312-1555 - ≡	Classic	*118*, 132
Cashion's Eat Place* Restaurant Bar	1819 Columbia Rd. NW (Biltmore St.) cashionseatplace.com	AM -	202-797-1819 - ≋	Chic	69
The Caucus Room* Cigar Bar	401 Ninth St. NW (D St.) thecaucusroom.com	PQ -	202-393-1300 - ▬	Classic	*118*, 132
Charlie Palmer Steak* Restaurant Bar	101 Constitution Ave. NW (First St.) charliepalmer.com/steak_dc	CH -	202-547-8100 - ▬	Classic Politico Sightings	132 38
Chi-Cha Lounge Lounge	1624 U St. NW (16th St.) latinconcepts.com/chicha/	US -	202-234-8400 - ≡	Hip	*85*, 103
Chief Ike's Mambo Room Dance Club	1725 Columbia Rd. NW (17th St.) chiefikes.com	AM C	202-332-2211 - ≡	Hip	103
Chloe Bar	2473 18th St. NW (Columbia Rd.) chloedc.com	AM C	202-265-6592 - ≡	Chic Singles Scenes	70 45
Cobalt Gay Bar	1639 R St. NW (17th St.) cobaltdc.com	DC C	202-462-6569 - ≡	Chic Gay Bars	70 24
D.C. Improv Comedy Club	1140 Connecticut Ave. NW (M St.) dcimprov.com	DC C	202-296-7008 - ≡	Hip	103
DC9 Bar	1940 Ninth St. NW (U St.) dcnine.com	US C	202-483-5000 - ≡	Hip	*85*, 104
Degrees Hotel Bar	3100 South St. NW (31st St.) ritzcarlton.com/hotels/georgetown	GT -	202-912-4100 - ≋	Chic Hotel Bars	*52*, 70 26
Dragonfly* Restaurant/Club	1215 Connecticut Ave. NW (Rhode Island Ave.) dragonflysushibar.com	DC -	202-331-1775 - ≡	Chic	*54*, 70
Duplex Diner Gay Bar	2004 18th St. NW (Florida Ave.) duplexdiner.com	AM -	202-265-7828 - ≡	Hip Gay Bars	104 24
18th Street Lounge Lounge	1212 18th St. NW (Jefferson Pl.) eslmusic.com	DC C	202-466-3922 - ≡	Hip Sexy Lounges	*86*, 104 44

Nightlife (cont.)

NAME TYPE	ADDRESS (CROSS STREET) WEBSITE	AREA COVER	PHONE FOOD/NOISE	EXPERIENCE 99 BEST	PAGE PAGE
Eyebar Bar	1716 I St. NW (17th St.) eyebardc.com	DT -	202-785-0270 - ≡	Chic Sexy Lounges	*54*, 70 44
Felix Bar	2406 18th St. NW (Columbia Rd.) thefelix.com	AM C	202-483-3549 - ≡	Chic	71
Finn macCool's Bar	713 Eighth St. SE (G St.) finnmaccoolsdc.com	CH -	202-547-7100 - ≡	Classic	133
Five Bar	1214 B 18th St. NW (Jefferson Pl.) fivedc.com	DC C	202-331-7123 - ≡	Hip Dance Clubs	*86*, 104 21
Fly Lounge Lounge	1802 Jefferson Pl. NW (18th St.) flyloungedc.com	DC C	202-828-4433 - ≡	Chic	71
Gazuza Lounge	1629 Connecticut Ave. NW (Q St.) latinconcepts.com/gazuza/	DC -	202-667-5500 - ≡	Chic Outdoor Drinking	*52*, 71 36
Habana Village Bar	1834 Columbia Rd. NW (Mintwood St.) habanavillage.com	AM C	202-462-6310 - ≡	Classic Dance Clubs	*117*, 133 21
Halo Gay Bar	1435 P St. NW (14th St.) halodc.com	US -	202-797-9730 - ≡	Chic Gay Bars	71 24
Helix Lounge* Hotel Lounge	1430 Rhode Island Ave. NW (14th St.) hotelhelix.com/heldini	DC -	202-462-9001 - ≡	Hip Hotel Bars	*85*, 104 26
Home Lounge	911 F St. NW (Ninth St.) homenightclub.net	PQ C	202-638-4663 - ≡	Hip	105
HR-57 Cabaret	1610 14th St. NW (Q St.) hr57.org	US C	202-667-3700 - ≡	Hip	105
IMAX Jazz at the National Museum of Natural History Jazz	Constitution Ave. NW (10th St.) mnh.si.edu/jazz/	NM C	202-633-7400 - ≡	Classic	133
IndeBleu* Restaurant Lounge	707 G St. NW (Seventh St.) bleu.com/indebleu/	PQ -	202-333-2538 - ≡	Chic	72
JR's Bar & Grill Gay Bar	1519 17th St. NW (Church St.) jrswdc.com	DC -	202-328-0090 - ≡	Classic	133
K Street Lounge Lounge	1301 K St. NW (14th St.) kstreetdc.com	DT C	202-962-3933 - ≡	Chic Sexy Lounges	*53*, 72 44
The Kennedy Center Roof Terrace Restaurant & Bar Bar	2700 F St. NW (25th St.) kennedy-center.org/visitor/restaurant_terrace.cfm	FB -	202-416-8555 - –	Classic Drinks with a View	134 22
Kinkead's* Restaurant Bar	2000 Pennsylvania Ave. NW (20th St.) kinkead.com	FB -	202-296-7700 - ≡	Classic	*119*, 134
Le Bar Bar	806 15th St. NW (H St.) sofitel.com	DT -	202-737-8800 - –	Classic	*117*, 134
LeftBank* Lounge	2424 18th St. NW (Columbia Rd.) leftbankdc.com	AM -	202-464-2100 - ≡	Chic	72
Lima* Restaurant Lounge	1401 K St. NW (14th St.) limarestaurant.com	DT -	202-789-2800 - ≡	Chic	72
Local 16 Bar	1604 U St. NW (16th St.) localsixteen.com	US -	202-265-2828 - ≡	Chic Outdoor Drinking	73 36

NAME	ADDRESS (CROSS STREET)	AREA	PHONE	EXPERIENCE	PAGE
TYPE	WEBSITE	COVER	FOOD/NOISE	99 BEST	PAGE
Logan Tavern*	1423 P St. NW (15th St.)	US	202-332-3710	Hip	*84*, 105
Restaurant Bar	logantavern.com	-	- ≡		
Love	1350 Okie St. NE (Kendall St.)	NE	202-636-9030	Chic	*53*, 73
Dance Club	lovetheclub.com	C	- ≡	Dance Clubs	21
Lucky Strike	701 Seventh St. NW (G St.)	PQ	202-347-1021	Chic	*52*, 73
Bowling Alley/Lounge	bowlluckystrike.com		- ≡		
Madam's Organ	2461 18th St. NW (Columbia Rd.)	AM	202-667-5370	Hip	*84*, 105
Bar	madamsorgan.com	C	- ≡	Live Music	30
Mantis	1847 Columbia Rd. NW	AM	202-667-2400	Hip	105
Lounge	(Mintwood Pl.)	-	- ≡		
Matchbox*	713 H St. NW (Seventh St.)	PQ	202-289-4441	Hip	106
Restaurant Bar	matchboxdc.com	-	- ≡		
Maté	3101 K St. NW (31st St.)	GT	202-333-2006	Chic	*54*, 73
Lounge	matelounge.com	C	- ≡	International Scenes 29	
MCCXXIII	1223 Connecticut Ave. NW	DC	202-822-1800	Chic	*54*, 74
Lounge	(Rhode Island Ave.) 1223dc.com	C	- ≡	Singles Scenes	45
Mie N Yu*	3125 M St. NW (31st St.)	GT	202-333-6122	Chic	*53*, 74
Restaurant Bar	mienyu.com	-	- ≡		
Modern	3287 M St. NW (33rd St.)	GT	202-338-7027	Chic	74
Lounge	primacycompanies.com	C	- ≡		
Off the Record	One Lafayette Sq. NW (H St.)	DT	202-638-6600	Classic	*117*, 134
Bar	hayadams.com/Dining/off_record.htm		- ≡	Politico Sightings	38
Old Ebbitt Grill*	675 15th St. NW (G St.)	DT	202-347-4801	Classic	134
Restaurant Bar	ebbitt.com	-	- ≡		
Old Glory BBQ*	3139 M St. NW (Wisconsin Ave.)	GT	202-337-3406	Classic	134
Bar	oldglorybbq.com	-	- ≡		
Oya*	777 Ninth St. NW (H St.)	PQ	202-393-1400	Chic	74
Restaurant Lounge	oyadc.com	-	- ≡		
Ozio Restaurant & Lounge	1813 M St. NW (18th St.)	DC	202-822-6000	Chic	*53*, 74
Restaurant Bar	oziodc.com	C	- ≡		
Pearl	901 Ninth St. NW (I St.)	PQ	202-371-0681	Chic	*52*, 75
Bar	dcpearl.com	C	- ≡		
Play Lounge	1219 Connecticut Ave. NW	DC	202-466-7529	Chic	*52*, 75
Lounge	(Jefferson Pl.) playloungedc.com	C	- ≡		
Republic Gardens	1355 U St. NW (14th St.)	US	202-232-2710	Chic	75
Bar	republicgardens.com	C	- ≡		
Rosa Mexicano*	575 Seventh St. NW (F St)	PQ	202-783-5522	Chic	*51*, 75
Restaurant Bar	rosamexicano.info	-	- ≡		
Round Robin	1401 Pennsylvania Ave. NW	DT	202-628-9100	Classic	*117*, 135
Hotel Bar	(14th St.)	-	- —	Hotel Bars	26
Russia House	1800 Connecticut Ave. NW	DC	202-234-9433	Classic	*117*, 135
Bar	(Florida Ave.) russiahouselounge.com		- ≡	International Scenes 29	
Saki	2477 18th St. NW (Columbia Rd.)	AM	202-232-5005	Hip	106
Lounge	sakidc.com	C	- ≡		

Nightlife (cont.)

NAME TYPE	ADDRESS (CROSS STREET) WEBSITE	AREA COVER	PHONE FOOD/NOISE	EXPERIENCE 99 BEST	PAGE PAGE
Science Club Lounge	1136 19th St. NW (L St.) scienceclubdc.com	DT -	202-775-0747 - ☰	Hip	85, 106
Sequoia Bar	3000 K St. NW (30th St.) arkrestaurants.com	GT -	202-944-4200 - ☰	Chic Outdoor Drinking	75 36
Sky Terrace at the Hotel Washington Hotel Bar	2800 Pennsylvania Ave. NW (28th St.) 	WH -	202-342-0444 - ☰	Classic Drinks with a View	117, 135 22
Sonoma Restaurant and Wine Bar* Wine Bar	223 Pennsylvania Ave. SE (Second St.) sonomadc.com	CH -	202-544-8088 - ☰	Chic	76
Spank Lounge	1223 Connecticut Ave. NW (M St.)	DC C	202-822-1800 - ☰	Chic	76
Tabaq Bistro* Lounge	1336 U St. NW (13th St.) tabaqbistro.com	US -	202-265-0965 - ☰	Chic Drinks with a View	76 22
Tabard Inn Lounge* Hotel Bar	1739 N St. NW (17th St.) tabardinn.com	DC -	202-785-1277 - ☰	Classic	135
Tapatinis Bar	711 Eighth St. SE (G St.) tapatinis.com	CH -	202-546-8272 - ☰	Hip	106
Tonic* Restaurant Bar	3155 Mt. Pleasant St. NW (Kilbourne Pl.) tonicrestaurant.com	MP -	202-986-7661 - ☰	Hip	106
Top of the Hill Bar	319 Pennsylvania Ave. SE (Third St.) politiki-dc.com/top.php	CH -	202-546-7782 - ☰	Classic	135
Town and Country Lounge Bar	1127 Connecticut Ave. NW (Desales St.)	DC -	202-347-3000 - ☰	Classic	136
Trio's Fox and Hound Dive Bar	1537 17th St. NW (Church St.)	DC -	202-232-6307 - ☰	Hip	107
Tryst* Cafe	2459 18th St. NW (Columbia Rd.) trystdc.com	AM -	202-232-5500 - ☰	Hip	84, 107
U-topia* Cabaret	1418 U St. NW (14th St.) utopiaindc.com	US -	202-483-7669 - ☰	Classic	119, 136
Vegetate* Restaurant Bar	1414 Ninth St. NW (O St.) vegetatedc.com	US -	202-232-4585 - ☰	Hip	107
Warehouse Bar/Theater	1021 Seventh St. NW (New York Ave.) warehousetheater.com	PQ C	202-783-3933 - ☰	Hip	107
The Wonderland Ballroom Dive Bar	1101 Kenyon St. NW (11th St.) thewonderlandballroom.com	UN -	202-232-5263 - ☰	Hip Local Favorites	85, 107 31
Zaytinya* Restaurant Bar	701 Ninth St. NW (G St.) zaytinya.com	PQ -	202-638-0800 - ☰	Chic	54, 76
Zengo* Restaurant Bar	781 Seventh St. NW (H St.) modernmexican.com/zengodc	PQ -	202-393-2929 - ☰	Chic	76
Zola* Restaurant Bar	800 F St. NW (Eighth St.) zoladc.com	PQ -	202-654-0999 - ☰	Chic	76

D.C. BLACK BOOK

Attractions

NAME / TYPE	ADDRESS (CROSS STREET) / WEBSITE	AREA PRICE	PHONE	EXPERIENCE / 99 BEST	PAGE / PAGE
African American Civil War Museum / Museum/Site	1200 U St. NW (12th St.) afroamcivilwar.org	US -	202-667-2667	Hip	108
Albert Einstein Memorial / Site	Constitution Ave. NW (22nd St.)	NM -	n/a	Hip	84, 108
Art Museum of the Americas / Art Museum	201 18th St. NW (Constitution Ave.) museum.oas.org	NM -	202-458-6016	Hip	83, 108
Artefacto / Store	3333 M St. NW (Bank St.) artefacto.com	GT -	202-338-3337	Chic	77
The Bead Museum / Museum	400 Seventh St. NW (D St.) beadmuseumdc.org	PQ -	202-624-4500	Hip	108
Betsy Fisher / Store	1224 Connecticut Ave. NW (Jefferson Pl.) betsyfisher.com	DC -	202-785-1975	Classic	137
Bike the Sites / Sport/Tour	Old Post Office Pavilion, 1100 Pennsylvania Ave. NW (12th St.) bikethesites.com	PQ $$$$	202-842-2453	Hip	84, 109
Cady's Alley / Shopping	3318 M St. NW (33rd St.) cadysalley.com	GT -	n/a	Chic	53, 56
Corcoran Gallery of Art / Art Museum	500 17th St. NW (New York Ave.) corcoran.org	WH $-	202-639-1700	Classic / Art Museums	116, 137 / 18
DownDog Yoga / Sport	1046 Potomac St. NW (M St.) downdogyoga.com	GT $	202-965-9642	Hip	86, 109
Dumbarton Oaks Gardens / Garden	R St. NW (32nd St.) doaks.org	GT $-	202-339-6400	Chic / Romantic Trysts	77 / 43
Dupont Circle Art Galleries / Galleries	Various	DC -	n/a	Chic / Insider D.C. Exp.	77 / 28
East Potomac Golf Course / Sport	972 Ohio Dr. SW golfdc.com	SW $$	202-554-7660	Hip	109
Eastern Market / Market	Seventh St. SE (North Carolina Ave.) easternmarketdc.com	CH -	202-544-0083	Hip / Insider D.C. Exp.	85, 109 / 28
Embassy Row / Neighborhood	embassy.org	DC -	n/a	Classic	137
Flight Simulators / Sport	National Air and Space Museum, Independence Ave. SW (Seventh St.) nasm.si.edu	NM $-	202-633-1000	Hip / Rainy Day Exp.	83, 110 / 40
Folger Shakespeare Library / Site/Garden	201 E. Capitol St. SE (Second St.) folger.edu	CH -	202-544-4600	Hip	85, 110
Franklin Delano Roosevelt Memorial / Site	West Basin Dr. SW (Independence Ave.) nps.gov/fdrm	SW -	202-426-6841	Classic	119, 137
Freer Gallery of Art / Art Museum	Jefferson Dr. SW (12th St.) asia.si.edu	NM -	202-633-1000	Chic	54, 77
The Grooming Lounge / Barber Shop	1745 L St. NW (Connecticut Ave.) groominglounge.com	DT	202-466-8900	Chic	78
Grounds of the U.S. Capitol / Park	aoc.gov	CH -	202-225-6827	Classic	137

Attractions (cont.)

NAME TYPE	ADDRESS (CROSS STREET) WEBSITE	AREA PRICE	PHONE	EXPERIENCE 99 BEST	PAGE PAGE
Hillwood Museum & Gdns. Museum/Garden	4155 Linnean Ave. NW (Tilden St.) hillwoodmuseum.org	UN $	202-686-5807	Classic	138
Hirshhorn Museum Art Museum	Independence Ave. SW (Seventh St.) hirshhorn.si.edu	NM -	202-633-1000	Chic Art Museums	52, 78 18
I Spa at the Willard Spa	1401 Pennsylvania Ave. NW (14th St.) washington.interconti.com	DT $$$$	202-942-2700	Classic Luxury Spas	117, 138 32
IMAX Films Museum/Entertainment	National Air and Space Museum, Independence Ave. SW (Seventh St); National Museum of Natural History, Constitution Ave. NW (10th St.) nasm.si.edu, mnh.si.edu	NM $	202-633-4629	Hip Rainy Day Exp.	83, 110 40
Indian Craft Shop Store	1849 C St. NW (18th St.) indiancraftshop.com	NM -	202-208-4056	Hip	84, 111
International Spy Museum Museum	800 F St. NW (Eighth St.) spymuseum.org	PQ $	866-779-6873	Chic Rainy Day Exp.	51, 78 40
International Spy Museum Gift Shop Store	800 F St. NW (Eighth St.) spymuseum.org	PQ -	202-654-0950	Chic	78
Jefferson Memorial Site	Ohio Dr. SW (Tidal Basin) nps.gov/thje	SW -	202-426-6841	Classic Monumental Sculp.	119, 138 33
Kennedy Center Site	2700 F St. NW (New Hampshire Ave.) kennedy-center.org	FB -	202-467-4600	Classic	118, 138
Kreeger Art Museum Art Museum	2401 Foxhall Rd. NW (Reservoir Rd.) kreegermuseum.org	GT $-	202-338-3552	Chic	53, 78
Library of Congress Site	101 Independence Ave. SE (First St.) loc.gov	CH -	202-797-8000	Classic	117, 139
Lincoln Memorial Site	Western end of the National Mall (23rd St.) nps.gov/linc	NM -	202-426-6842	Classic Monumental Sculp.	119, 139 33
Meeps Vintage Fashionette Store	1520 U St. NW (15th St.) meepsonu.com	US -	202-265-6546	Hip	111
Meridian Internat'l Center Art House	1630 Crescent Pl. NW (16th St.) meridian.org	UN -	202-667-6800	Chic	79
Miss Pixie's Furnishings and Whatnot Store	2473 18th St. NW (Columbia Rd.) misspixies.com	AM -	202-232-8171	Hip	111
Muléh Store	1831 14th St. NW (T St.) muleh.com	US -	202-667-3440	Hip	111
Nana Store	1528 U St. NW (16th St.) nanadc.com	US -	202-667-6955	Hip	111
National Archives Site	Constitution Ave. NW (Seventh St.) archives.gov	NM -	202-357-5000	Classic Patriotic Adventures	116, 139 37
National Building Museum Museum	401 F St. NW (Fourth St.) nbm.org	PQ -	202-272-2448	Chic	85, 79
National Gallery of Art & Sculpture Garden Art Museum	Constitution Ave. NW (Seventh St.) nga.gov	NM -	202-737-4215	Classic Art Museums	118, 140 18
National Geographic Museum Museum	17th St. NW (M St.) nationalgeographic.com/museum	DC -	202-857-7588	Chic	79

D.C. BLACK BOOK

NAME	ADDRESS (CROSS STREET)	AREA	PHONE	EXPERIENCE	PAGE
TYPE	WEBSITE	PRICE		99 BEST	PAGE
National Mall	Bounded by Constitution Independence Aves. and the Lincoln Memorial and the Capitol.	NM			
Site	-			Outdoor Activities	35
National Museum of the American Indian Museum	Independence Ave. SW (Fourth St.) americanindian.si.ed	NM -	202-633-1000	Hip	83, 112
National Museum of Women in the Arts Art Museum	1250 New York Ave. NW (H St.) nmwa.org	PQ $-	202-783-5000	Hip	85, 112
National Postal Museum Museum	2 Massachusetts Ave. NE (N. Capitol St.) postalmuseum.si.edu	CH	202-633-5555	Hip	85, 112
National World War II Memorial Site	17th St. NW (Constitution Ave.) wwiimemorial.com	NM -	202-619-7222	Chic	79
Nusta Spa Spa	1129 20th St. NW (M St.) nustaspa.com	DC -	202-530-5700	Hip	86, 112
Old Post Office Pavilion Tower Site	1100 Pennsylvania Ave. NW (12th St.) oldpostofficedc.com	PQ -	202-289-4224	Hip Views of D.C.	84, 113 48
Pedal Boats Sport	Raoul Wallenberg Pl./15th St. SW (Independence Ave.) tidalbasinpeddleboats.com	SW $-	202-479-2426	Hip Outdoor Activities	84, 113 35
Phillips Collection Art Museum	1600 21st St. NW (Q St.) phillipscollection.org	DC $-	202-387-2151	Chic Rainy Day Exp.	54, 79 40
Pink November Store	1529 Wisconsin Ave. NW (Volta Pl.) -	GT	202-333-1121	Chic	80
Potomac Riverboat Co. Boat Tour	Washington Harbour (31st St.) potomacriverboatco.com	GT $$	703-548-9000	Chic Views of D.C.	53, 80 48
Relish Store	3312 Cady's Alley NW (34th St.) relishdc.com	GT -	202-333-5343	Chic	80
Renwick Gallery Art Museum	1661 Pennsylvania Ave. NW (17th St.) americanart.si.edu	WH -	202-633-2850	Classic	116, 140
Rizik's Store	1100 Connecticut Ave. NW (L St.) riziks.com	DC -	202-223-4050	Classic	140
Rock Creek Park Park	From the Potomac River nr. the Kennedy Center, NW through the city into Maryland nps.gov/rocr	VA -	202-895-6070	Classic Outdoor Activities	118, 140 35
Rowing on the Potomac Sport	3500 K St. NW (35th St.) jacksboathouse.com	GT $	202-337-9642	Chic Romantic Trysts	80 43
Sherman Pickey Store	1647 Wisconsin Ave. NW (Reservoir Rd.) shermanpickey.com	GT -	202-333-4212	Classic	140
Smithsonian American Art Museum / National Portrait Gallery Art Museum	F St. NW (Eighth St.) americanart.si.edu, npg.si.edu	PQ -	202-275-1500	Chic Patriotic Adventures	51, 81 37
SomaFit Spa and Fitness Center Spa/Health Club	2121 Wisconsin Ave. NW (35th St.) somafit.com	GT $$$$	202-965-2121	Chic Luxury Spas	53, 81 32
Spa at the Mandarin Oriental Spa	1330 Maryland Ave. SW (12th St.) mandarinoriental.com.washington	NM $$$$	202-787-6100	Chic Luxury Spas	81 32

215

BLACK BOOK

Attractions (cont.)

NAME TYPE	ADDRESS (CROSS STREET) WEBSITE	AREA PRICE	PHONE	EXPERIENCE 99 BEST	PAGE PAGE
Supreme Court Site	One First St. NE (E. Capitol St.) supremecourtus.gov	CH -	202-479-3000	Chic	52, 81
Textile Museum Museum	2320 S St. NW (24th St.) textilemuseum.org	DC -	202-667-0441	Hip	86, 113
A Tour de Force Tour	Various atourdeforce.com	VA $$$$	703-525-2948	Classic Romantic Trysts	118, 141 43
Union Station Site/Store	50 Massachusetts Ave. NE (First Ave.) unionstationdc.com	CH -	202-289-1908	Classic Insider D.C. Exp.	141 28
U.S. Botanic Garden Garden	100 Maryland Ave. SW (Independence Ave.) usbg.gov	CH -	202-225-8333	Classic	117, 141
U.S. Capitol Site	E. Capitol St. (First St.) aoc.gov	CH -	202-225-6827	Classic Patriotic Adventures	117, 141 37
U.S. Dept. of Interior Musm. Museum	1849 C St. NW (18th St.) doi.gov/museum	NM -	202-208-4743	Hip	83, 113
U.S. Holocaust Mem. Museum Museum	100 Raoul Wallenberg Pl. SW (Independence Ave.) ushmm.org	SW -	202-488-0400	Classic	119, 142
Vietnam Veterans Memorial Site	Constitution Ave. NW (21st St.) nps.gov/vive	NM -	202-426-6841	Hip	84, 114
Washington Monument Site	National Mall (15th St.) nps.gov/wash	NM -	202-426-6841	Classic Monumental Sculp.	142 33
Washington National Cathedral Site/Garden	Massachusetts Ave. NW (Wisconsin Ave.) cathedral.org	UN -	202-537-6200	Classic Views of D.C.	142 48
The White House Site	1600 Pennsylvania Ave. NW (17th St.) whitehouse.gov	WH -	202-456-7041	Classic	116, 142

D.C. Black Book By Neighborhood

Adams Morgan (AM)
R	Bardia's New Orleans Café		92
	Cashion's Eat Place*	16	62
	The Diner		94
	L'Enfant Café		95
	LeftBank*		64
	Mama Ayesha's Restaurant	47	96
	Meskerem		97
	Perrys	19	98
	Tryst*		99
N	Bedrock Billiards		100
	Bossa		101
	Cashion's Eat Place*		69
	Chief Ike's Mambo Room		103
	Chloe	45	70
	Duplex Diner	24	104
	Felix		71
	Habana Village	21	133
	LeftBank*		72
	Madam's Organ	30	105
	Mantis		105
	Saki		106
	Tryst*		107
A	Miss Pixie's Furnishings and Whatnot		111

Capitol Hill (CH)
H	The Hotel George		57
R	Belga Café		92
	Bistro Bis	16	60
	Bread and Chocolate		93
	Charlie Palmer Steak*	38	125
	Johnny's Half-Shell	17	95
	Market Lunch		96
	The Monocle	34	127
	Montmartre		128
	Sonoma Restaurant and Wine Bar*	46	66
N	Capitol Lounge		103
	Charlie Palmer Steak*	38	132
	Finn macCool's		133
	Sonoma Restaurant and Wine Bar*		76
N	Tapatinis		106
	Top of the Hill		135
A	Eastern Market	28	109
	Folger Shakespeare Library		110
	Grounds of the U.S. Capitol		137
	Library of Congress		139
	National Postal Museum		112
	Supreme Court		81
	Union Station	28	141
	U.S. Botanic Garden		141
	U.S. Capitol	37	141

Downtown (DT)
H	Willard InterContinental		123
R	Cafe Asia*		93
	Lima*	41	65
	The Occidental	39	128
	Old Ebbitt Grill*		129
	Palette		98
	The Willard Room	34	131
N	Cafe Asia*		102
	The Capitol Steps		132
	Eyebar	44	70
	K Street Lounge	44	72
	Le Bar		134
	Lima*		72
	Off the Record	38	134
	Old Ebbitt Grill*		134
	Round Robin	26	135
	Science Club		106
A	The Grooming Lounge		78
	I Spa at the Willard	32	138

Dupont Circle (DC)
H	Hotel Helix		89
	Hotel Madera		89
	Hotel Palomar		57
	Hotel Rouge		90
	Tabard Inn		90
	Topaz Hotel		90
R	Afterwords Cafe		92
	Bistrot du Coin		92
	Dragonfly*		63

Code: H-Hotels; R-Restaurants; N-Nightlife; A-Attractions. Blue page numbers denote listings in 99 Best. Black page numbers denote listings in theme chapters. The D.C. Neighborhoods Map is on p.223.

Dupont Circle (DC) (cont.)
- R Firefly 94
- Hank's Oyster Bar 94
- Helix Lounge* 95
- Komi 64
- Lauriol Plaza 64
- Obelisk 23 128
- The Palm 130
- Pesce 66
- Tabard Inn 130
- Vidalia 131
- N The Big Hunt 101
- The Brickskeller Saloon 31 101
- Café Citron 102
- Cobalt 24 70
- D.C. Improv 103
- Dragonfly* 70
- 18th Street Lounge 44 104
- Five 21 104
- Fly Lounge 71
- Gazuza 36 71
- Helix Lounge* 26 104
- JR's Bar & Grill 133
- MCCXXIII 45 74
- Ozio Restaurant & Lounge 74
- Play Lounge 75
- Russia House 29 135
- Spank 76
- Tabard Inn Lounge* 135
- Town and Country Lounge 136
- Trio's Fox and Hound 107
- A Betsy Fisher 137
- Dupont Circle Art Galleries 28 77
- Embassy Row 137
- National Geographic Museum 79
- Nusta Spa 112
- The Phillips Collection 40 79
- Rizik's 140
- Textile Museum 113

Foggy Bottom (FB)
- R Agua Ardiente* 60
- Kinkead's* 126
- Marcel's 23 127
- N Agua Ardiente* 29 69
- The Kennedy Center Roof
  Terrace Restaurant & Bar 22 134
- Kinkead's* 134
- A Kennedy Center for the
  Performing Arts 138

Georgetown (GT)
- H Four Seasons Hotel 57
- The Ritz-Carlton, Georgetown 59
- R Bangkok Bistro 60
- Café Bonaparte 93
- Café Milano* 38 61
- Citronelle 25 125
- La Chaumiere 126
- Leopold's Kafe & Konditorei 64
- Mendocino Grille and Wine Bar 65
- Mie N Yu* 65
- Old Glory BBQ* 129
- 1789 Restaurant 42 130
- Sushi-Ko 130
- N Blue Gin 45 69
- Blues Alley 30 132
- Café Milano* 69
- Degrees 26 70
- Maté 29 73
- Mie N Yu* 74
- Modern 74
- Old Glory BBQ* 134
- Sequoia 36 75
- A Artefacto 77
- Cady's Alley 56
- DownDog Yoga 109
- Dumbarton Oaks Gardens 43 77
- Kreeger Art Museum 78
- Pink November 80
- Potomac Riverboat Company 48 80
- Relish 80
- Rowing on the Potomac 43 80
- Sherman Pickey 140
- SomaFit Spa & Fitness Center 32 81

Mount Pleasant (MP)
- R Tonic* 99
- N Tonic* 106

National Mall (NM)
- R Mitsitam 27 97
- National Gallery of Art Cafes 128
- N IMAX Jazz at the National
  Museum of Natural History 133
- A Albert Einstein Memorial 108

BLACK BOOK BY NEIGHBORHOOD

A	Art Museum of the Americas		108
	Flight Simulators	40	110
	Freer Gallery of Art		77
	Hirshhorn Museum and Sculpture Garden	18	78
	IMAX Films	40	110
	Indian Craft Shop		111
	Lincoln Memorial	33	139
	National Archives	37	139
	National Gallery of Art and Sculpture Garden	18	140
	National Mall	35	
	National Museum of the American Indian		112
	National World War II Memorial		79
	Spa at the Mandarin Oriental	32	81
	U.S. Department of the Interior Museum		113
	Vietnam Veterans Memorial		114
	Washington Monument	33	142

Northeast (NE)

N	Love	21	73

Penn Quarter (PQ)

H	Hotel Monaco		89
R	Acadiana	17	60
	Butterfield 9	42	61
	Café Atlantico	19	61
	The Capital Grille	39	124
	The Caucus Room*	39	125
	Ceiba		62
	Chinatown Express		93
	IndeBleu*	41	63
	Jaleo		95
	Les Halles		127
	Marrakesh		96
	Matchbox*		97
	Minibar at Café Atlantico	20	97
	Oceanaire Seafood Room		129
	Oya*	41	65
	Poste		98
	Rasika	46	66
	Rosa Mexicano*		66
	Teaism		99
	TenPenh		67
	Tosca	23	67
	Zaytinya*	46	68

R	Zengo*		68
	Zola*	17	68
N	Avenue		100
	The Caucus Room*		132
	Home		105
	IndeBleu*		72
	Lucky Strike		73
	Matchbox*		106
	Oya*		74
	Pearl		75
	Rosa Mexicano*		75
	Warehouse		107
	Zaytinya*		76
	Zengo*		76
	Zola*		76
A	The Bead Museum		108
	Bike the Sites		109
	International Spy Museum	40	78
	International Spy Msm. Gift Shop		78
	National Building Museum		79
	National Museum of Women in the Arts		112
	Old Post Office Pavilion Tower	48	113
	Smithsonian American Art Museum/ National Portrait Gallery	37	81

Southwest (SW)

H	Mandarin Oriental		58
R	Café MoZU		124
	CityZen	25	62
A	East Potomac Golf Course at Hains Point		109
	Franklin Delano Roosevelt Mem.		137
	Jefferson Memorial	33	138
	Pedal Boats	35	113
	U.S. Holocaust Mem. Museum		142

Upper Northwest (UN)

R	Dino		63
	Domku Bar & Café		94
	Indique	27	63
	Lebanese Taverna		64
	Palena	25	65
N	Bardeo		69
	The Wonderland Ballroom	31	107
A	Hillwood Museum and Gardens		138
	Meridian International Center		79
	Washington National Cathedral	48	142

U Street Corridor (US)

- R Al Crostino 60
- Ben's Chili Bowl 34 92
- Café Saint-Ex* 93
- Creme Cafe 94
- Logan Tavern* 95
- Love Café 96
- Merkado 97
- Rice 98
- Tabaq Bistro* 67
- U-topia 131
- Vegetate* 47 99
- Viridian 47 99
- N Bar Nun 100
- Bar Pilar 100
- The Black Cat 30 101
- Bohemian Cavern's 101
- Busboys and Poets 102
- Café Saint-Ex* 31 102
- Capital City Records 102
- Chi-Cha Lounge 103
- DC9 104
- Halo 24 71
- HR-57 105
- Local 16 36 73
- Logan Tavern* 105
- Republic Gardens 75
- Tabaq Bistro* 22 76
- U-topia 136
- Vegetate* 107
- A African American Civil War Museum and Memorial 108
- Meeps Vintage Fashionette 111
- Muléh 111
- Nana 111

Various (VA)

- A Rock Creek Park 35 140
- A Tour de Force 43 141

West End (WE)

- H Park Hyatt Washington, DC 58
- The Ritz-Carlton, Washington, D.C. 123
- R Blue Duck Tavern 61
- Galileo 16 126
- Laboratorio del Galileo 20 127
- The Prime Rib 130
- N The Bar at the Ritz-Carlton, Washington, D.C. 132

White House (WH)

- H Hay-Adams Hotel 122
- The Jefferson 122
- The Renaissance Mayflower Hotel 122
- Sofitel Lafayette Square 123
- R The Bombay Club 27 124
- BreadLine 124
- DC Coast 62
- Equinox 125
- Gerard's Place 42 126
- Lafayette Room 19 127
- The Oval Room 129
- Taberna del Alabardero 131
- Teatro Goldoni 20 67
- N Sky Terrace at the Hotel Washington 22 135
- A Corcoran Gallery of Art 18 137
- Renwick Gallery 140
- The White House 142

D.C. Unique Shopping Index

NAME	(202) PHONE	AREA	PRODUCTS	PAGE
Appalachian Spring	337-5780	GT	American crafts	121
Artefacto	338-3337	GT	Brazilian furniture emporium	56, 77
Beadazzled	265-2323	DC	Beads and gems	56
Betsy Fisher	785-1975	DC	Designer women's apparel	121, 137
Botanica Yemaya-Chango	462-1803	AM	Candles, herbs, and statues	88
Brooks Brothers	659-4650	DC	High-end women's apparel	121
Cady's Alley	(no phone)	GT	Design district with 50 shops	56
Carbon	986-2679	US	Funky shoes	88
Chocolate Moose	463-0992	DC	Eclectic gifts and accessories	56
Crooked Beat Records	483-2328	AM	Records and posters	88
The District Line	558-5508	AM	British clothing designers	88
Fornash	338-0774	GT	Preppy accessories	121
Galerie L'Enfant	625-2873	GT	Antiques	121
Georgetown Tobacco	338-5100	GT	Cigars, pipes, and humidors	121
Go Mama Go	299-0850	US	Gifts and glassware	88
Gore Dean	625-9199	GT	Antiques/contemporary furnishings	121
The Grooming Lounge	466-8900	DC	Men's razors, skin care products	56, 78
Hu's Shoes	342-0202	GT	High-end shoes	56
Indian Craft Shop	208-4056	NM	Native American crafts, jewelry	111
International Spy Museum Gift Shop	654-0950	PQ	Unusual souvenirs	78
K Baby	333-3939	GT	High-end baby store	121
Meeps Village Fashionette	265-6546	US	Edgy women's apparel	88, 111
Millennium Decorative Arts	483-1218	US	Retro home décor, accessories	88
Miss Pixie's Furnishings and Whatnot	232-8171	AM	Eclectic mix of home décor	88, 111
Muléh	667-3440	US	Edgy women's apparel	88, 111
Nana	667-6955	US	Vintage/modern women's apparel	88, 111
Oya's Mini Bazaar	667-9853	AM	Eclectic mix of accessories	88
Pink November	333-1121	GT	Edgy women's apparel	56, 80
Proper Topper	842-3055	DC	Hats, gifts, and accessories	56
Pulp	462-7857	US	Edgy gifts	88
Relish	333-5343	GT	High-end men's and womenswear	56, 80
Rizik's	223-4050	DC	High-end women's apparel	121, 140
Secondi Consignment Clothing	667-1122	DC	High-end secondhand apparel	56
Sherman Pickey	333-4212	GT	Preppy women's apparel	121, 140
Sugar	333-5331	GT	Chic women's apparel	56
Tiny Jewel Box	393-2747	DC	Vintage and contemporary jewelry	121
Wink	338-9465	GT	Casual feminine fashions	56

For Neighborhood (Area) Key, see p.202.

ACTION CENTRAL D.C.

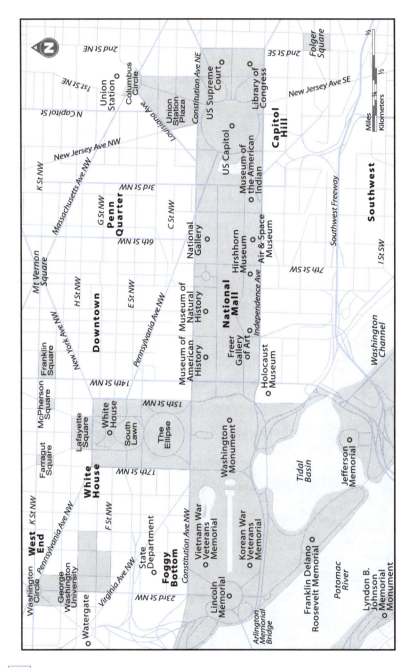

D.C. NEIGHBORHOODS

New. It's You.
Night+Day online
@ pulseguides.com

a travel web site designed to complement your lifestyle

Today's urbane, sophisticated traveler knows how fast things change in the world. What's hot, and what's not? Now you have access to the insider information you need, whenever you need it **Night+Day**—at pulseguides.com.

We're committed to providing the latest, most accurate information on the hottest, hippest, coolest and classiest venues around the world, which means keeping our listings current—even after you've purchased one of our **Night+Day** guides.

Visit pulseguides.com and browse your way to any destination to view or download the most recent updates to the **Night+Day** guide of your choice.

Online and in print, **Night+Day** offers independent travel advice tailored to suit your lifestyle, capturing the unique personality of each city. From uptown chic to downtown cool, our guides are packed with opinionated tips, and selective, richly detailed descriptions geared toward the discerning traveler.

Enhance your travel experience online:
- Zero in on hot restaurants, classic attractions and hip nightlife
- Print out your favorite itinerary to keep in your purse or pocket as you travel
- Update your **Night+Day** guide with what's new
- Read news and tips from around the world
- Get great deals on all the titles in our Cool Cities series

Night+Day—online now at pulseguides.com.

"Perfect for the business person or jet-setter."
—*Sacramento Bee*

"Focus[es] their information to attract vacationers who don't want cookie-cutter itineraries."
—*Wall Street Journal*

"Delivers pithy comments and frank opinions."
—*Salt Lake Tribune*

"Count on trendy, hip, and hot tips, smart clubs, and fashionable fun."
—*Physicians Travel Monthly*

"Refreshingly different ... It's amazing how much information is crammed into a handy 230-page paperback format."
—Anthony Dias Blue, *KCBS Radio*